A Collector's History
of
BRITISH
PORCELAIN

Portobello Road.

A Wedgwood vase and cover in Classical style, with a border showing signs of the Zodiac. In glazed Parian with enamelled ground. 'Victoria Ware', 1875

A Collector's History

of

BRITISH PORCELAIN

John and Margaret Cushion

Antique Collectors' Club

Dedication

This book is dedicated to the late Mrs Patricia Fay, O.B.E.
Founder of the National Association
of the Decorative & Fine
Arts Society

© 1992 John and Margaret Cushion
World copyright reserved
First published 1992

ISBN 1 85149 155 4

Published for the Antique Collectors' Club
by the Antique Collectors' Club Ltd.

British Library CIP Data

Cushion, John P.
   Collector's History of British Porcelain
   I. Title II. Cushion, Margaret
   738.2

Printed in England by the Antique Collectors' Club Ltd.
Woodbridge, Suffolk

A Collector's History

of

BRITISH PORCELAIN

John and Margaret Cushion

Antique Collectors' Club

Dedication

This book is dedicated to the late Mrs Patricia Fay, O.B.E.
Founder of the National Association
of the Decorative & Fine
Arts Society

© 1992 John and Margaret Cushion
World copyright reserved
First published 1992

ISBN 1 85149 155 4

Published for the Antique Collectors' Club
by the Antique Collectors' Club Ltd.

British Library CIP Data

Cushion, John P.
    Collector's History of British Porcelain
    I. Title II. Cushion, Margaret
    738.2

Printed in England by the Antique Collectors' Club Ltd.
Woodbridge, Suffolk

Antique Collectors' Club

The Antique Collectors' Club was formed in 1966 and now has a five figure membership spread throughout the world. It publishes the only independently run monthly antiques magazine *Antique Collecting* which caters for those collectors who are interested in widening their knowledge of antiques, both by greater awareness of quality and by discussion of the factors which influence the price that is likely to be asked. The Antique Collectors' Club pioneered the provision of information on prices for collectors and the magazine still leads in the provision of detailed articles on a variety of subjects.

It was in response to the enormous demand for information on ''what to pay'' that the price guide series was introduced in 1968 with the first edition of *The Price Guide to Antique Furniture* (completely revised, 1978 and 1989), a book which broke new ground by illustrating the more common types of antique furniture, the sort that collectors could buy in shops and at auctions rather than the rare museum pieces which had previously been used (and still to a large extent are used) to make up the limited amount of illustrations in books published by commercial publishers. Many other price guides have followed, all copiously illustrated, and greatly appreciated by collectors for the valuable information they contain, quite apart from prices. The Antique Collectors' Club also publishes other books on antiques, including horology and art reference works, and a full book list is available.

Club membership, which is open to all collectors, costs £17.50 per annum. Members receive free of charge *Antique Collecting,* the Club's magazine (published ten times a year), which contains well-illustrated articles dealing with the practical aspects of collecting not normally dealt with by magazines. Prices, features of value, investment potential, fakes and forgeries are all given prominence in the magazine.

Among other facilities available to members are private buying and selling facilities, the longest list of ''For Sales'' of any antiques magazine, an annual ceramics conference and the opportunity to meet other collectors at their local antique collectors' clubs. There are over eighty in Britain and more than a dozen overseas. Members may also buy the Club's publications at special pre-publication prices.

As its motto implies, the Club is an amateur organisation designed to help collectors get the most out of their hobby: it is informal and friendly and gives enormous enjoyment to all concerned.

For Collectors — By Collectors — About Collecting

The Antique Collectors' Club, 5 Church Street, Woodbridge, Suffolk

Acknowledgements

In the 'Further Reading' at the end of each entry we have listed the relevant books and articles written over recent years together with the names of the authors involved, who are sometimes porcelain enthusiasts interested in one particular factory or type of ware and are so generous with their knowledge. The fear with acknowledging the help we have received over the past two years in the preparation of this volume is of course that a name has unintentionally been omitted, one could of course just say 'thank you all' but that would not really express our thanks sufficiently. When on the staff of the Ceramics Department of the Victoria & Albert Museum it was comparatively easy to illustrate wares from the collection, but many readers we are sure are all too familiar with 'V. & A.' pieces. To gather the nine hundred or so photographs illustrated in this book we have had the help and co-operation of over forty museum curators, salerooms, major dealers in the field of antique porcelain, collectors and other authors, all of whom have been so patient and generous in providing pictures of the elusive pieces we were sometimes lacking, so thank you to: Elizabeth Adams, Paul Atterbury, John Austin (Curator of Ceramics at Colonial Williamsburg Foundation, Virginia, U.S.A.), Valerie Baynton (Curator of the Sir Henry Doulton Gallery), Bearne's Auction House, Torquay, Michael Berthoud of Micawber Antiques, Bridgnorth, Gilbert Bradley, *Ceramics Review*, Christie's, Robert Copeland, Charmaine Cox, Doulton's Ltd., Robin Emmerson (Curator of Ceramics, Norwich Castle Museum), Ann George of Amor Antiques, Miranda Goodby (Museum Curator of the Newcastle under Lyme Museum & Art Gallery), Ronald Govier, Robin Gurnett, Pat Halfpenny (Keeper of Ceramics, City Museum & Art Gallery, Hanley), Andrew Hartley Fine Arts, Ilkley, Dr. J. Hendry, Roderick Jellicoe, Joan Jones (Curator of Minton Museum, Stoke), Jimmy Jones, Sir Leslie Joseph, Kathie & Sydney Kear, Terence A. Lockett (Chairman of the Northern Ceramic Society), Micawber Antiques, Mr. & Mrs. Phillip Miller, John P. Moulton, Museum of London, Archaeology Department, Kathy Niblett (Senior Assistant Keeper of Ceramics, City Museum & Art Gallery, Hanley), Nicholas Pine of Goss Crested China Ltd, Roger Pomfret, Michael Ransom-Witt of Leigh Gallery, Gaye Blake Roberts (Curator of the Wedgwood Museum, Barlaston), Mr. & Mrs. D. Roberts, John Sandon (Director of European Ceramics at Phillips Auction House), Mrs Margaret Sargeant of the Royal Crown Derby Museum, Simon Spero Antiques, Spode Ltd, John Twitchett (Curator of Royal Crown Derby Museum), Venner's Antiques, Victoria & Albert Museum, Trustees of The Wedgwood Museum, and Jack Whyte (Ceramics Department of Bearne's of Torquay).

Contents

CONTENTS

List of Colour Plates

Introduction

Today there are many excellent books available which discuss in great depth the porcelains produced in Britain from the mid-eighteenth century to the present day, some devoted to wares produced by well-known factories, some to the work of individual painters and others to wares of more recent artist or studio potters.

It will doubtless be said 'not another book on English porcelain', but it is in the field of ceramics that opinions are frequently changing, often due to excavations on former factory sites becoming available and there are few books produced on the subject of late which do not contain some errors of attribution due to finds and research taking place whilst the volume is in the course of preparation, often making a 'stop-press' addenda necessary.

John Cushion, the co-author of this new volume, has for the past thirty years lectured on the history and appreciation of decorative ceramics to English speaking groups all over the world, where his audiences invariably include many people to whom he is opening up a new field of interest. The most common question asked following such meetings is: 'Have you written a book which will give us the necessary guidance to the recognition and appreciation of decorative porcelain, especially catering for the beginner?' This volume will certainly fill the need for such a book, aiming to help the newcomer to this field of collecting in every possible way, with the obvious exception of actually handling examples.

The new collector will first have to learn how to decide whether an object is of porcelain, earthenware or stoneware, if the former, then what type of porcelain, hard-paste, soft-paste, bone china or one of the many hybrid materials? What is the manner of decoration, moulded, incised, impressed or hand carved? Is the painting of high temperature colours, enamel colours or transfer printed, are any indicative colours used in the palette and what type of gilt decoration has been used? These and many other aids all help the collector to form an opinion as to when and where the piece in question was made, bearing in mind that some of the most interesting examples are entirely devoid of makers' or other helpful marks, whilst often what appears to be an acceptable mark is not always genuine. Perhaps the best practice for the collector to adopt is to refrain from immediately seeking a mark, but to carefully study every other available clue as to the provenance of the piece in question, study the material, the glaze, the style and manner of decoration and finally having formed an opinion, then to check whether an applied mark of some type will prove the accuracy, or otherwise, of the decision made.

There are many ways in which the collector can pursue his or her interest apart from illustrated books, which at times can be unreliable if published several years ago. There are many local antique societies where the new collector is as much welcomed as the more knowledgeable collector of long standing. Some such societies embrace the study of the entire range of antiques or collectables of more recent times, whilst there are also those where the research and lectures are devoted entirely to ceramics in general or those of a particular factory, type or country, such as The Oriental Ceramic Society, The Spode Society, or The Friends of Blue, whose members are concerned only with British ceramic wares decorated with underglaze blue transfer prints. Many other groups and societies are listed later in this volume.

Handling pieces can prove difficult, but it is unfortunately only through close examination that it is possible to appreciate the differences between the various materials. Ideally one should aim to acquire a modest collection, which includes at least one example of each ceramic material, in order to train the eye, as the true collector is not too concerned with perfect pieces, providing they are not over-priced!

There are of course the many auction houses and antique fairs, especially those devoted entirely to the sale of ceramics, where one can handle, with great care, the items to be sold or on offer; remember the knowledgeable antique dealer will always welcome a potential new customer and readily give valuable advice.

Materials and Techniques

Following excavations over recent years on the sites of Ding kilns, in the province of Hebei, China, it has been proved that the Chinese potter was using china clay and china stone to produce a high quality white porcellaneous ware, of the so-called 'Samarra' type, from at least the ninth century. The great advantage of the hard-paste porcelain body was that it could be glazed with the feldspathic china stone (*petuntse*), enabling the body, any underglaze decoration and the glaze itself, to be fired in a single kiln firing.

The various European spellings of the word 'porcelain' are all thought to be derived from the word 'porcella', a Portuguese word meaning a cowrie shell, the texture of which was likened to this new and exciting material, first imported to Europe by the trading vessels of the Portuguese from around the middle of the sixteenth century. One of the most admired features of porcelain is that of translucency, which is normally a simple, but not entirely reliable, method of deciding whether a ceramic object is of a form of porcelain, or earthenware or stoneware, the latter two usually being quite opaque. This test can be a dangerous guide if an object is excessively thick, or underfired, which is often the case with late Bow, which at times is seen to be quite opaque if held to a transmitted light.

The Chinese potters guarded their secret of the making of a hard-paste porcelain so closely that it was 1710 before a somewhat similar hard-paste porcelain was produced at Meissen, primarily to serve the court of Augustus II, the Elector of Saxony and King of Poland, at Dresden, a factory that was to dominate the styles of most European porcelain during the entire baroque period.

There were minor productions of imitation, or soft-paste porcelains, made in both Italy and France during the sixteenth and seventeenth centuries, usually the work of potters who were normally employed in the production of tin glazed earthenwares (*maiolica* or *faience*). The very rare 'Medici' porcelain was made in Florence between 1575 and 1587; it was a very glassy body containing a small proportion of china clay from Vicenza, usually decorated in underglaze blue with an occasional purple derived from manganese. Only about sixty examples of these rare museum pieces have been recorded.

In 1673 a patent was granted to Louis Poterat in Rouen for the manufacture of a form of porcelain, but wares attributed to this potter are extremely rare and usually subject to differences of opinion among the specialists and they cannot be regarded as an important development towards the making of true porcelain. Further various forms of artificial or soft-paste porcelain were made in France from the late seventeenth century, first at St. Cloud and later at Chantilly and Mennecy, but it was from about 1745 that the really beautiful French soft-paste was made at Vincennes, a production that was moved to the new building at Sèvres in 1756, where their wares excelled those of Meissen in the new and fashionable rococo styles.

Whilst it is not the intention of the authors to endeavour to teach the reader the art of practical potting, knowing how the piece of porcelain received its shape often helps to decide the place of manufacture. The most common method, which is so often seen being demonstrated is 'throwing' on a potter's wheel, a technique dating back to ancient Egypt, where the ball of moist, malleable clay is centralised on the wheel-head with wet hands, which are then used to hollow out and draw up the required walls of clay, so easy to the skilled potter, but so frustrating to the learner. If repetitive shapes are desired, templates of wood or metal are used as a guide. The vulnerable soft clay form is then removed from the wetted wheel-head by cutting by means of a 'cheese-wire', before being slid to an adjacent shelf to partially dry, when it is again centred upside-down on the wheel to have the surplus clay removed from the base with the aid of a turning tool, which is also sometimes used to pare away the marks made by the potter's fingers during 'throwing'. It is at this stage that any additional claywork in the form of decoration, handles or spouts must be added to achieve uniform shrinkage. It must be remembered that during the initial firing all types of ceramic bodies shrink approximately one-sixth to one-seventh, some, such as that used at Belleek, as much as twenty-five percent, enabling them to often produce a so-called 'eggshell' porcelain.

In the industry today many of the simple forms required for domestic wares are produced almost entirely by machine. It is obvious that only shapes in the round can be produced by the potter with the aid of a wheel, although of course after 'throwing' the clay can, if wished, be distorted by hand to an irregular form, but normally if an oval, or other shape, is required then a mould is used. Having decided the design, a master-model of the required article is produced, usually in clay. This master-model has of course to be oversize, bearing in mind the question of shrinkage, already mentioned. From this master model earthenware or plaster-of-Paris moulds are made, into which the prepared sheets of clay or clay slip are pressed or poured.

The main two methods of manufacture are press moulding or slip casting. In the case of the latter, as used at the Chelsea factory, the clay is watered down to a thick cream or batter consistency, which is then poured into the hollow plaster mould, which in absorbing the water in which the particles of clay are suspended, builds up a thin layer of clay on the inside wall of the mould, when by experience the potter knows a wall of clay of adequate thickness is adhering to the inside of the mould, the surplus slip is poured off and within a short period the mould can be opened and the cast carefully removed.

Bow usually preferred to use the same method favoured by the early German factories, that of press moulding, where the clay can best be compared to thin sheets of dough, which is then pressed by hand into the walls of the mould, a technique which usually results in the finished wares being much heavier and subject to 'fire-cracks' due to the irregular thickness of the walls of clay.

In both processes figures would almost certainly call for several separate moulds, made from sections of the master model, such as heads, torso, arms,

Those of us who have attempted to form a pot on a rotating wheel can well appreciate the skill of the professional thrower who, with the aid of gauges and profiles was able to produce large numbers of almost identically shaped wares within a short period, usually under far from ideal conditions
Courtesy the Wedgwood Museum Trustees, Barlaston, Stoke-on-Trent

After a wheel-made pot had been thrown it was often attached to a lathe, which enabled the potter to make refinements to the surface and the foot rim by the use of metal tools, with the lady assistant controlling the turning of the lathe to his instructions
Courtesy the Wedgwood Museum Trustees, Barlaston, Stoke-on-Trent

and legs. It is only the simple Staffordshire 'flat-back' figures of the nineteenth century which can at times be produced from a simple two-piece mould. Any seam marks left by the mould joints were usually removed from the finer wares with the aid of a piece of wet leather.

Assuming all the necessary clay work has been completed the ware is now ready for firing. Hard-paste porcelain, as the name implies, is a very hard brittle material, fired in the region of 1300°C and if chipped can be seen to have a conchoidal, or glassy, appearance. It was the practice of the Oriental potter to fire the body and the glaze of a hard-paste porcelain in a single kiln firing, whereas the majority of European potters such as the German, some Italian and later French, preferred to first fire the body to a 'biscuit' at a lower temperature, then add the glaze and again fire to the full 1300-1400°C. The glaze on a hard-paste porcelain is very hard and scratches or wear through the use of cutlery is rarely seen on table wares. On figures the tight-fitting glaze is seen to advantage, leaving the underlying modelling clear and crisp, especially noticeable on the hands and features. If

One of the worst health hazards encountered by the potters was lead poisoning, contracted by those engaged in the application of the liquid glaze to the biscuited wares. Not until the beginning of this century was the high lead content of the glaze eliminated through the use of compounds of boron, and in consequence the highly skilled dipper invariably suffered. Here the dipper and his assistant are applying the glaze to teapots previously decorated with an underglaze transfer. The opaque glaze clarifies during the firing

cracked, the area surrounding the damage usually remains clean and does not absorb impurities and so discolour, as is often the case with a soft-paste. It is also rare for the glaze on a hard-paste porcelain to 'craze' or 'crackle', a technical fault seen in the form of a fine mesh of cracks. There are exceptions, when the Chinese potter, dating from the Song dynasty, deliberately applied an ill-fitting glaze to produce a 'crackle' to give the appearance of antiquity.

As we will learn, it was not until 1768 that an English potter, William Cookworthy, established a factory at Plymouth, Devon, for the manufacture of a hard-paste porcelain, moving to Bristol in 1770, where Richard Champion was to continue the production until 1781, when he sold the remaining years of his patent to a group of Staffordshire potters, who formed the New Hall factory. When the patent finally expired in 1796, other English potters are now known to have produced various hybrid hard-paste porcelain bodies which included china clay and china stone.

Unlike hard-paste porcelain, there is a wide variety of artificial, or soft-paste, ceramic bodies, some including various proportions of bone, others of soapstone or steatite, whilst Chelsea, Derby and Longton Hall favoured a percentage of frit (a form of powdered glass). The ingredients used by the known English factories were rarely consistent, changes were constantly taking place in their endeavours to improve their wares and minimise kiln losses. Use was often made of much of the hard-paste Oriental porcelains imported by the East India Company, which were found to be broken on arrival or by accident later. Several grinding mills were located around London to recycle this material for use by various factories.

During the initial 'biscuit' firing the wares are placed in circular refractory clay saggars, recently aptly described by Prof. Alan Smith as the shape of a Victorian hat-box, which are then stacked high within the oven, the inner chamber of the kiln, and then cemented together with clay to prevent smoke and other impurities coming into direct contact with the porcelain during the firing.

Whilst a hard-paste porcelain could be used without a glaze, due to the biscuit being non-porous, a glaze was very necessary to most of English wares of a soft-paste, except perhaps at Derby, where from about 1770 figures and groups were left unglazed to appear as miniature statuary. This is also the case with the nineteenth century Parian wares of Spode, Minton and several other manufacturers. The body of a soft-paste porcelain, even after firing to between 1050°C and 1150°C, is still slightly porous and easily stained, so a thin layer of liquid glass, or glaze, is applied, mostly by dipping into the solution, which on application looks like white emulsion paint, but on being fired clarifies to a colourless glaze. During this 'glost-firing' precautions have to be taken against the wares touching each other or coming into contact with the base or inner walls of the saggar. Glaze is either removed from likely areas of contact or various gadgets in the way of kiln furniture are used to support the wares in a minimal manner, such as the 'knife-edge' of triangular rods of fired clay, or pin-like points of spurs or stilts. Derby frequently used small pads of clay under the base, resulting in three or more small blemishes or 'pad-marks'.

It is during these two initial firings that the production is most prone to kiln losses in the form of 'wasters', or 'shards', when the wares often 'slumped' or cracked. Such losses were usually broken and dumped at a nearby tip. It is these tips, which today are at times becoming available through rebuilding, that are frequently providing the keen researcher with clear evidence as to just what type of wares a factory was producing (*see* Vauxhall p.103). It is rare to find such 'wasters' with decoration, other than underglaze blue, as most wares safely survive the 'muffle-kiln' when enamel colours or on-glaze prints are being fired. The new student is cautioned that only wasters that have been discarded through manufacturing faults can be regarded as positive evidence as fragments of finished wares of other factories or countries have frequently been found on sites.

Today there are many collectors of 'blue-and-white', where the painted or printed decoration is sandwiched between the body and the protective glaze, a form of decoration used initially by the Chinese potter from about 1320AD, when they discovered the metallic oxide of cobalt could withstand the high firing temperature of hard-paste. The decoration of English wares by this method is well covered by Dr. Bernard Watney in his book on *English Blue and White Porcelain of the 18th Century* (Faber & Faber, London, Revised Edition, 1973).

Similar engraved copper plates used for printing on the biscuit in underglaze blue could be used for transferring designs in enamel colour on to the fired

The placing of the wares in the bottle oven ready for the firing, was a very skilled and dangerous task. The porcelain to be biscuited or glazed was placed in a saggar, a container made from refractory clay, with as many as 2,000 methodically placed under the direction of the cod placer, using a ladder, known as an 'oss, or horse, into piles or bungs, some as high as sixteen feet. When filled, the wicket or clammins (doorway), was sealed with firebricks, after which the coal in each fire-mouth was lit Courtesy the Wedgwood Museum Trustees, Barlaston, Stoke-on-Trent

The highest paid employee and almost certainly the most important in the production was the fireman, as bad firing could result in the loss of the contents of as many as 2,000 saggars. First he would kindle the coal in the fire-mouths, then light and build up to the required temperature aided by various temperature measuring devices and dampers, the complete firing cycle requiring his attention for as long as seventy-two hours, during which an average sized biscuit firing would use as much as twelve tons of coal. Even a highly skilled fireman could not sometimes avoid a loss of as much as thirty per cent. Such primitive methods of firing were only slowly replaced by the use of tunnel kilns from about 1950 Courtesy the Wedgwwod Museum Trustees, Barlaston, Stoke-on-Trent

glaze. These lower fired enamel colours were fired in a muffle-kiln at temperatures ranging from 700°C – 800°C and frequently used to provide easy to follow guidelines for unskilled decorators, who merely applied further enamel decoration by brush; note for example how frequently the flower sprays applied at intervals on the rims of plates are identical in outline.

Not all enamel decoration was so easily applied and in the following chapters the reader will learn of talented porcelain painters whose work is only found on some of the most sought after wares of today. Regrettably present-day porcelain manufacture offers less opportunities for the skilled ceramic decorator, although there are a few highly qualified ceramic artists, most of whom are working independently on private commissions.

The last stage in the decoration of porcelain is that of applying gilding, seen at its best on the French eighteenth century wares of Vincennes and Sèvres. The earliest form of gilding was composed of gold powder or gold leaf, ground up in honey prior to being painted on to the glazed wares and then fired at approximately 600°C. This form of gilding, which was very durable, was soft in tone and could be applied in sufficient depth to permit tooling and chasing. There were a few early factories that used unfired gold leaf, but this was a form of decoration which usually had a fairly short life and soon wore away. After firing it was necessary to burnish the gilding, which now had a dull metallic appearance, with a bloodstone or agate to bring about the admired brilliance. In about 1790 the honey was replaced with mercury, producing a mixture which was similarly painted on to the glaze and fired. This form of gilding when burnished has a much brassier appearance and often shows a distinct copper coloured tint.

The contrast of the dull and burnished gilding was often used very effectively on expensive nineteenth century wares, where the design on the rims of plates had previously been etched with acid, leaving part of the design in relief. In consequence the gilding in the slightly sunken areas remained matt in contrast to the burnished gilding on the slightly higher ornamentation.

The collector seeking old wares should avoid the 'bright-gold' which was introduced about 1875, this gilding, often seen on late Staffordshire figures, did not require burnishing and was soon adopted by firms wishing to produce inexpensive wares, perhaps best described as 'fairground' gilding.

During the eighteenth century gilding was much favoured by 'outside decorators' such as James Giles, who was able to acquire from the Worcester factory either white glazed wares or pieces to which only some underglaze blue ground colour had been applied. Giles's gilding on these pieces is often much superior to that applied at the Worcester factory.

The potters involved with the industrially made ceramics today have few of the arduous labours of their predecessors, as a machine has been invented for almost every stage in the manufacture of modern ceramics, with the exception of some ornamental wares and figures.

The former laborious task of preparing the liquid clay (slip) from the various ingredients is today carried out by machines and stored in large containers (arks), in readiness for either producing clay for the various shape forming machines or for pouring into plaster moulds. The old process of making hollow wares by roughly lining a mould with clay and then operating a simple arm to bring down a profile to shape the interior and remove surplus clay, called 'jollying' has today been replaced by a machine which completes this entire stage of manufacture in one operation, even to partially drying the cast and automatically removing it to have the edges smoothed (fettled).

A similar automatic process, for the making of flatwares (plates, etc.) called

From around the middle of the 18th century decoration of ceramic wares by means of transfer printing became increasingly popular. Here the operator is applying pressure by means of flannel attached to the roller, to the paper tissue which has been carefully laid upon a heated copper plate into which the required design has been engraved, after the engraving has been filled with the necessary colour. This action transfers the design to the tissue, which is then soaked off and after drying is ready to apply to the ware, either before or after glazing, depending whether the colour is underglaze or enamel
Courtesy the Wedgwood Museum Trustees, Barlaston, Stoke-on-Trent

'jiggering' is also in use today, in which a thin slab of clay is accurately placed on a moulded form mounted on a turntable, the clay is then 'sandwiched' by the lowering of a metal profile, which shapes the reverse.

Although no machine has as yet been invented to replace the talents of the ceramic painter, the application of colour prints has progressed immensely since the multicoloured prints were first introduced at the end of the nineteenth century, using lithographic stones. Today four-colour prints can be produced with the use of an off-set stainless steel screen and then applied to the glazed ware with a silicone pad, in a single print. A further computer controlled machine enables an item, such as a mug, to be decorated with a range of five separate quick-drying thermoplastic colours, which are superimposed one upon the other, whilst a new machine now under development will enable a full colour design to be directly printed on to the glaze, by means of a silicone pad in a single operation.

An attractive, and easily understood, process can be seen today at the Wedgwood Visitor Centre, where 'Water Slide-on Printing' is demonstrated. The coloured image of up to sixteen colours is produced by lithography or silk-screen printing and applied on to the gummed side of a special paper, then coated with a thin plastic film. After being soaked with water, the print, or decal, is skilfully slid on to the warm glazed pot by hand, and water, air and wrinkles smoothed out with a rubber tool in readiness for firing. Today there is even a machine for applying the lines or bands of colour or gilt used as decoration to wares of any shape, not only circular.

In Stoke alone half the people employed in potting towards the end of the 19th century were women, who were very poorly paid. Many of these young girls, as pictured, were apprentices, seen here applying the decoration under the watchful eye of a supervisor, in what appears to be a far from comfortable workshop

Courtesy the Wedgwood Museum Trustees, Barlaston, Stoke-on-Trent

The early coal-fired bottle kilns were eventually replaced by electric, gas or oil-fired tunnel kilns, as first used by Josiah Wedgwood & Co. Ltd. in their new factory at Barlaston in 1940. In 1955 a new, yet simple, type of intermittent kiln was also introduced, called a Top Hat Kiln, where a bottomless box-like oven was lowered over the wares to be fired, which were stacked in readiness on a fixed base, thus eliminating the risk of movement and 'toppling' during firing.

Today in some tunnel kilns the refractory material, lining the kiln, has been replaced with a ceramic fibre, which can be more quickly heated and therefore more economic in fuel consumption, enabling bone china to be biscuited from start to finish in two hours. A replacement for the old type 'muffle' kiln has also been introduced in which the wares to be decorated are simply placed on a wire mesh belt to move them through the kiln, requiring only thirty minutes to produce the completed articles.

Regretfully the production of industrially produced porcelains today calls for very few skilled personnel, with the obvious exception of designers and modellers, but only by the acceptance of these necessary changes, can the British industry hope to compete with increasingly fierce competition.

FURTHER READING:
Chandler, Maurice, *Ceramics in the Modern World,* Aldus Books Ltd, 1967.
French, Neal, *Industrial Ceramics: Table-ware,* Oxford University Press, 1972.
Wolliscroft, Terence, *Bottle Ovens,* Gladstone Pottery Museum, 1979.
Niblett, Kathy, *Dynamic Design, The British Pottery Industry 1940-1990, Exhibition,* City Museum & Art Gallery, Stoke-on-Trent, 1990.

21

Chapter 1

British Porcelain Factories
from the mid - late 18th Century

THE POMONA POTWORKS

Newcastle under Lyme, c.1744-c.1754

This pottery, so named after a later inn built on the site, was originally in the hands of Samuel Bell Junior, who was producing earthenware and red stoneware from *c.*1724. He died in 1744, and his brother John, who was in business in London, came into possession of the factory, but by 1746, it is known to have been in the hands of a Mr. William Steers, from Hoxton in Middlesex. William Steers had taken out a patent on the 29th October 1744, for producing a 'Transparent earthenware in imitation of China ware after a method entirely new'. It seems, however, that he encountered difficulties with his production, and by June 1748, we know that he had returned to Hoxton, leaving the business in the hands of Joseph Wilson, whom it is thought, may have been previously concerned with the Limehouse Factory in London. He may well have seen John Bell's advertisement in London, for the letting of the house and pottery at 'Newcastle-under-Lime', in 1746, which was at that time in the possession of Mr. Steers.

It was not until 1970, when Mr. Paul Bemrose, Curator of the Newcastle Museum, with members of his staff, were excavating on the old site in Lower Street, that they discovered the foundations of two kilns, and some 2,000 porcelain wasters. Among the wasters was a fragmented bowl with the underglaze inscription '25th July 1746', as illustrated; it is possible that this date may have been applied to commemorate the first day's firing, which was unfortunately doomed to failure, for most of the wasters seem to have come from only one or two unsuccessful kiln firings.

The porcelain body was of the 'frit' or 'glassy' type, which seems to have been unstable. Sherds also showed that there was much bubbling of the glaze. Press

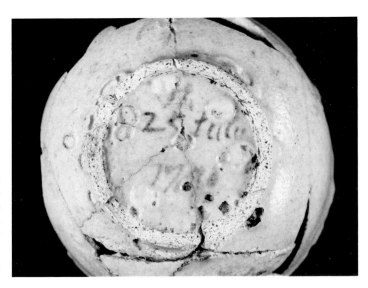

An important documentary bowl found on the Pomona Works site, where William Steers was endeavouring to produce a soft-paste porcelain, c.1744-7. The inscription on the base in underglaze blue reads '25th July 1746', the earliest known dated piece of English porcelain using underglaze blue. H. 48cm.

Courtesy Newcastle under Lyme Museum
& Art Gallery

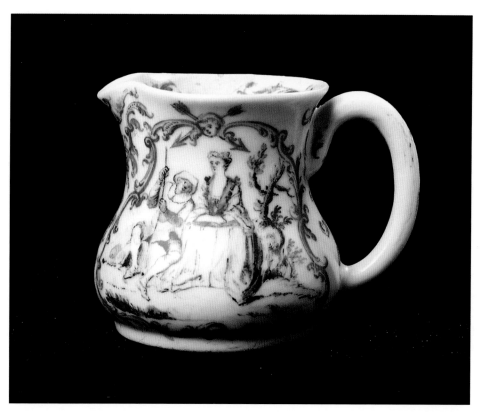

Small cream jug, thickly potted hybrid hard-paste porcelain, painted in enamel colours. Over thirty pieces have now been recorded, but no firm attribution has as yet been decided upon. Mark, 'A' incised. H. 5.7cm.
Courtesy The Victoria & Albert Museum

A large and impressive tureen in the Victoria & Albert Museum on lion mask and paw feet, a typical feature of the Limehouse factory, c.1745-8, decorated in underglaze blue with excellent painted scenes depicting a harbour scene, an ostrich hunt and a mythological group. H. 18.7cm.
Courtesy The Victoria & Albert Museum

moulded, cast, and thrown and turned wares were found, mostly in typical Staffordshire shapes, but in a few exceptions following the forms of Meissen. Decoration was found in underglaze blue, and mainly falling into two groups, one using a peony motif, and the other showing a Chinese pavilion set on an island, with rocks and a willow tree. Many sherds of useful wares were found, including tea wares, bowls, jugs, tankards, pickle trays, mustard pots and spittoons.

It is problematical whether or not Joseph Wilson was producing porcelain wares after the departure of William Steers, or whether after the disastrous kiln failures it was decided to abandon the project. Certainly no perfect porcelain wares have been definitely assigned to this factory, although during the excavations on the Pomona site a lid of a tea jar in the form of a boy's head was sighted, but proved impossible to retrieve. This tea jar is now thought to have been made at the Limehouse factory, under which it is illustrated, despite the fact that no matching sherds were recovered on the recently excavated Limehouse site. There does, however, seem to have been a link between the two factories. A porcelain cup moulded with a prunus design, and with a crabstock handle, on show in the Godden reference collection at the Hanley Museum, appears to closely resemble a sherd from the Newcastle site, in stoneware, and similar fragments of handles of this crabstock type in porcelain, have been discovered at Limehouse. Also the badly fired figure of a hound on a square base, possibly used as a seal, was discovered at Limehouse, and a similar sherd, but again of stoneware, was found on the Pomona site.

Two soft-paste porcelain jugs decorated in underglaze blue painting, reconstructed from fragments excavated on the site of William Steers factory at Newcastle under Lyme, c.1744-7. This site is referred to today as the Pomona Works. H. 12.7cm and 14cm.
Courtesy Newcastle under Lyme Museum & Art Gallery

(Above) A soft-paste porcelain spittoon and mug decorated with underglaze blue painting, reconstructed from fragments excavated on the site of the Pomona Works, Newcastle under Lyme. Made by William Steers, c.1744-7. H. 9.8cm and 13.4cm.

Courtesy Newcastle under Lyme Museum & Art Gallery

(Left) Soft-paste porcelain teapot decorated in underglaze blue painting, made up of fragments excavated on the site of the Pomona Works, Newcastle under Lyme, c.1970. Made by William Steers, c.1744-7. H. 12.1cm.

Courtesy Newcastle under Lyme Museum & Art Gallery

Two examples of translucent soft-paste porcelain, decorated in the manner of Whieldon-type earthenware with high temperature oxides in blue, brown and green. Excavated on the Pomona Works site and attributed to William Steers, c.1744-7. H. 7.8cm and 10.9cm.

Courtesy Newcastle under Lyme Museum & Art Gallery

Although not a commercial success, there seems little doubt that this early attempt to produce a soft-paste porcelain, must at present rank as the first step to produce such wares in Staffordshire.

The wasters of this factory are on display at both the Newcastle under Lyme and the Hanley Museums.

FURTHER READING:
Bemrose, Paul, 'The Pomona Potworks, Newcastle, Staffs.', *The English Ceramic Circle Transactions,* Vol. 9, Part 1, 1973.
Mountford, Arnold, *Staffordshire Porcelain,* (Ed. G. Godden), Chapter 2, Granada Publishing, 1983.
Barker, David, and Halfpenny, Pat, *Unearthing Staffordshire,* City of Stoke-on-Trent Museum & Art Gallery, 1990. Catalogue of an exhibition sponsored by Christie's.

'A' MARKED WARES
1740s?

With the current wave of new discoveries in the ceramic field, evidence resulting in the sure attribution of this mysterious class of wares could well come to light between the writing and the publishing of this book.

This so termed 'A' marked group, which would appear to have been made during the 1740s, is based on the fact that they are decorated in polychrome enamel painting taken from engravings published in London at that time, which tends to rule out the possibility that they are Italian, which in general appearance they might well be.

The limited number of pieces bearing the as yet unaccountable capital 'A' in either blue enamel or incised, are of a hybrid hard-paste and so far various researchers have suggested three possibilities: Scottish, with the 'A' for the Duke of Argyll as being a possible patron, Chelsea, made by a group of workers who seceded from Sprimont's factory or Italian.

This interesting group was commented on at an English Ceramic Circle meeting as long ago as 1937, attended by many ceramic researchers, many of whom are no longer with us, including the late Arthur Lane, later the Keeper of the Ceramics Department of the Victoria & Albert Museum, who had a special interest in Italian wares and wrote the Faber Monograph on Italian porcelain. He favoured that country as a possible source on the grounds of the similarity of the material and the manner in which the mark was applied, an opinion shared much later by one of the foremost experts on European porcelain today, whose opinions are constantly being sought. The majority argued against the Italian attribution due to one example decorated after an engraving showing children playing a game of cricket, after a work by the French engraver Hubert François Gravelot, who was working in London between 1733 and 1745, where his work as a draughtsman-illustrator was greatly admired.

This French engraver seemed to favour showing children at play and his work to help decorate the supper rooms at the Vauxhall Pleasure Garden illustrates 'Children building houses with cards'.

The subject of Gravelot's engravings is discussed in full detail by R.J. Charleston and J.V. Mallet in their paper read to the English Ceramic Circle in March, 1970, when they made out a very good case for giving this class, which at the time of their paper numbered twenty-eight examples, as being English.

FURTHER READING:
Charleston, R.J., and Mallet, J.V.C., 'A Problematic Group of Eighteenth Century Porcelains', *E.C.C. Transactions,* Vol. 8, Part 1, 1971.

LIMEHOUSE
London, c.1745-1748

The history of this factory is somewhat fragmentary and speculative, and has been under discussion among learned researchers for many years. Archaeological excavations have been eagerly awaited, the possible site, for even this seems to have been uncertain, has been uncovered, and at last the secrets of at least some of the wares have been revealed.

The site we are discussing is at number 20 Fore Street, now renamed Dunbar Wharf 110-116 Narrow Street, Limehouse, London, and it is due to the redevelopment of the docklands area, that in March 1990 the site was cleared, and the Museum of London archaeologists, with the kind permission of the developers, were allowed to move in.

We know that the site was occupied by Joseph Wilson & Co., who arrived there between July 1744 and March 1745, and left between June 1747 and August 1748. This information was taken from Land Tax Returns, which did not mention that the site was a pottery. The first mention of a factory on the site, is taken from a book by John Ward writen in 1843, *The Borough of Stoke-on-Trent,* in which a letter is quoted dated 28th December 1745, addressed to a William Tams, believed to be from Staffordshire, and sent to him at the Potwork in Fore Street, 'night Duke Store [Shore] in Limehouse, London'. On 22nd September 1746, we know from the *Daily Advertiser,* that pot-painters were wanted to work at the 'Pot Works at Limehouse'. We also know from another advertisement dated 4th October 1746 that a Mr. Wilson was at the pottery, for he was advertising for '. . . Pot, Fan, or Box Painters, wanting employment'. By 1st of January 1747 we know that the factory was in production, because of an advertisement in the same paper 'To the Dealers in China and Earthenware. The Proprietors of the Limehouse Ware give notice, that they now have a large assortment at their Manufactory, near Dick Store [Duke Shore] in Limehouse'. By 20th June 1747, they were advertising, 'The new invented Limehouse Ware. . .being now greatly improved. . .', and offering '. . .all reasonable

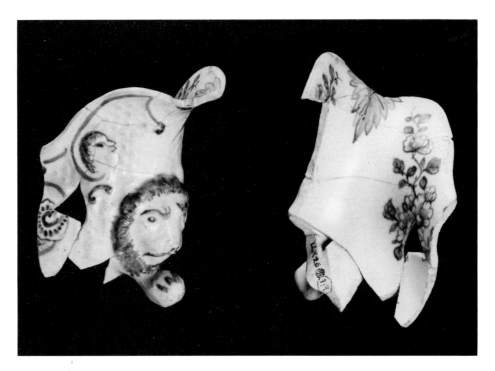

*Two wasters from the site
of the Limehouse factory,
c.1745-8, showing a lion
mask and paw from part of
a sauce boat. Note the
painted human head. The
sherd on the right shows the
blue painted flowers on the
interior*
Courtesy the Museum
of London

*This sauce boat from the
factory at Limehouse,
c.1745-8, showing the lion
mask and paw feet is
identical to the sherds found
during the excavations on the
site, as illustrated above*
Courtesy Colonial
Williamsburg Foundation

encouragement...' to Dealers. On 11th November 1747 it seems that they had been successful with their advertisement, for again they were advertising 'said Ware is to be met with at the Principal Dealers in China and Glass, both in Town and Country'. However, by 13th May 1748, once again from the *Daily Advertiser,* the notice appeared '...now selling off cheap at Mr. Underwood's, the upper end of Pall Mall...the Price being greatly reduced. All the Goods in Trade of the Limehouse Manufactory, commonly called English China, consisting of great variety of Sauce-boats. Tea-Pots etc...' This obviously heralded the closure of the factory. We know for certain, that in the Land Tax Assessment of 5th August 1748, Joseph Wilson & Co. were no longer in Limehouse.

The potters concerned are a little difficult to establish. We know from the

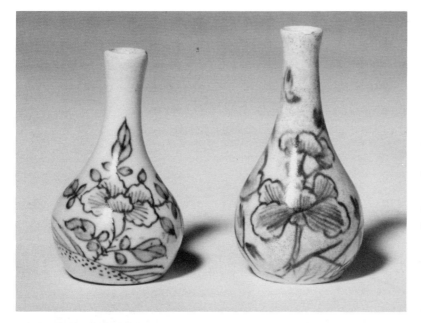

A pair of miniature pear shaped bottles from the Limehouse factory, c.1745-8. The flowering plant on the vase on the left is painted in blue with leaves in a pale blue wash. H. 6cm. The vase on the right is painted in blue with a design of flowers coming from a band of grasses. H. 6.5cm.
Formerly Gilbert Bradley Collection

A cream boat from the Limehouse factory, c.1745-8, with a moulded body and painted in blue with a European scene of a gentleman sitting beneath a tree with a large house in the background
Courtesy Simon Spero Antiques

A flared beaker vase from the Limehouse factory, c.1745-8, painted in blue with an oriental lady with a feather in her hat, holding a fan and standing against a fence with flowering shrubs. On the reverse is a baluster vase filled with flowers. H. 11cm.
Formerly Gilbert Bradley Collection

A shell shaped pickle dish painted in underglaze blue with a border of entwined ribbons which is often a feature of the Limehouse factory, c.1745-8. H. 10cm.
Courtesy Phillips, London

A pair of pickle dishes attributed to the Limehouse factory, c.1745-8. The dish on the left painted in underglaze blue with a house and grasses behind which appear two hills; it has a border of ribbons and feathers, which is a typical decorative feature of this factory, and on the reverse are two trailing branches. W. 10.5cm.

The dish on the right has a similar border and a central motif of a vase containing two feathers standing against a scroll, another feature typical of this factory; the reverse has two trailing branches. W. 9.6cm.

Most of these wares have very little translucency, which may be due to the slightly opaque glaze, which at times contained a small percentage of tin oxide.

Pickle dishes appear to have been made in several sizes and a variety of shapes

Formerly Gilbert Bradley Collection

research of Dr. Bernard Watney, that the site had been occupied by Joseph Wilson & Co., it is the '& Co.', which still remains in doubt. The movements of potters are of great interest to historians, and we note that our great correspondent, Dr. Pococke, in a letter to his mother, dated 14th July 1750, wrote that in '...Newcastle-on-Lime [Newcastle under Lyme]...There are some few Potters here and one I visited whom I saw at Limehouse, who promised to make the best china ware, but disagreed with his Employers...'. Dr. Pococke also wrote in November 1750, of the Bristol porcelain works having been founded by '...one of the principal manufacturers at Limehouse which failed'. We know that the founders of the Bristol Porcelain Factory were Benjamin Lund and William Miller, and of the two, Benjamin Lund seems more likely to have been the person in question. Lund was a Quaker and copper merchant who, in March 1749 had been granted a licence to mine soap-rock in Cornwall. William Miller was a banker, and possibly the financial backer for the concern.

Another potter who is considered for the role of '& Co.', is William Ball. A William Ball is known from the Land Tax Assessments discovered by Mrs. Elizabeth Adams, to have been in the district from 1745 to 1746, and according to Dr. Watney, he lived in 46 Fore Street Limehouse, near to the pottery from 1747 to 1748. It is possible that he may be the same William Ball who was later known to be managing the porcelain factory of William Reid & Co. (1755-61) in Liverpool; he was certainly known to have been employed there in 1761 when the firm went bankrupt.

Three pickle dishes from the Limehouse factory, c.1745-8. The dish on the left is one of three sizes, painted in blue. L. 10cm. The centre dish has incised veins on the leaf shape with the flowers painted in blue. L. 12cm. The dish on the right, also painted in blue, shows speckling due to imperfections. L. 6.7cm.
Courtesy Simon Spero Antiques

Three pickle dishes from the Limehouse factory, c.1745-8. The central dish is of leaf shape with incised veins and painted in blue with a flowering branch against a background of birds in flight. It has six pad feet. W. 10cm.
   The pair of dishes on either side are painted in blue with flowering plants amidst grasses. W. 7.5cm.
Formerly Gilbert Bradley Collection

At the time of writing, we have a certain knowledge of the production of this early factory from sherds discovered on the site. We know that sauce boats were produced, some with distinctive lion mask and paw feet, as illustrated. Pickle trays were made, a comma-shaped foot on a part-base was found, handles, including a crabstock handle, which appears to match a prunus cup, and two finely potted tea bowls. The bases of two dry mustard pots were found, and also the figure of a hound seated on a small square base, possibly for use as a seal.

Designs in blue and white include an interesting motif of a stylised peacock feather bound by a ribbon, also patterns including the Chinese precious objects, and European designs, including a group of houses.

A pair of tea canisters in the shape of a boy's head painted in underglaze blue, c.1746. These may be a product of the factory at Limehouse, but there is a possibility that they could have been made at the Pomona factory in Newcastle under Lyme; they are, however, far superior to the wasters so far discovered on the site of this factory and until definite evidence becomes available they remain a mystery. H. 13.4cm.

Courtesy Colonial Williamsburg Foundation

It is believed that polychrome decoration was also used at this factory, in a limited amount, but it is rare to find coloured wasters on sites, as having survived the earlier high temperatures there would have been less danger of failure in the enamelling kilns.

At a seminar held at the museum of London in March 1991, entitled 'The Limehouse Link: Archaeology & Porcelain', Mavis Bimson of the British Museum Research Laboratory, disclosed that after analysis of samples of the sherds, she had evidence that two types of porcelain had been made at the factory. It has been suggested by John Potter a member of the Morley College Ceramic Circle, who has been involved with the Limehouse porcelain factory research from prior to the excavation, that one of the bodies produced, may well have been of a proto-porcelain type, and probably experimental.

Known wares are very rare, even in museums, and may still occasionally be wrongly exhibited as the wares of Messrs. Reid & Co. of Liverpool, to which they had been formerly attributed.

It was suggested by Lawrence Pontin, lately Senior Archaeologist, Department of Greater London Archaeology, Museum of London, that one of the reasons for the closure of this early factory, was the rising of the waters of the Thames, which finally made the kilns unusable.

FURTHER READING:

Valpy, Nancy, 'Extracts from London Newspapers', *English Ceramic Circle Transactions,* Vol. 11, Part 3, 1983.

Watney, Dr. Bernard, 'Limehouse in the Limelight', *Antique Collecting,* September, 1983; 'A Report on Recent Excavations on London Porcelain Sites', *English Ceramic Circle Transactions,* Vol. 14, Part 1, 1990.

Latham, J.P., 'Some thoughts on Limehouse and other early English Factories', *English Ceramic Circle Transactions,* Vol. 13, Part 1, 1987; 'Limehouse Inhabitants 1744-1749', *English Ceramic Circle Transactions,* Vol. 13, Part 2, 1988.

Godden, Geoffrey, A., *Encyclopaedia of British Porcelain Manufacturers,* Barrie & Jenkins, London, 1988.

Spero, Simon, 'Pomona-related ware', *Collectors' Guide,* May 1989.

CHELSEA

1745-c.1770

As eighteenth century Meissen porcelain is to Germany, so the wares of the London factory in Chelsea are to England and today the porcelain of both these factories is hard to find and generally very expensive. They were sought at the time of production as objects of beauty, prior to their becoming collectable as antiques and were included in such famous eighteenth century collections as that of Horace Walpole at Strawberry Hill.

The history and knowledge of the porcelains produced at Chelsea between about 1745 and 1769 is a comparatively easy study compared with some of the later English factories. As early as March, 1745, the *London Advertiser* was praising the quality of 'the China made at Chelsea', which at the time was being produced in insufficient quantities to meet the demand. From the beginning Chelsea porcelains showed very little originality in style, owing a great deal to the earlier exports from both China and Japan and the baroque fashions of Meissen, changing in about 1756-8 to the new rococo styles popularised by Sèvres.

The creator of the Chelsea concern was Nicholas Sprimont, a silversmith born at Liège in 1716 and seemingly pursuing his craft in London as early as 1739, registering his mark at Goldsmiths' Hall in 1743 and continuing as a goldsmith until about 1747, by which time he must have felt confident that his new venture into the manufacture of porcelain was to flourish.

Sprimont's Chelsea China Manufactory was certainly in production by 1745, the date sometimes incised into the base of one of his early models, the so-called 'goat and bee' jugs. These and other early examples made c.1745-9 are referred to as being of the 'incised triangle period', and often show a small triangle scratched into the clay whilst it is still in a moist condition. This mark on close inspection shows the clay as having been displaced with the resultant ridges alongside; the keen observer will clearly see the difference when a 'triangle' has been added at a later date to a reproduction by grinding the mark into the previously fired body.

Chelsea, in common with early Sèvres, produced only a soft-paste porcelain, which in this early period consisted of white non-fusible clay together with a form of powdered glass (frit), which was necessary to produce the desirable translucency of porcelain. These early wares in the main have a warm white appearance, but do vary a little due to the tinting of the glaze, which has to be applied at the second kiln firing. Another pointer to 'triangle period' Chelsea are the so-called moons, seen when a piece is held to a transmitted light, in the form of extra bright specks, now known to be minute pockets of air trapped in the clay. This same feature can at times also be seen on the wares made at the Staffordshire factory of Longton Hall.

During this period many of the shapes were fashioned after Sprimont's earlier silver wares, including salts, sauce boats and cups, often moulded in relief as if to suggest repoussé decoration and after glazing subjected to yet a third firing

Chelsea shell shaped dish of soft-paste porcelain painted in enamel colours with flowers and insects, some of which hide a blemish in the paste. Mark an incised triangle of c.1745-9. L. 12.5cm.
Private Collection

Chelsea 'Goat and bee' jug, soft-paste porcelain of the triangle period, c.1745-9. Mark on base 'Chelsea 1745' incised. No early prototype of this shape in silver that might be attributed to Nicholas Sprimont has as yet been seen. H. 11cm.
Private Collection

to add a range of enamel colours, which at times were used to disguise slight firing faults.

The influence of Chinese *blanc-de-chine* can clearly be seen in the rare figures of the Goddess Guanyin (*Kuan-Yin*) and the teapots in the form of rotund Orientals with snake or parrot-like spouts.

Towards the end of the triangle period a mark in underglaze blue consisting of a trident through a crown, was sometimes used, a rather strange mark for a factory which only rarely used this colour for their decoration. No acceptable explanation has been suggested as to why Sprimont used such a mark, but what an ideal mark this device would make for the factory which is thought to have existed at Greenwich, which at the time was a flourishing seaport and the site of a royal palace.

From about 1749 a new mark in the form of a small anchor in relief on an applied oval medallion was adopted and often used until about 1752, resulting in the second phase of the Chelsea production being referred to as the 'raised-anchor' period. The quality of their paste improved at this time and chemical analysis has proved that the slight whitening of the glaze was due to the addition of a small quantity of tin oxide. An advertisement in the *Daily Advertiser* of 1750 drew attention to a forthcoming sale of Chelsea wares which included a whole variety of tea services and other useful table wares. At this time Sprimont was fortunate in acquiring the services of a skilled sculptor, Joseph Willems, born in Brussels about 1715. It was Willems who made the original oversize models in

Chelsea salt in the form of a crayfish, probably painted in enamel colours by William Duesbury. Made in the incised triangle period, c.1745-9. An original Sprimont silver model, once belonging to Frederick, Prince of Wales, is in the Royal Collection. W. 12.7cm.
Private Collection

Rare soft-paste porcelain figure of Hogarth's pug, Trump, painted in sparse enamel colours, from the triangle period, c.1745-9. Modelled after an original model in terracotta by L.F. Roubiliac. L. 28cm.
Courtesy Sotheby's

Group in soft-paste porcelain made at Chelsea, c.1749-50 and attributed to the modeller Joseph Willems. Marked with a crown and trident in underglaze blue. H. 22.9cm.

Courtesy British Museum

Chelsea soft-paste porcelain teapot, marked with an incised triangle under the glaze, c.1745-9. H. 17.5cm.
Courtesy Colonial Williamsburg Foundation

either clay or wax, from which so many delightful figures were to be produced over many years, sometimes after those originals made at Meissen, which were made available from the collection of Sir Charles Hanbury-Williams, which he acquired whilst British Ambassador at Dresden in Saxony, and at the time were stored in Holland House, London.

The form of many useful wares made during the raised-anchor period continued to remind one that Sprimont was formerly a silversmith, but at this same time the charming oriental shapes decorated in the enamel colours of the so-called Japanese Kakiemon were introduced, a style previously used at both Meissen and Chantilly. It was during the raised-anchor period that tea bowls, cups, saucers, plates and dishes began to be decorated with strong enamel colours depicting a wide range of the popular *Aesop's Fables;* today these are usually considered to be the work of 'the fable painter' Jefferyes Hamett O'Neale, who later did similar work at the Worcester factory.

Today it is generally accepted that the Chelsea productions were at their best between about 1752-58, the 'red anchor' period. This mark in the form of a small red anchor is a dangerous mark to rely on, as enamels which are only fired to a maximum temperature of 800°C can always be added to porcelain at a later date, although there is a far greater risk subjecting any soft-paste porcelain to a

Chelsea soft-paste porcelain cream jug in the form of a peach, decorated in enamel colours. Mark an applied oval pad with a raised anchor, dating c.1750-2. H. 6.4cm.
Courtesy Colonial
Williamsburg Foundation

Chelsea teabowl and saucer of soft-paste porcelain, painted in enamel colours in the Japanese Kakiemon style with Lady and Pavilion pattern (also used at Bow). Marked on bowl and saucer with the raised anchor, dating c.1750-2. D. (saucer) 11cm.   Courtesy Albert Amor Ltd

later firing than there is to a hard-paste. The so-called 'moons' previously mentioned are still often to be seen on the earlier wares of this period, together with the partially opaque glaze, but from about 1756 a more glassy transparent glaze was used, which was often very prone to crazing.

Chelsea plate of silver shaped moulded form, painted in enamel colours with the Japanese Kakiemon Tiger and Dragon pattern. Made in the raised anchor period, c.1750-2. D. 22.6cm.
Courtesy Albert Amor Ltd

Chelsea porcelain dish of silver form, soft-paste porcelain painted in enamel colours. Made in the raised anchor period, c.1750. D. 24cm. Courtesy Bearnes, Torquay

Chelsea soft-paste porcelain plate of silver form, painted in enamel colours with Aesop's Fable of the Lion and the Mice, attributed to the hand of Jeffereys Hamett O'Neale, c.1752-6, during the red anchor period. D. 22.9cm. Courtesy Albert Amor Ltd

Chelsea teabowl and saucer, soft-paste porcelain decorated with Aesop's Fables in enamel colours, c.1753-4, during the red anchor period. D. (saucer) 13.7cm.
Courtesy City Museum & Art Gallery, Stoke-on-Trent

Chelsea soft-paste porcelain teapot of oriental form, painted in enamel colours with Fable decoration, c.1752-3 during the red anchor period. H. 11.2cm.
Courtesy City Museum & Art Gallery, Stoke-on-Trent

Although the styles of decoration to be seen first on Meissen, then a little later those popularised at Sèvres, continued to be used at Chelsea, a new range of dishes, plates and other useful wares showing much more originality were now produced, wares which for many years have been wrongly termed 'Sir Hans Sloane'. These beautifully painted botanical specimens had little to do with Sir Hans, who was a patron of the Chelsea Physic Garden, whereas the original engravings were published by Philip Miller and were in many instances the work of Georg Dionysius Ehret; these wares are in great demand by collectors today.

From about 1758-69 the factory used an anchor painted in gilt as their mark

Chelsea soft-paste porcelain tea bowl and saucer painted in enamel colours with Meissen type landscapes, c.1753, during the red anchor period. D. (saucer) 14.8cm.
Courtesy Albert Amor Ltd

(the gold anchor period) and together with the clear transparent glaze they began to use a more stable paste which contained calcined animal bone, producing bone porcelain as had been used from the start of the Bow factory.

It was at about this same time that the baroque style made fashionable by Meissen became outdated and the Chelsea designers, modellers and painters looked towards Sèvres in the new age of rococo. Whilst this was a style easily adapted for table wares, the now highly decorated figures became too large and less animated, often perched on high rococo style bases with lavish gilding and often backed with a leaf and flower bocage, which limited their use to chimney-piece or sideboard decoration, due of course to the now very unattractive reverse. Increasing use was now also made of the various ground colours, but by comparison the quality was far poorer than those of Sèvres.

Similar gold anchors are often to be seen on entirely modern hard paste Continental wares and figures, which bear very little resemblance to eighteenth century Chelsea, whereas the hard-paste reproductions made by the French

Chelsea porcelain group of Tyrolean Dancers, based on an original Meissen model, c.1750. Marked with an anchor in red enamel dating c.1755. H. 44.1cm.

Chelsea soft-paste porcelain saucer dish, painted in enamel colours with a botanical specimen of a spotted lily. A type erroneously associated with Sir Hans Sloane, who died in 1752, prior to the production of these wares. Made during the red anchor period, c.1755. D. 12cm.

Courtesy Albert Amor Ltd

Chelsea soft-paste porcelain plate painted in imitation of a Japanese, (so-called Imari) pattern. Mark an anchor painted in blue, c.1755. D. 24.9cm. Courtesy Colonial Williamsburg Foundation

Chelsea soft-paste porcelain miniature dish, painted in enamel colours, made during the red anchor period, c.1755. W. 11cm.

Courtesy Bearnes, Torquay

Chelsea soft-paste porcelain table decoration in the form of a river god, derived from the marble figures by Edmé Bouchardon on the fountain of Grenelle in Paris. Mark a red anchor, c.1755. H. 14.1cm.

Courtesy British Museum

Chelsea scent bottle of soft-paste porcelain painted in enamel colours, mounted in gold, c.1755, during the red anchor period

Courtesy Venner's Antiques

Chelsea tureen and cover in the form of a rabbit of soft-paste porcelain painted in enamel colours, c.1755, during the red anchor period, and described in the Chelsea sale catalogue of that year as 'big as life, in a fine oval dish'. L. 36.9cm. Courtesy Sotheby's

Chelsea soft-paste porcelain dish painted in enamel colours with the so-called Warren Hastings pattern — this politician once owned a similarly decorated service. The four reserves illustrating Aesop's Fables are attributed to the painter Jefferyes Hammett O'Neale, c.1756, during the red anchor period. W. 33.5cm.

Courtesy Albert Amor Ltd

Plate of Chelsea soft-paste porcelain, painted in enamel colours and gilt. Made in the gold anchor period, c.1765. Mark, an anchor in gilt. D. 22.7cm. Private Collection

firm of Samson from 1845, were at least modelled after the originals and are today considered highly collectable.

From the early 1760s Sprimont's continuing success was marred by his ill health, production was limited and may well have consisted primarily of stock in hand. The factory was sold to a jeweller, James Cox, in 1769, but changed hands again the following year when it was purchased by the proprietor of the Derby porcelain factory, William Duesbury. The wares which may well have been produced at Chelsea from this time until the final closure of the concern in about 1783 are discussed in the chapter dealing with Derby wares, known from 1770-*c*.1783 as 'Chelsea-Derby'. Nicholas Sprimont, the founder of this most important English undertaking died in 1771, a time that might well be regarded as the end of the age of rococo and the beginning of the neo-classical.

Rare Chelsea vase, painted in enamel colours and gilt, with an underglaze blue ground, described by Nicholas Sprimont as the 'inimitable Mazarine blue'. (Exotic birds on reverse.) Made at Chelsea, c.1756-8. Unmarked. H. 44.1cm.
R.H. Williamson Bequest, Tullie House, Carlisle

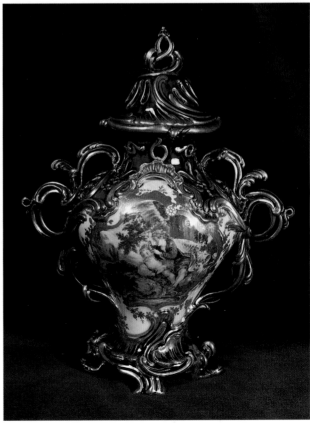

One of a pair of pot-pourri vases and covers of Chelsea soft-paste porcelain. Gold anchor period, c.1765.
Courtesy The Victoria & Albert Museum

Chelsea soft-paste porcelain figure of the conductor of the Monkey Band, modelled after that of Meissen. Marked with a red anchor on reverse, c.1756-8. H. 20.3cm.

Courtesy Colonial Williamsburg Foundation

Chelsea cup and saucer, soft-paste porcelain decorated with a translucent green enamel over black outlined landscapes, with gilt dentil rim on cup and saucer. Made during the gold anchor period, c.1760. D. (saucer) 13.3cm.

Courtesy Albert Amor Ltd

Soft-paste porcelain moulded dish of rococo form, painted in enamel colours and gilt. Made at the Chelsea factory during the gold anchor period, c.1765. W. 35cm.

Courtesy Albert Amor Ltd

Pair of Chelsea candlesticks, with groups illustrating two Aesop's Fables, *'The Dog in the Manger' and 'The Selfish Ass'. Mark, an anchor in gold, c.1765-70. H. 32.2cm and 30.9cm.*
R.H. Williamson Bequest, Tullie House, Carlisle

One must remember when considering the eighteenth century porcelains of England and perhaps comparing them unfavourably with the sophisticated productions of their Continental contemporaries, that those in this country were striving as commercial concerns with limited means, unlike such factories as Meissen and Sèvres who had the great advantage of Royal patronage. Not only was the money supplied for the production of the porcelain, but there was also a ready market for the finished wares they produced, within the Royal Courts of Europe.

FURTHER READING:
Adams, Elizabeth, *Chelsea Porclain,* Barrie & Jenkins, 1987.
Austin, John C., *Chelsea Porcelain at Colonial Williamsburg,* 1977.
Legge, Margaret, *Flowers & Fables. A survey of Chelsea Porcelain,* National Gallery of Australia, Victoria, 1984.
Synge-Hutchinson, Patrick, 'G.D. Ehret's Botanical Designs of Chelsea Porclain', *Connoisseur,* October, 1958.

Tureen in the form of a bunch of asparagus, as made originally at the Meissen factory, in soft-paste porcelain painted in natural colours and made at the Chelsea factory, c.1755. Mark, on base, an anchor in red enamel. L. 17.5cm. Courtesy Christie's

Chelsea soft-paste porcelain figure of a female hen harrier, c.1752, based on an engraving by George Edwards in his Natural History of Uncommon Birds, *published in 1743. Mark, an anchor in relief, picked out in red enamel on an applied oval medallion. H. 17.2cm.*
Courtesy Christie's

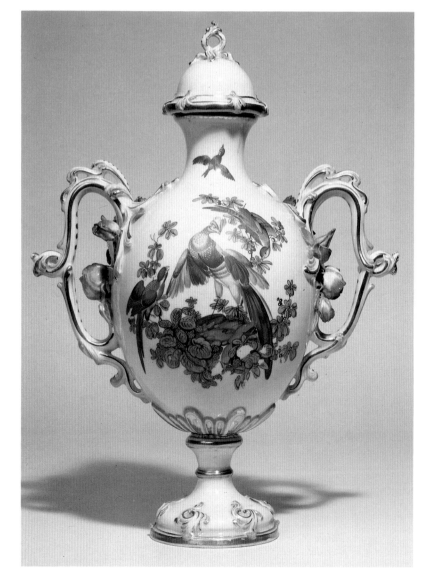

Vase and cover of Chelsea soft-paste porcelain painted in enamel colours with full relief flowers applied to reverse, probably inspired by Sèvres, of rococo form, c.1760-5. Unmarked. H. 38.6cm.
Courtesy Christie's

THE 'GIRL-IN-A-SWING' FACTORY

c.1750-1754

This group of wares which for many years was considered as part of the output of the major Chelsea factory, is named after a white porcelain figure of a girl in a swing, of which there is a copy in the Victoria & Albert Museum, in London, and another in the Museum of Fine Arts, Boston, Massachusetts.

Over recent years various writers have endeavoured to prove when and where, these charming, but comparatively naïve wares were produced, now thought to be between about 1750 and 1754. Chemical analysis has been used to show that this family of porcelains usually contain a much higher percentage of 'frit' in their makeup, resulting in a far less stable body, which was often inclined to collapse or 'slump' during the kiln firing. Neither the now recognised table wares or figures bear the Chelsea factory marks previously

Pair of very rare Chelsea 'Girl-in-a-Swing' groups, painted in enamel colours, which have probably been added at a later date by an 'outside decorator'. H. 12.6cm.

R.H. Williamson Bequest, Tullie House, Carlisle

49

Figure of a Girl-in-a-Swing, a group of figures and wares made in London, c.1750-4, about which conflicting opinions still range as to where they were actually produced, the paste used having a much higher percentage of lead oxide to those attributed to Nicholas Sprimont's factory in Chelsea. The Victoria & Albert Museum also has a similar figure. H. 15.3cm.

mentioned, the modelling is very inferior to that of Joseph Willems and the palette of colours used very distinctive.

Until more proof comes to light one must still accept the opinion of the majority of collectors, which is that these wares were produced by the group of Staffordshire potters, who are known to have come to London initially to work at the Chelsea China Manufactory under Sprimont. These potters would doubtless have been very knowledgeable as far as ceramic firing and the technique of slip-casting was concerned, but appear to have had very little artistic ability, being more conversant with the less refined earthenwares being made at the time in Burslem and other pottery towns in the area.

The Chelsea-type figures produced at this still puzzling concern are of a very limited variety and only few of each of the twenty odd examples recorded are known to exist, which is also the case with the even scarcer group of small vases, creamers and cups and saucers now attributed to the 'girl-in-a-swing' group. The major part of their output was seemingly devoted to small slip-cast scent bottles, often found to have very superior gold mounts, compared to those found on the slightly later 'toys' of Sprimont's own production. This feature could well be explained if one accepts the fact that the Staffordshire employees of Sprimont left to start their own factory under the direction of Charles Gouyn, a jeweller, who appears to have been with Sprimont as a partner, or manager,

Soft-paste porcelain figure of a hound, attributed to the Girl-in-a-Swing factory, c.1750-4. H. 11.4cm.   Courtesy the Victoria & Albert Museum

Soft-paste porcelain scent bottle decorated in the typical Girl-in-a-Swing palette of enamel colours including a strong yellow and pink and doll-like outlined eyes, c.1750. H. 8.6cm.
Courtesy Albert Amor Ltd

up until about 1749 and continued to be involved in the sale of porcelain up to the time of his death in 1783.

This 'Girl-in-a-Swing' factory appeared to have failed in 1754, which could well account for the fact that Sprimont at that time put into auction in 'Mr. Ford's great Room in the Hay-Market' an entire stock of CHELSEA PORCELAIN TOYS, drawing attention to the fact that some were mounted in gold, others unmounted (or unfinished) and that such 'Snuff-boxes, Smelling-Bottles and Trinkets for watches' had not been offered by him for sale before, all suggesting that Sprimont took over the entire remaining stock of his unsuccessful competitors.

FURTHER READING:
Adams, Elizabeth, 'The Sites of the Chelsea Porcelain Factory', *Ceramics,* November, 1985.
Lane, Arthur, and Charleston, R.J., 'Girl-in-a-Swing Porcelain & Chelsea', *English Ceramic Circle Transactions,* Vol.5, Part 3, 1962.

Bow porcelain figure emblematic of 'Earth' from a set of The Elements. Painted in enamel colours, unmarked and dating to c.1760-5. H. 27.5cm.
R.H. Williamson Bequest, Tullie House, Carlisle

BOW
c.1747-1774

The first approach to the manufacture of Bow porcelain was in 1744, when Edward Heylyn, a Bristol clothier and Thomas Frye, an Irish artist, took out a patent for the manufacture of a porcelain body, not for the actual making of porcelain wares. It was not until 1749 that a further patent was taken out, this time in Frye's name alone and apparently about two years after the actual production had commenced in about 1747. At this time there were five partners involved, the two named, together with John Weatherby and John Crowther, who were both involved with the ceramic and glass trade and George Arnold, a wealthy alderman of the City of London.

The site of this new porcelain factory, known as New Canton, was on what is now Stratford High Street, across the River Lea in the County of Essex.

Bow porcelain figure emblematic of 'Smell' from a set illustrating 'The Five Senses'. Painted in enamel colours, unmarked and dating to c.1760-5. H. 13.2cm.
R.H. Williamson Bequest, Tullie House, Carlisle

Group of Bow soft-paste porcelain decorated in the Japanese Kakiemon fashion in enamel colours, with the popular 'quail' or 'partridge' pattern. D. (basket) 15.8cm.
Courtesy Albert Amor Ltd

Pair of Bow soft-paste porcelain busts, referred to as 'The Chinese Heads', 'Mongolian Heads' or 'The Roumanian Minister and his Wife'. Unmarked, c.1750. H. 26.7cm and 26.5cm.
Courtesy Albert Amor Ltd

According to Thomas Craft, an early painter of Bow porcelain, 'the model of the building was taken from that of Canton in China', and that three hundred persons were employed there. Bow porcelain was obviously very popular and soon justified the opening of a London warehouse, with sales of over £10,000 per annum by 1753.

Whilst the porcelains of the Chelsea factory catered primarily for the wealthier client, who was not so concerned with their functional use as with their beauty, the wide range of tablewares made at Bow to compete with the mass of Chinese porcelain being brought to England by the vessels of the East India Company, appealed to the middle classes. The porclain made at New Canton was the first to our knowledge to contain a high percentage of calcined animal bone, and in his second patent, Frye had claimed he was able to make '...a certain ware which is not inferior in beauty and fineness and is rather superior

Bow soft-paste porcelain figure of the actress Kitty Clive as 'The Fine Lady' in David Garrick's farce Lethe, *c.1750. H. 26.5cm.*
Courtesy Albert Amor Ltd

Bow soft-paste porcelain figure of an owl, painted in enamel colours, c.1755. H. 19cm.
Private Collection

The Bow factory produced seven figures in bone porcelain of the Muses; they are very primitive and are attributed to the early years of c.1747-50. Seven of the Nine Muses have been recorded, the figures of Calliope and Thalia are still missing. The 'family likeness' in all their features suggests a single modeller. This figure of Erato is inscribed on the back 'Eraton for the Love' and probably modelled from a French source. The Muses were probably sold 'in the white' and then decorated with fired, or unfired, colours by such outside decorators as William Duesbury. H. 16.5cm.
Courtesy The Victoria & Albert Museum

Bow figure of a musician in soft-paste porcelain, c.1765. Marks, a large 'A' in underglaze blue and an anchor and dagger in red enamel. H. 21.5cm.   Private Collection

Bow soft-paste porcelain figure of Water, made during the 1760s when the fashion for rococo called for the typical Bow table-like bases with S-shaped feet, painted in enamel colours. H. 26.5cm.

Courtesy Bearnes, Torquay

The list of orders drawn up in 1756 by John Bowcocke, general clerk to the Bow factory, often helps in the recognition of models, the female cook shown here being one of a pair of 'a pair of cooks carrying dishes'. A further clue to Bow figures is that they frequently have small square holes cut into the back of the base, which were intended if the purchaser so wished, for the insertion of metal branches to support candle sconces or to form a bocage with the addition of porcelain flowers at the end of the branches. These additions are rarely seen today. H. 17.7cm.

Courtesy The Victoria & Albert Museum

in strength than the earthenware that is brought from the East Indies and is commonly known by the name of China, Japan, or porcelain ware'.

The wares produced at Bow tended to vary in both paste and glaze. The early being of a creamy tint, under a slightly blue glaze, it was usually heavily potted but still translucent. When underglaze blue decoration was used the glaze often appears to have been deliberately underfired, to prevent the glaze becoming too fluid and merging with the painting: this immature glaze can often be recognised by the presence of minute bubbles. At a later period the body of the wares is sometimes so underfired as to appear as opaque as earthenware, whilst

Bow soft-paste porcelain group of a cock and hen, painted in enamel colours, c.1754-8. H. 10.8cm.

Courtesy Albert Amor Ltd

Three of the Four Seasons, Summer, Spring and Autumn, press-moulded bone porcelain, painted in enamel colours and made at the Bow factory, on the Essex side of Bow Bridge, not strictly London. Unmarked. H. c. 12.5cm.

Courtesy Phillips, London

Bow porcelain figure of a cat, holding either a small rat or a large mouse, painted in enamel colours, c.1753-8. H. 7.4cm.
Courtesy Venner's Antiques

Bow soft-paste porcelain stand for a finger bowl, painted in underglaze grey-blue, c.1750. Mark a workman's mark in the form of an incised 'R'. D. 15.3cm.
Formerly in the Gilbert Bradley Collection

Pair of Bow porcelain pickle dishes in the form of leaves with relief moulding of veins on reverse, painted in polychrome enamels, c.1755. W. 11cm.
Courtesy Bearnes, Torquay

the glaze was fired to the full temperature, often resulting in a blurred decoration. As with all bone porcelains (phosphatic) all their wares were prone to a light-brown staining, especially when cracks or chips have allowed impurities or moisture to penetrate the body.

Much of the charm of the early Bow figures is their obvious appeal to the Londoner of the day, featuring such characters as Henry Woodward as the Fine Gentleman and Kitty Clive as the Fine Lady, the actor and actress in David Garrick's farce *Lethe,* or the figure of the Thames Waterman, sometimes bearing on his sleeve the fouled anchor badge of the Admiralty barge, or rather

Porcelain figure of a boy, painted in enamel colours and known as the 'New Dancer'. Made at Bow, London, c.1760-5, marked with a red enamel anchor alongside a dagger. H. 19cm.

R.H. Williamson Bequest, Tullie House, Carlisle

Figure of a parrot, porcelain, painted in enamel colours. Made at the Bow factory, c.1760-5. Unmarked. H. 18cm.

R.H. Williamson Bequest, Tullie House, Carlisle

Bow soft-paste porcelain dish moulded in the form of a vine leaf, painted in underglaze blue, c.1760. L. 22.5cm.

Courtesy Bearnes, Torquay

Bow soft-paste porcelain dish, decorated in underglaze blue with a popular landscape often seen on Bow reserves in a powder blue ground, c.1760. Mark (on reverse) six imitation Chinese characters (see right). L. 26.5cm. Courtesy Allan Weaver Collection

Six imitation Chinese characters on the reverse of the Bow octagonal dish (above), one in the form of the crossed swords of Meissen, all in underglaze blue Courtesy Allan Weaver Collection

Bow soft-paste porcelain dish moulded with vine leaves and grapes and painted in underglaze blue, c.1760. Mark on reverse of four imitation Chinese characters. L. 21cm. Private Collection

more rarely the Doggett's badge of the white horse of Hanover, the prize for the competition instituted in 1715 by Thomas Doggett. These figures were usually very heavy in relation to their size, due to the Bow modellers using the technique of press moulding, rather than slip casting, resulting in much thicker walls of clay. One feature which is almost unique to Bow figures is a small square hole cut into the back, intended if the purchaser so wished, to locate a metal candle holder or a bocage of metal green enamelled stems capped with porcelain flowers.

With such an output it is not surprising that many examples of Bow blue and white useful wares are still available to collectors, as their obvious aim was to compete with the vast numbers of oriental imports, and in many instances the decoration was directly copied from Chinese hard-paste wares, even to applying illiterate forms of reign marks. The sure identification of the wide range of English porcelain decorated in underglaze blue is a great challenge to collectors, many, as is the case with Bow, only rarely has some positive form of mark been

Bow soft-paste porcelain figure painted in enamel colours, emblematic of Autumn, c.1760-5. H. 14cm.
Courtesy Bearnes, Torquay

Bow figure of a boy selling fish, soft-paste porcelain, painted in enamel colours. Unmarked, c.1760. H. 15.9cm.
R.H. Williamson Bequest, Tullie House, Carlisle

applied, and so it is necessary to study the many recurring painted or printed designs attributed to the factory by the specialists in the field.

Enamel decoration is known to have been applied at the factory to both useful wares and figures. The Chinese so-called *famille rose* style of painting is seen on the rare circular inkwells, inscribed 'MADE AT NEW CANTON 1750' or '1751', a form also known with the same inscription, in underglaze blue. An interesting range of Bow figures was obviously sold in the white glazed state to independent outside decorators, such as William Duesbury, and in his London account book, 1751-3, the prices are stated for decorating with unfired colours, which soon flaked off, or for a higher charge the figure could be in his words 'inhamild', meaning the more permanent fired colours.

One of the most successful uses of enamel colours on Bow wares is seen on those pieces decorated in one of the well-known Japanese Kakiemon styles. Perhaps because of their lack of highly skilled painters they succeed in recapturing the seemingly free manner of painting seen on the oriental wares, as opposed to the more painstaking copies on some Continental and English porcelains.

From about 1760 until the factory closed in 1774, both the figures and useful

Three Bow soft-paste porcelain figures painted in enamel colours, the figure with a cornucopia emblematic of Earth, c.1755-60, Juno with eagle emblematic of Air, c.1760-5, and Neptune with dolphin emblematic of Water, c.1752-5. All three are unmarked. H. 19.7cm, 25.4cm, 20.2cm.

Courtesy Albert Amor Ltd

wares made at Bow tended to follow the more fashionable gold anchor styles of the Chelsea concern; figures were perched on four-footed scrolled bases and the table wares were overdecorated, so well described by Arthur Lane in his *English Porcelain Figures of the Eighteenth Century* (Faber & Faber) as 'its now seedy Rococo style'.

Although for many years it has been suggested by various writers that William Duesbury, of the Derby factory, purchased the stock and material of the Bow China Works when it closed in 1774, there is not as yet any evidence to support this.

FURTHER READING:
Adams, Elizabeth and Redstone, David, *Bow Porcelain,* Faber & Faber, Revised Edn., 1991.
Amor (Ann George), *Bow Porcelain,* Exhibition Catalogue, 1980.
Gabszewicz, A., Freeman, G., *Bow Porcelain (Freeman Collection),* Lund Humphries, 1982.
Tait, H., *Bow Exhibition,* British Museum, 1959.
Handley Collection, Joseph M., *18th Century English Transfer Printed Porcelain & Enamels,* Mulbery Press, Carmel, California, 1991.

LONGTON HALL & WEST PANS
c.1750-1760   *c.1764-1777*

With the obviously skilled potters and modellers available in the Staffordshire potteries by the mid-eighteenth century, who were capable of producing finely thrown, moulded and often enamel decorated useful wares of earthenware or stoneware, it is surprising that their early attempts to produce a soft-paste porcelain were initially such a failure.

The exact date of the establishment of the more successful Staffordshire porcelain factory at Longton Hall is a little vague, but today 1750 is regarded as an acceptable year when William Jenkinson rented a fairly remote Hall from Obadiah Lane and in the following year took into partnership William Nicklin, a lawyer, and the very experienced potter, William Littler, who had previously been engaged in the production of salt glazed stoneware.

Good evidence of the porcelain produced at Longton Hall has been provided by the numerous excavations carried out on the site from 1955 by Dr. Bernard Watney, Dr. Geoffrey Blake, the staff of the City Museum & Art Gallery at Hanley and further groups of archaeologists. The large number of 'wasters' found again proved that so many early attempts to manufacture soft-paste porcelain resulted in a very high percentage of kiln losses through firing difficulties.

The early figures produced at Longton Hall are aptly described as 'snowmen', with the thick white glaze usually obscuring any crisp detail of the modelling on figures which were frequently inspired by Chinese, Continental or Chelsea originals. The soft-paste porcelain body used at Longton Hall had a lot in common with that used at the so-called 'Girl-in-a-Swing' factory, they both contained a high proportion of 'frit', resulting in many 'slumped' pieces, sometimes not too obvious due to their preference for so many naturalistic shapes, as popularised by the Saxon factory at Meissen; various leaf forms were especially popular, such as tureens in the form of cabbages or lettuces.

Figure of a horse, an early type of Longton Hall model, with very thick glaze, a feature of the so-called 'snowman' pieces. This model was also produced in salt glazed stoneware. L. 17.5cm.   Courtesy Sotheby's

Longton Hall sauce boat, c.1755, made from a mould that would appear to have been made initially for the production of salt glazed stoneware, when the modelling would have been far crisper. The decoration is applied in purple enamel. L. 19.3cm.   Courtesy the Victoria & Albert Museum

Coffee pot in soft-paste porcelain, decorated with deep underglaze so-called 'Littler blue'. Once thought to be of Longton Hall manufacture, but today thought to be among the wares made by William Littler after his move from Staffordshire to West Pans in Scotland, c.1764-70. Mark, crossed L's in underglaze blue   Courtesy Simon Spero Antiques

The finds during the excavations on the site of the 'Longton Porcelaine China Factory' (Longton Hall) proved that during its early years the manufactory had a high rate of kiln wastage. This illustration shows a collapsed figure of a soft-paste porcelain dog, fused into the saggar in which it was being fired. L. (dog) 9.5cm.   Courtesy City Museum & Art Gallery, Stoke-on-Trent

Pair of dishes in the form of leaves, painted in natural colours. Made at Longton Hall, Staffordshire, c.1755. L. 15.5cm.
Courtesy Bearnes, Torquay

Pair of groups, soft-paste porcelain painted in enamel colours, copied with slight modifications from Meissen originals modelled by J.J. Kaendler, c.1750. Made at Longton Hall, c.1755. H. 20.5cm.
Courtesy Sotheby's

Pair of soft-paste porcelain sauce boats in the form of ducks, decorated in enamel colours. Made at Longton Hall, c.1755.
Courtesy Christie's

Rare Longton Hall soft-paste porcelain jug, moulded in relief and painted with enamel colours, including group of roses by the so-called 'trembly-rose' painter, c.1755-60. H. c.21cm.
Courtesy Colonial Williamsburg Foundation

Jug in soft-paste porcelain of quatrefoil shape, moulded in relief with carnations, strawberry leaves and auricular plant, with twisted branch handle and decorated in underglaze blue. Made at Longton Hall, c.1755. Unmarked. H. 20.4cm.
Courtesy Sotheby's

Dish moulded in the form of leaves, with pierced decoration and painted with enamel colours. Made at Longton Hall, c.1755
Courtesy Christie's

Longton Hall soft-paste porcelain dish in the form of a leaf, painted in enamel colours, c.1756-60. L. 21.5cm.
Courtesy Bearnes, Torquay

Pair of soft-paste porcelain pug dogs, decorated in high temperature colours. Made at Longton Hall, c.1756-60. Pug dogs, or 'mops', were adopted as a symbol of a German secret society which was opposed to the attempt to ban Freemasonry by Pope Clement XII in 1738. H. 9.5cm.

Courtesy City Museum & Art Gallery, Stoke-on-Trent

A rare shell-shaped moulded sauce boat made at the Longton Hall factory and painted in enamel colours, c.1755-6. It will be noted that enamel painting has been used to help disguise the fact that both the foot rim and the rim near the handle had minor fire cracks

Courtesy Simon Spero Antiques

A distinct branch of the potters' training was concerned with the design and application of handles, but those used on so many Longton Hall vessels are best described as 'ill-fitting', but however they are a distinct aid to the collector aiming to correctly attribute these wares. The various forms of decoration used at this early Staffordshire factory are also rather distinctive, first the well-known underglaze 'Littler blue', which was inclined to 'bleed' into the glaze, a colour he had used more successfully on his salt glazed stonewares. By the mid-1750s some excellent enamel flower painting was applied to a variety of wares, again often bearing a marked similarity to the flowers seen on the slightly earlier and rare table wares now attributed to the 'Girl-in-a-Swing' factory. Some very finely painted landscapes which include buildings, are thought to be the work of John Hayfield, the appropriately named 'Castle Painter', who used a rather

A well-known form of Longton Hall teapot. Wasters found on the factory site confirm the shape of the handle; the acorn knob is also a good pointer to the form. The decoration is painted in underglaze blue. Unmarked but dating to c.1755-8. H. c.14cm.

Courtesy Simon Spero Antiques

Porcelain sauce boat made at Longton Hall, the name of a large mansion of late 17th century date, near Stoke-on-Trent, demolished in 1939. The manufacture was under the direction of William Littler, who had previously been making salt glazed stoneware. The sauce boat, made c.1755-6, is decorated with enamel colours. L. 15cm.
Courtesy Phillips, London

Soft-paste porcelain jug with moulded decoration and painted with underglaze blue floral sprays. Made c.1757-60 at the Longton Hall porcelain factory. Matching sherds have been excavated on the early site. H. 24.5cm.
Courtesy Newcastle under Lyme Museum & Art Gallery

Longton Hall mug decorated with underglaze blue painting, c.1758. Unmarked, but again easily identified by the form of the handle. H. c.16cm.   Courtesy The Victoria & Albert Museum

A typical Longton Hall mug of c.1759, decorated with a black enamel transfer print of the arms of the Society of Bucks, which bears the signature of John Sadler of Liverpool. Whether he purchased Longton Hall blanks to decorate to sell himself, or whether they were decorated to order is not known. Note the unusual form of the handle — a good guide to Longton Hall wares. H. 16.5cm.
Courtesy The Victoria & Albert Museum

Soft-paste porcelain loving cup made at Longton Hall, c.1755. The decoration is painted in underglaze blue. Note the form of the handle which appears to be unique to this factory. H. 10.2cm.
Courtesy City Museum & Art Gallery, Stoke-on-Trent

The ill-shaped handle is a sure indication of the Longton Hall factory, which was having difficulty with its wares slumping due to the high content of the lead oxide. Painted in underglaze blue and dating c.1755-8. H. c. 15.5cm.   Courtesy Simon Spero Antiques

Longton Hall soft-paste porcelain mug, painted in enamel colours in the Chinese famille-rose *style. H. 11.2cm.*   Courtesy Bearnes, Torquay

detailed manner of painting buildings which has a lot in common with that seen on some of the larger pieces of salt glazed stoneware, such as punch pots. It is rather surprising that some of the more finely potted items, which were probably awaiting decoration at the time of the closure of the factory, should have found their way to Liverpool for the addition of enamel prints by the firm of John Sadler. The late date of decoration is proven by one example of a mug, featuring the bust of Queen Charlotte under a crown, for the actual marriage to George III was not until a year after the closure of the factory. This decoration poses the question of why Sadler should have obtained these undecorated pieces from Staffordshire, when so much Liverpool porcelain must have been more readily available; was it to the order of a retailer or were the Longton Hall pieces being sold cheaply?

Despite their obviously difficult beginnings, William Littler, the factory manager, considered that by 1758 the quality of the wares justified the opening of a London China Warehouse at 'the Corner of St. Paul's Churchyard next Watling Street', but the competition of the porcelains being produced at that time at Bow, Chelsea, Derby and Worcester proved too great and the warehouse was closed after only nine months. The factory closed in 1760 after

Longton Hall figure of a Vegetable Seller, a frit porcelain painted in enamel colours. Unmarked, c.1755. H. 20cm. R.H. Williamson Bequest, Tullie House, Carlisle

Longton Hall figure of Britannia, holding a shield with a relief profile of George II, painted in enamel colours. Unmarked, c.1757-60. H. 28.5cm.
R.H. Williamson Bequest, Tullie House, Carlisle

the dissolving of the partnership and in the same year the sale of over 90,000 pieces of Longton Hall porcelain was so praised by the auction house advertising in the *Salisbury Journal,* that one cannot understand why they had remained unsold previously.

It is now about thirty years since evidence came to light proving that following the failure of the Longton Hall factory, William Littler and his wife had moved to West Pans, near Musselburgh in Scotland, to start yet another new production of soft-paste porcelain, stoneware and cream coloured

Model of a seated tiger in soft-paste porcelain decorated in enamel colours. Made at Longton Hall, c.1755   Courtesy Christie's

earthenware, a venture started in about 1764, probably with the help of a local patron of high rank, enabling Littler to hold a seven day sale of porcelain in 1765 in the Royal residence of Holyrood Palace, Edinburgh. Whether some of these wares were pieces he had brought with him at the closure of Longton or from his recently established West Pans factory is a difficult problem to answer, as it was initially thought that all the wares associated with West Pans were from the old stock of Longton Hall, but it is now accepted that he was in fact producing the various ceramic wares in Scotland, and in most instances the porcelain was almost identical in many ways to that which he had produced at the Staffordshire factory. Advertisements in the *Glasgow Journal* in 1767 and 1768 listed a wide range of wares for sale 'At. Mr. John Parlane's at the Sign of the White Hart in the Gallowgate Glasgow'.

Due to the fact that no wasters were found on the Longton Hall site bearing the mark of the comparatively rare crossed 'L' device, which was probably suggested by the crossed sword mark of the Meissen factory, it is now thought that this mark was only at times used by Littler whilst he was at West Pans.

After a vain attempt to find a financial backer for his ailing factory, the venture came to a close in 1777 and Littler returned to Staffordshire, where it is now suggested that he may well have become manager for Ralph Baddeley at Shelton, producing a variety of wares from a soft-paste porcelain, again almost identical to that which he had used at Longton Hall and West Pans. He may

Longton Hall soft-paste porcelain figure of a shepherd, painted in enamel colours and deep underglaze blue, referred to as 'Littler's blue', c.1756-60. H. 20cm.
Courtesy City Museum & Art Gallery, Stoke-on-Trent

Large porcelain jug of Longton Hall shape. These wares were formerly thought to have been taken by William Littler to West Pans in Scotland at the time of the closure of the Staffordshire factory, but it is now recognised that wares such as this jug with crests or armorial bearings for the Scottish nobility, were not merely decorated at West Pans, but made there between 1764 and 1777 when Littler returned to Staffordshire. H. 22.8cm.

Courtesy The Victoria
& Albert Museum

Tea bowl and saucer, most probably made by William Littler at West Pans, near Edinburgh in Scotland, c.1764-77. The decoration consists of underglaze blue, referrerd to as 'Littler's blue' and enamel decoration including an armorial bearing for the third Duke of Rutland or his son

Courtesy The Victoria & Albert
Museum

Plate of soft-paste porcelain, moulded in relief with strawberry leaves and fruit, painted in enamel colours. Made at Longton Hall, Stoke-on-Trent, c.1751-60. Matching sherds were found during excavations on the factory site in 1970. D. 21.5cm.

Courtesy City Museum & Art Gallery, Stoke-on-Trent

well have continued to work at Shelton until his death in 1784, but this last phase of Littler's life as a potter still requires further research.

FURTHER READING:

Lane, Arthur, *English Porcelain Figures of the 18th Century,* Faber, London, 1961.
Mountford, Arnold, 'Porcelain Comes to the Potteries', *Staffordshire Porcelain* (Ed. G. Godden), Granada, London, 1983.
Watney, Dr. Bernard, *Longton Hall Porcelain,* Faber, London, 1961.
Barker, David and Halfpenny, Pat, *Unearthing Staffordshire,* City of Stoke-on-Trent Museum & Art Gallery, Catalogue of Exhibition sponsored by Christie's, 1990.

Soft-paste porcelain vase of rococo form with stopper of hand modelled flowers, the flower and insect painting in overglaze enamel colours. Attributed to the Longton Hall factory, Stoke-on-Trent, but matching sherds have not as yet been excavated although a number of similarly modelled flowers were found, c.1751-60. H. 19.5cm. Courtesy City Museum & Art Gallery, Stoke-on-Trent

BRISTOL (SOAPSTONE PORCELAIN)
c.1749-1752

Among the many pioneers of research into the history of British porcelain was the late Aubrey Toppin C.V.O., who was a frequent visitor to the ceramic department of the Victoria & Albert Museum. Prior to the publishing of his paper to the English Ceramic Circle in 1954, the early porcelain factory at Bristol was erroneously termed 'Lowdin's', but since that time the correct term 'Lund's-Bristol' has been used when referring to a production of porcelain made at William Lowdin's glass works in Bristol by Benjamin Lund and William Miller. It was Lund who in 1749 obtained a licence to mine the important Cornish ingredient of soap-rock at £5 per ton, which was to enable him to produce a fine porcelain which had so many advantages normally expected only of a hard-paste, such as initially produced by the Chinese potter.

A few documentary examples which were produced by the moulding technique bear the mark of 'Bristol' or 'Bristoll' in relief; the even rarer figure taken from a Chinese original depicts Lü Tung-pin, one of the Eight Taoist Immortals, this also bears the date of 1750. The theory that only the pieces marked 'Bristol' can be accepted as such is unacceptable as there are far too few so marked examples to account for at least three years' successful production before the concern was taken over by Dr. Wall and his fourteen partners of the newly established Worcester factory.

Inspired by the current popularity of Chinese porcelain decorated with underglaze blue, many of the unmarked wares attributed to early Bristol follow this fashion and are painted with Chinese style landscapes, often marred by the tendency for the rather pale blues to merge into the glaze. These early decorations are inclined to be rather repetitive, enabling the collector to recognise certain peculiarities of a painter, the best example being the so-called 'three-dot' painter, who so frequently included a group of three small 'blobs' in his compositions.

Soapstone porcelain cream jug, painted in underglaze blue with a popular pattern which sometimes includes a cluster of three dots. The painting is very blurred, as is often the case with such pieces, which at times are marked with the word 'Bristoll' in relief on the base and attributed to the factory of Benjamin Lund at Bristol, dating to c.1750. Courtesy Phillips, London

Two soapstone porcelain teacups painted in enamel colours. As it is difficult to say for certain whether such pieces were made at Lund's Bristol factory or in the earliest years of Worcester, they are usually referred to as Bristol/Worcester, c.1750-4. A matching 'waster' was found on the Warmstry House site. H. 6.3cm.
Courtesy Phillips, London

Pair of soapstone porcelain vases, painted in colours in the Kakiemon style. Made at either Lund & Miller's Bristol factory or at Worcester, dating to c.1750. H. 12cm.
Courtesy Bearnes, Torquay

The early factory obviously had many production problems and seemingly preferred the technique of moulding their small table wares, rather than the more traditional 'throwing' of wares in the round. There is no sure evidence that enamel colours were applied to Lund's porcelains and there is quite a large group that must be considered to have been made at either Bristol or during the early days at Worcester after the takeover in 1752.

The new collector must remember that there were two Bristol porcelain factories: the one just discussed, producing a soapstone porcelain and the later hard-paste porcelain factory of William Cookworthy, transferred from Plymouth in 1770 and remaining in production until 1781.

FURTHER READING:
Barrett, Franklin A., *Worcester Porcelain and Lund's Bristol,* Faber & Faber, 2nd Edn., 1966.
Watney, Dr. Bernard, *English Blue and White Porcelain of the 18th Century,* Faber & Faber, Revised Edn., 1973.

WORCESTER

1751-c.1783

In 1751 Dr. Wall and his fourteen partners formed their company to acquire the then flourishing Bristol concern of Lund and Miller. The claim of Dr. Wall and one of the partners, William Davis, to have invented the formula for the production of soapstone porcelain which was to be used at their 'Worcester Tonquin Manufacture' cannot be accepted. If any porcelain was being made at the Worcester factory during 1751, it could not have been of a body which included soapstone, as this did not become available to them prior to 1752, after the 'stock, utensils and effects and the process of manufacture' moved from Bristol to Worcester, accompanied by Benjamin Lund, who was employed by the new partnership during their early years.

Worcester tea bowl and saucer, painted in colours in Chinese famille rose *style, c.1754-5; the porcelain is extremely thin and of a creamy tone. D. (saucer) 12.4cm.*   Private Collection

80

Worcester bowl of soapstone porcelain, decorated with a version of the 'Lord Henry Thynne' pattern, painted in underglaze blue, enamel colours and gilt, with a small riverside landscape inside. Mark, an open crescent, c.1775. D. 17.5cm.
Private Collection

Very rare and early Worcester soapstone porcelain coffee cup, painted in underglaze blue in naïve fashion. Mark a cross in underglaze blue on inside of foot rim, probably a painter's mark, dating to c.1753. H. 6.8cm.
Private Collection

Three examples of early Worcester porcelain painted in enamel colours, c.1753-4. Worcester at this time were having difficulty in producing a stable porcelain and the vase is leaning to one side. H. (vase) 11.5cm.
Courtesy Simon Spero Antiques

81

Worcester sauce boat and pickle dish decorated with enamel colours. The sauce boat on the left is in the form of a cos lettuce and dates to 1754-5; the rare pickle dish, painted in the Chinese famille verte *style, marked with an incised cross, is of the same date, the sauce boat on the right is of a silver shape produced at Bristol, it is unmarked and dates to c.1753-5. L. (sauce boats) 19cm.*
Courtesy Albert Amor Ltd

Pair of early soapstone porcelain Worcester sauce boats, decorated in underglaze blue, made during the Dr. Wall period, c.1755. L. 18cm.
Courtesy Phillips, London

It is rare in the field of ceramics that one can quote a unique example, but such is the case with the small cream boat, now in the Dyson Perrins Museum at Worcester, which bears the relief moulded word on the base 'Wigornia' (the Latinised name of Worcester). This rare piece was first seen by the author in a fine private collection of porcelain in Halifax, Nova Scotia, in 1963. In 1973 this same piece was offered for sale in a London auction house and was sold for the then fabulous amount of £20,000.

The Worcester porcelain concern is the only English porcelain factory to have continued with an unbroken history from 1751 to the present day and apart from some rather poor quality blue and white wares made around 1785, has always been of a high quality. In this chapter we will discuss the wares made from 1751 to c.1776, the so-called Dr. Wall Period and from 1776-1793, during which time the factory continued under William Davis alone, until the factory was purchased by Thomas Flight in 1783, who then also continued alone until joined by Martin Barr in 1793. These very workable divisions were suggested by Henry Sandon, a former curator of the Dyson Perrins Museum and have today been generally accepted by collectors, dealers and the salerooms.

The nice easy guides to the recognition of much Worcester porcelain, as often suggested in early books on the subject are now known to be very misleading.

Worcester soapstone porcelain teapot, painted in underglaze blue with the 'Prunus Root' pattern, popular from c.1752-70. Lowestoft, Bow and Longton Hall also used this pattern. Mark an open crescent in underglaze blue, c.1760. H. 10cm. Private Collection

Worcester soapstone porcelain saucer, printed in underglaze blue with the very rare 'Two Swan Precipice', seemingly only used on saucers, c.1757-60. D. 11.4cm. Private Collection

A rare Worcester coffee cup, showing on one side a portrait bust of the King of Prussia and on the reverse the armorial crest of the Marquis of Bute, printed in black and tinted in with colour, c.1757. H. 6cm. Private Collection

Worcester soapstone porcelain mug, printed in black enamel with added washes of translucent enamel colours. The print is known as 'Milking Scene No. 1'; a similar scene called 'The Rural Lovers' is usually applied on the other side, c.1760s. H. 8.5cm.
Private Collection

Teapot and cover, coffee cup and saucer of Worcester porcelain, purchased 'in the white' with enamel and gilt decoration added in the London workshop of James Giles, c.1770-5. H. (teapot) 14.7cm.
R.H. Williamson Bequest, Tullie House, Carlisle

An outstanding example of the work of James Giles' London workshop painted in enamels and gilt on a Worcester porcelain 'blank', c.1765-70. The earliest work of James Giles (1718-1780) is almost certainly that found on Chinese porcelain which was purchased either 'in the white' or with sparse underglaze blue decoration, but from the 1760s most of the work carried out at his atelier was on Worcester wares, some of which already had underglaze blue grounds applied enabling his painters to paint in the reserves and apply very high quality gilding. H. approx. 16cm.
Courtesy Micawber Publications, Bridgnorth

True the translucency of most Worcester wares made during the Dr. Wall period shows a pleasing pale green, but some wares of the rival Caughley factory show a similar tint, and certainly not always a 'straw colour' as previously suggested. From about 1760 most Worcester examples have a narrow unglazed margin in the right-angle formed by the base and the foot rim, where the glaze has been removed to prevent any excess running down the foot rim and fusing the article to the kiln furniture used as a support within the saggar during the glost firing. This feature was at one time attributed to 'glaze shrinkage', which never happens. The same feature can also be seen on some Caughley and some Liverpool porcelains.

Worcester porcelain cream jug, painted in underglaze blue and showing part of the so-called 'Cannonball' pattern, a very common pattern c.1755-80. Mark, an open crescent. H. c.8cm.
Allan Weaver Collection

Fine Worcester porcelain mug, decorated with transfer prints in puce. The print of George III is by Robert Hancock after an original by Jeremiah Meyer; on the reverse the portrait bust of Queen Charlotte, also by Hancock, is after the original by Germain Aliamet, c.1760. H. 15cm.
Courtesy Venner's Antiques

Pair of salt cellars and coffee cup and saucer in Worcester soapstone porcelain. The shells are sparsely decorated with enamel colours and gilt, one marked 'To' impressed, probably for repairer John Toulouse, c.1770. W. 7.6cm. The cup and saucer, unmarked, are moulded with flowers and foliage in relief with enamel decoration, c.1760-5

Courtesy Albert Amor Ltd

Lozenge-shaped dessert dish with reserves decorated in enamel colours on a maroon ground with gilding of the quality of the work associated with James Giles, c.1770. L. 32cm.

Courtesy Bearnes, Torquay

Detail of a painting by Jeffryes Hamett O'Neale, the 'Fable' painter, in a Worcester basket. Mark, the fretted square in blue, c.1768. D. 19.7cm.   Courtesy Albert Amor Ltd

Worcester porcelain teacup and saucer of fluted form, painted by James Giles in turquoise, red, royal blue and yellow in Japanese style with a dragon among oriental plants. A pattern today called the 'Jabberwocky', but described in the 1769 catalogue as 'the rich dragon'. Mark, a fretted square in underglaze blue, c.1770.

Courtesy Bearnes, Torquay

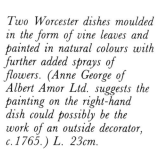

Two Worcester dishes moulded in the form of vine leaves and painted in natural colours with further added sprays of flowers. (Anne George of Albert Amor Ltd. suggests the painting on the right-hand dish could possibly be the work of an outside decorator, c.1765.) L. 23cm.

Courtesy Albert Amor Ltd

Old mark books are always a source of danger, but especially so in the case of Worcester and Caughley. Much of the porcelain made at Worcester between 1780 and 1790 was marked with the so-called 'disguised Chinese numerals', numbers one to nine written to imitate Chinese characters in underglaze blue. These pieces are of a very inferior quality compared to the earlier Worcester and consequently were always dismissed by the collectors of Worcester as being 'obviously Caughley', but following excavations on the early sites of both factories, wasters were found which proved them wrong. No such marked pieces

Tankard and coffee cup and saucer painted with bouquets of enamel flowers with apple green grounds, c.1765-70. The mark on cup and saucer, crossed swords and '9'. H. (tankard) 11.5cm.
Courtesy Albert Amor Ltd

A miniature or 'toy' soapstone porcelain service made at the Worcester factory, c.1770 (note that these miniature services did not include a teapot stand or spoon tray). The decoration is entirely in gilt and is of a very high quality of the type usually associated with the work of the London decorator, James Giles. H. (teabowl) c.3cm.
Courtesy Colonial Williamsburg Foundation

Pair of shell-shaped dishes and a plate in Worcester soapstone porcelain, decorated with enamel flower sprays within reserves on an underglaze blue scale ground, c.1768-76. Mark, the fretted square

Courtesy Bearnes, Torquay

Group of Worcester soapstone porcelain tea wares, decorated in the so-called 'dry' blue enamel and gilt, c.1770. Marked with a version of the Meissen crossed-swords and numeral. D. (saucer) 18.8cm.

Courtesy Bearnes, Torquay

were found on the Caughley site in Shropshire, but many were discovered at Worcester, a find which raised the general standard of the Salopian wares and lowered, at least for a short period, the quality of Worcester during the Flight period. During this same period many pieces were decorated with underglaze blue transfer prints and marked with a printed version of their crescent mark, filled with fine lines. If not of the quality to please the Worcester collector, it was suggested that this was a letter 'C' for Caughley, but the wasters proved otherwise and the 'C' for Caughley is a distinct capital letter, not a crescent.

Prior to 1757, the fine porcelains made at Worcester were decorated with either underglaze blue or enamel colours in a variety of styles, sometimes influenced by the well established Continental factories of Meissen or Sèvres, and frequently with the palette and designs of Chinese *famille-verte,* with the predominating tones of green, or the *famille-rose,* which included the wide range

Worcester teapot in soapstone porcelain decorated with transfer prints in underglaze blue of 'The Man in the Pavilion' pattern, popular c.1757-85. H. 14.5cm.
Courtesy Bearnes, Torquay

Three Worcester soapstone porcelain vases, decorated in relief with garlands of flowers and a surround of moulded shells, all painted in enamel colours and gilt, c.1765. The two larger vases are marked with 'To' impressed. Today these letters are thought to refer to a modeller named John Toulouse, rather than the former attribution to a 'Mr. Tebo'. H. 40.6 and 21.6cm.
Courtesy Albert Amor Ltd

Worcester soapstone cream boat painted with the 'Prunus Root' pattern in underglaze blue, c.1760. Workman's mark → in underglaze blue. H. 6cm.
Allan Weaver Collection

Worcester teapot and miniature tea bowl and saucer, printed in underglaze blue with the very common design of 'The Fence', used c.1765-85. Mark, a hatched crescent on teapot. D. (saucer) 10cm.
Private Collection

of pale pinks to deep crimsons. The painting of the underglaze blue decoration on the early wares of Worcester did not have the same tendency as at Bristol to 'bleed' into the glaze, resulting in a hazy image, this minor fault was prevented at Worcester by subjecting the biscuit decorated piece to a low kiln firing to 'harden' on the colour, prior to glazing and firing to the full temperature. Decoration by over glaze transfer printing was used somewhat unsuccessfully during their early years and generally described as 'smoky primitives', but following the arrival of the accomplished engraver, Richard Hancock, in 1757, their wares decorated by this technique were unsurpassed.

Worcester soapstone porcelain teapot, painted in underglaze blue with the uncommon 'Two Quails' pattern, c.1775-80. Mark, an open crescent. H. 14.5cm.

Courtesy Phillips, London

A unique Worcester trio, once owned by the Edwardian hostess Mrs. Arthur James at West Dean, Sussex. The enamel decoration includes a rare pink and lilac palette. Unmarked but dating to c.1775

Courtesy Albert Amor Ltd

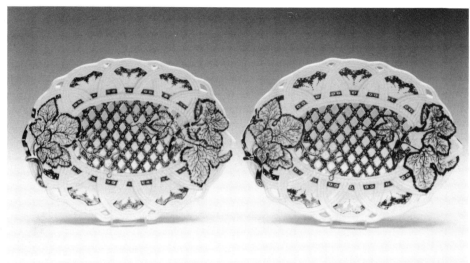

Pair of Worcester dessert dishes with pierced decoration, painted in underglaze blue, matching wasters found during the excavation of the Warmstry House site in 1968, c.1770-5. L. 29.5cm.
Courtesy Bearnes, Torquay

Worcester soapstone porcelain trio, decorated with prints in black enamel with 'The Milkmaids', after a 1766 engraving by Robert Sayer, c.1770s. D. (saucer) 12cm.
Private Collection

Some of the finest Worcester enamel painted decoration was produced from the mid-1750s in a style associated with a painter, James Rogers, who applied his name and '1757' on a documentary mug in the British Museum. Similar scenes of birds in landscapes are to be found on large jugs moulded in the form of cabbage leaves, which must have presented a very irregular surface to the painter. These same large jugs often have a pouring lip in the form of a bearded face mask; careful examination of the moulding again helps to distinguish those made at Caughley or Lowestoft.

The fact that soapstone porcelain was not so liable as some other soft-paste bodies to shattering or crazing when filled with hot liquid, made it ideal for the many varieties of teapots produced, frequently with the attractive, but easily damaged knob in the form of a flower. Teething troubles were obviously experienced in their early years with plates and dishes, which were often

Trio, tankard and teacup and saucer in Worcester porcelain, all decorated in the 'Orange Japan' pattern popular at Worcester, c.1765-75. The manner of painting on the white ground owes much to Kakiemon, whilst the orange panels are derived from the so-called Imari. The teacup and saucer are marked with the crossed swords and '9'. H. (tankard) 12.7cm. Courtesy Albert Amor Ltd

Pair of Worcester soapstone porcelain dishes, painted in underglaze blue, enamel colours and gilding in the Japanese Imari style. Mark, a pseudo oriental character. This design is called 'old mosaick Japan pattern' in the 1769 Worcester catalogue. D. 21.5cm. Courtesy Bearnes, Torquay

Worcester porcelain plate, tea bowl and saucer painted in enamel colours and gilt with the so-called 'Hop' or 'Earl Manvers' pattern, derived from Sèvres. Unmarked but dating to c.1775. D. (plate) 20.4cm.
Courtesy Albert Amor Ltd

Worcester teacup and saucer, painted in enamel colours by the so-called 'spotted fruit painter', with apple green ground with gilt decoration laid alongside, c.1775. Gilding would not adhere to this particular green enamel. Mark, crossed swords and '9'.
Courtesy Bearnes, Torquay

inclined to warp in the firing and in consequence, the condiment rims were kept very narrow or reinforced with raised, moulded decoration. Their early wares did not bear a recognised factory mark but a variety of small underglaze blue marks are to be found which were applied by the decorators as 'tally' marks, to identify their work. The well-known marks of the crescent, the cursive 'W', the 'W' formed by two overlapping 'V's and the fretted square, do not appear to have been adopted until about 1760.

Underglaze blue transfer printing, an easy, cheap and popular method of decorating ceramics, was used from about 1760; these pieces are usually marked, whereas the overglaze printed wares, a technique used until about 1770, were only rarely marked in any way.

From about 1760 the Worcester painters relied a great deal on the popularity of the Oriental wares of the type being exported to England via the vessels of the East India Company, these designs were at times applied entirely in enamel colours, but frequently on reserves left within an underglaze blue ground, which was sometimes applied as a plain blue ground, but more frequently in the so-called 'scale-blue' manner. Other colour grounds were used from about 1760, including the now very much sought after yellow. Sky blue, pea green (now called apple green), pink and purple ground colours were used, obviously inspired by those at Sèvres. A fine collection of coloured Worcester wares may be seen in the Rissik Marshall Collection in the Ashmolean Museum, Oxford.

Worcester chamber candlestick, painted with underglaze blue flower sprays, c.1770-80; unglazed wasters of this form were found in excavations on the factory site. Mark, an open crescent in blue. D. 13cm. Courtesy The Victoria & Albert Museum

Worcester moulded cabbage leaf jug with mask spout in soapstone porcelain, printed with bouquets in underglaze blue, c.1770-5. Mark, a hatched crescent in underglaze blue. H. 17.7cm.
Private Collection

Pair of Worcester soapstone porcelain plates, printed in underglaze blue with the 'Pine Cone' pattern, a very common subject c.1770-85. D. 25cm.
Courtesy Bearnes, Torquay

Following research over more recent years an increasing class of enamelled Worcester porcelain is considered to have been decorated in the atelier of the London decorator James Giles, whose work was often of a far higher quality than that applied by the painters and gilders employed at the factory. Giles's studio was seemingly very active decorating both porcelain and glass from about 1760 to 1776. The Victoria & Albert Museum possesses four very important

*Teapot, porcelain, painted
with enamel colours and
gilding with the Kylin pattern.
Made at Worcester,
c.1780-90, unmarked.
H. 14.7cm.*
R.H. Williamson Bequest,
Tullie House, Carlisle

documentary plates, once in the possession of Mrs Dora Edgell Grubbe, a direct descendant of James Giles. These plates show a wide variety of subjects and suggest that the very prolific output of his studio was only made possible by his employing many skilled painters and gilders.

By 1768 the Chelsea factory in London had become less active and several of their painters went to the more flourishing Worcester concern, these included Jeffreyes Hamett O'Neale; the so-called fable painter, James Donaldson, who excelled in flowers and rather voluptuous mythology and Fidelle Duvivier, a very nomadic painter, whose Continental style appears to owe a great deal to Teniers.

Following the death of Dr. Wall in 1776 the wares that were produced are very disappointing and hard for the collectors of the fine earlier wares to accept, this is probably due to the competition they were now suffering from the newly established factory at Caughley under Thomas Turner, compelling them to produce a wide range of cheaper underglaze blue printed wares, catering for a wider market of less wealthy customers. It is during this 1776-1793 period that so many of their underglaze blue printed patterns can be confused with many almost identical designs being used at Caughley. Geoffrey Godden's book, *Caughley and Worcester Porcelains 1775-1800*, published after the excavations on the sites of both factories, goes into great depth on this subject, to help the collector correctly attribute the porcelains made by these two rivals during the last quarter of the eighteenth century.

FURTHER READING:

Godden, Geoffrey A., *Caughley & Worcester Porcelains 1775-1800.* Antique Collectors' Club, Woodbridge, Revised Edn., 1973.
Sandon, Henry, *Worcester Porcelain 1751-1793,* Barrie & Jenkins, 3rd Edn., 1980.
Branyan, Lawrence, French, Neal, and Sandon, John, *Worcester Blue and White Porcelain, 1751-1790,* Barrie & Jenkins, 1981.
Marshall, Rissik, *Coloured Worcester Porcelain of the First Period,* Ceramic Book Co., 1954.
Coke, G., *In Search of James Giles,* Micawber Publications, 1983.

THE VAUXHALL CHINA WORKS
1751-1764

The records of this factory have been painstakingly researched by a number of ceramic historians, and it is through their findings that we are able to piece together the interesting history of this concern.

We know that in 1751, a soap-rock licence was granted to Nicholas Crisp, listed as a London jeweller, and John Sanders [Saunders], a potter of Lambeth. The first shipment of soap-rock from Cornwall, for use in their porcelain body, did not arrive until 1752, but by 1753, the pottery was advertising for sale, 'a strong and useful Manufacture of Porcelaine ware...'. In 1755, according to a receipt discovered by Mrs. Nancy Valpy, a Samuel Martin 'pd. Mr. Crisp of Bow church yard for four small figures of Vauxhall china a guinea & a half as pr recd of Smith for Crisp & Co'. It was also recorded at the Haberdashers' Hall

Group of wares painted in underglaze blue from the Vauxhall factory, c.1751-64. The mug on the left has a grooved loop handle and is decorated with two rice planters in a paddy field. The tea bowl and saucer are painted with a fishing scene, the tea bowl of a flaring shape. The saucer to the right has a scalloped edge showing six indentations. H. (mug) 6cm.

Formerly Gilbert Bradley Collection

100

that on 6th June 1755 John Bacon was bound to Nicholas Crisp by indenture for seven years. John Bacon, later to become a member of the Royal Academy, received many awards for his sculptures, and according to the *Gentleman's Magazine* of 1799, which published his obituary, it was mentioned that 'In the year 1755, and at the age of 14, he was bound apprentice to Mr. Crispe of Bow church-yard, where he was employed in painting on porcelain. Mr Crispe had a manufactory of china at Lambeth, where Mr. B. occasionally went and assisted. His then occupation, indeed, was but a feeble step towards his future acquirements, as he was chiefly employed in forming shepherds, shepherdesses, and such like small ornamental pieces, yet, for a self-taught artist to perform even works like these with taste, and, in less than two years form (as he did) all the models for the manufactory, was to give indications of no ordinary powers...In attending the manufactory at Lambeth he had an opportunity of observing the models of different sculptors, which were sent to a pottery, on the same premises to be burnt...'.

John Sanders died in 1758, leaving the pottery side of the business to his son, and son-in-law, Henry Richards. On 1st January 1760, Viscount Falmouth transferred the soap-rock licence which had been granted to Crisp and Saunders in 1751, to John Baddeley of Shelton, and William Yates of Newcastle under Lyme. Nicholas Crisp carried on alone until November 1763 when he became bankrupt, the bankruptcy was not entirely due to the failure of the porcelain factory, as Crisp was also involved in other business. The remaining stock was sold the following year, as we learn from the sale notice in the *Daily Advertiser*, discovered by Mrs. Nancy Valpy. The sale took place in Taylor's Room, over the Royal Exchange in London, on 31st May and 1st June 1764, and consisted of '...curious Figures, all Sorts of ornamental Toys, Knife-Handles, and Variety of all Kinds of useful Sorts, etc...'.

We next hear of Crisp in Bovey Tracey in Devon, in about 1766, where it seems he was trying to establish a further pottery. He became involved with William Cookworthy, for whom, before Cookworthy had established his own hard-paste factory in Plymouth, Crisp was firing Cookworthy's experimental wares, but by December 1767, when Crisp's new venture appeared to be failing, Cookworthy noted in a letter to William Pitt, his principal partner, that 'Poor Crisp is quite aground', and that he had 'taken three of his head Servants off his hands'. These workmen were a modeller and a painter, who had formerly been employed at the Chelsea, Bow and Vauxhall China Potteries, and the other was a burner. None of the wares from the Bovey Tracey porcelain pottery have as yet been identified.

Nicholas Crisp was a most enterprising man of his time. He was a founding member of the Society of Arts, he was involved in assaying furnaces, enamels, paper suitable for engravers, and the production of cobalt, used in the application of underglaze blue decoration to ceramic wares; he also had interests in various vessels of the East India Company, in which he was also a shareholder (these interests have been fully covered by Mr. Geoffrey Godden in his

Sauce boat painted in blue and white of a similar shape to Bow, even to the heart-shaped terminal at the base of the handle. Thought at one time to be from a factory associated with William Ball at Liverpool, but now identified as Vauxhall, from the factory of Nicholas Crisp and John Sanders, c.1751-64. Wasters found on the factory site show painting which appears almost identical to the twin peaks and trees at top right. L. 22.5cm.   Formerly Gilbert Bradley Collection

Pickle dish from Vauxhall, c.1751-64. Painted in underglaze blue with a butterfly in the centre, these dishes have also been found with the butterfly painted in enamel colours. H. 10cm.

Courtesy Phillips, London

Encyclopaedia of British Porcelain Manufacturers). Nicholas Crisp died in Bovey Tracey in 1774.

Prior to 1980 there was no certain knowledge of the wares produced at Vauxhall; it was at this time that excavations were carried out by the Southwark & Lambeth Archaeological Committee under the supervision of Robin Densem, and further excavations were undertaken in 1987 for the Museum of London's Department of Greater London Archaeology under the direction of Derek Seeley. From the excavations of the site located on the east side of the Albert Embankment, London, delftware, stoneware and porcelain wasters were recovered, but the proportion of porcelain was small as only about sixty sherds were recovered; amongst these underglaze blue pieces, was a test piece for firing enamels, but no sherds of figures were found. From the analysis of these wasters carried out by Mavis Bimson of the British Museum Research Laboratory, it has been found that two types of porcelain were made at Vauxhall, one similar to the soapstone porcelain produced at the Worcester factory, and the other containing a mineral not normally found in English porcelains. These were limited trials, carried out on twenty of the sixty sherds recovered.

We do, however, have a group of wares which relate to the sherds recovered from the site, which have been closely studied by Dr. Bernard Watney, who published his findings in the *E.C.C. Transactions* of 1989 and 1990, in which he showed cream jugs with handles which he had matched with two handles found on the site, also cream jugs, tea bowls and cups and saucers decorated with underglaze blue decoration in Chinese style, which also matched wasters. Sherds were recovered bearing floral patterns which so far are unmatched to wares, as is the sherd of a sauceboat moulded with a cob nut and fish egg design.

Dr. Watney suggests that common motifs can be found linking Vauxhall to Plymouth, and also to Bow. This would seem probable as we know that two of the Vauxhall potters had previously been employed at the Bow factory and had later worked at Plymouth.

An unusual form of polychrome transfer printing is found on some Vauxhall porcelain, a form of decoration which is at times also found on Longton Hall figures, and it has been suggested by Dr. Watney that after the transfer of the soap-rock licence in January 1760, following the death of John Sanders, that Nicholas Crisp purchased figures of Longton Hall porcelain in the white and that he added the transfer prints at Vauxhall. It is known that a sale of Longton Hall porcelain was held on 10th and 11th July, 1760 at their London warehouse, at the corner of St. Paul's Church Yard, near Watling Street, and that this lay only a few minutes walk from Bow Church Yard where the Vauxhall factory was situated. This sale was held two months before the large sale of Longton Hall porcelain which was sold in Salisbury.

As mentioned previously, it is difficult to establish the whole output of a factory over thirteen years on the evidence of only sixty sherds and limited advertisements. At this time, further excavations are prevented by the existence of a nineteenth century railway viaduct which covers the most important part of the site, but perhaps sometime in the future rebuilding will again take place and further secrets of this interesting factory will be revealed.

Readers are reminded that in many earlier books, and in some museum collections, these wares will still be wrongly attributed to William Ball of Liverpool.

FURTHER READING:

Watney, Dr. Bernard, 'The Vauxhall China Works 1751-64', *English Ceramic Circle Transactions,* Vol. 13, Part 3, 1989; 'Interim report on excavations at Vauxhall', *E.C.C. Transactions,* Vol. 14, Part 1, 1990.

Valpy, Nancy, 'Nicholas Crisp: a newly-found Benefactor', *E.C.C. Transactions,* Vol. 13, Part 2, 1988.

Bimson, Mavis, 'The Composition of Vauxhall porcelain', *E.C.C. Transactions,* Vol. 13, Part 3, 1989.

Seeley, Derek, 'Description of Excavations on Vauxhall Site (38-46 Albert Embankment S.E.1.), *E.C.C. Transactions,* Vol. 13, Part 3, 1989.

Stevenson, Roy, 'Description of Ceramic Material found on the Vauxhall Site', *E.C.C. Transactions,* Vol. 13, Part 3, 1989.

Godden, Geoffrey, A., *Encyclopaedia of British Porcelain Manufacturers,* p.268, Barrie & Jenkins, London, 1988.

This plate is a rare example from the factory at Vauxhall, c.1751-64, showing a moulded shape decorated with an unusual form of polychrome printing which is an interesting feature of the pottery. D. 23.7cm.

Courtesy The Victoria & Albert Museum

This tea bowl and saucer is matched by a sherd found on the site of the Vauxhall factory, c.1751-64. Painted in underglaze blue, it was copied from an original design seen on Chinese porcelain of the Kangxi period (1662-1722), showing the eight horses of Mu Wang, the Emperor of China, 1001BC-946BC. D. (saucer) 12.2cm.

Courtesy The Victoria & Albert Museum

Two saucers painted in underglaze blue with added enamel in red with sparse gilding. The saucer on the left is painted with the same design as a tea bowl in the Williamson Art Gallery, Birkenhead, which bears the date 1764. The saucer on the right is of scalloped shape with six indentations. Both saucers have very shallow foot rings. Vauxhall, 1751-64. D. 14cm. D. 12cm. Private Collection

THE LIVERPOOL PORCELAIN FACTORIES

c.1754-1840

When discussing the porcelains made in Liverpool during the eighteenth century, one must approach the subject with some caution. In the light of new knowledge, attributions are changing. In 1980, and again in 1987 following excavations in London, a group of wares formerly thought to have been made by William Ball of Liverpool had to be reassigned to the factory of Nicholas Crisp and his partner John Sanders of Vauxhall. More exciting excavations have taken place, as recently as March 1990, which proved that wares long thought to have been made at another Liverpool factory, that of William Reid & Co., were indeed again from London, the pottery of Wilson & Co., of

Liverpool porcelain cider jug, painted in enamel colours, from Richard Chaffers' factory, c.1757.
H. 17.5cm. Courtesy Roderick Jellicoe Antiques

A fine example of a jug from the factory of Richard Chaffers of Liverpool, c.1755-65, decorated with a Chinese scene in underglaze blue and overglaze red with added gilding. H. 27cm.
Courtesy Colonial Williamsburg Foundation

Beaker attributed to Richard Chaffers, c.1755-65. Painted in underglaze blue with the 'Jumping Boy' pattern and a Chinese lady sitting on a rock. Four pseudo Chinese character marks. H. 6cm.
Courtesy Phillips, London

Tankard from the factory of Richard Chaffers of Liverpool painted in underglaze blue, c.1755-65
Courtesy Simon Spero Antiques

Limehouse. New discoveries are being made, and new theories are being offered, all of which tend to alter the scene. Bearing this in mind, however, we do have some firm ground, such as the evidence provided by insurance policies and newspaper advertisements, which are invaluable, and in some cases the discovery of wasters on former factory sites, all of which help researchers to further our knowledge. Thus a picture of the now diminished Liverpool manufacturers has been built up.

In the middle of the eighteenth century Liverpool was a thriving port, concerned mainly with the slave trade and the cotton industry, but not with the East India Company which was a monopoly of the Port of London. With the massive import of Chinese porcelain, a popular market was created and British potters were trying to emulate these wares, and break into this trade. The potters of Liverpool who were eager to take a share of this thriving business included **SAMUEL GILBODY JUN.** who in 1754 seems to have inherited his father's pottery, which had most probably originally been used solely for the production of tin-glazed earthenware (delftware). We know, however, that by 1758 Gilbody advertised in the *Liverpool Chronicle* and the *Marine Gazette,* that he was now selling 'CHINA-WARE of all SORTS equal for Service and Beauty to any made in ENGLAND'. Two years later he was presumably still doing well, enough to justify opening a warehouse in York. Unfortunately he appeared to have taken on too much, as one month later he was bankrupt, and in July 1761 his business was being offered for sale.

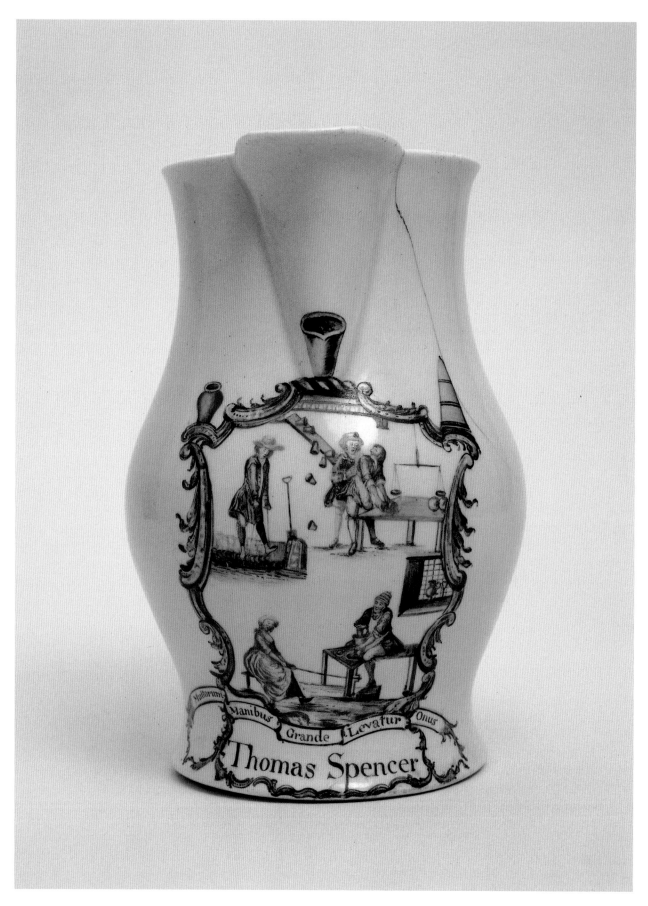

A group of Liverpool tea wares painted in enamel colours. The 'High Chelsea Ewer' shaped cream jug on the left (H. 8.5cm.) and the central teapot stand (D. 16.5cm) are both from the factory of Seth Pennington, c.1785. The cream jug to the right (H. 9cm.) is from that of Philip Christian, c.1775. All unmarked
Private Collection

An exceptionally interesting porcelain jug, painted in enamel colours. Made by Richard Chaffers, Liverpool. The lively scene depicted is best described by Dr. Maurice Hillis in 'The Liverpool Porcelains', Northern Ceramic Society Occasional Paper No. 1. 1985, *in which he writes, 'It is decorated with splendid enamel scenes of a potworks showing firstly the clay being cut from a weathering pit with a wire, then weighed out and finally thrown on a wheel. Along the top of the decoration, almost as if armorial crests, are displayed typical products of the potworks, from the left a storage jar, a crucible and a sugar mould. This exceptional piece would have been made for presentation to Thomas Spencer whose name appears near the base and who it is perhaps not too fanciful to identify as the gentleman knocking over the pot-board in the second scene. Thomas Spencer, potter, married Elizabeth Gibson at St. Peter's, Liverpool on the 23rd September, 1764. Joseph Mayer in his early work on Liverpool pottery records that Thomas Spencer ran the potworks at the bottom of Richard Row. It seems quite likely that this magnificent jug was presented on the occasion of his marriage and it is interesting that porcelain was considered appropriate rather than the coarse pottery made at Spencer's own potworks'. H. 20.7cm.*
Courtesy City Museum & Art Gallery, Stoke-on-Trent

Sauce boat decorated in polychrome enamels, c.1770-2. This shape also occurs in underglaze blue. From the factory of Philip Christian, Liverpool. L. 14cm.
Private Collection

Tea bowl and saucer painted in underglaze blue from the factory of Philip Christian, Liverpool, c.1765. D. (saucer) 12cm.
Private Collection

We are fortunate in having some evidence of the wares made by Samuel Gilbody, for during roadworks carried out in Liverpool in 1966, fragments of porcelain were recovered by Professor Alan Smith which matched wares previously attributed to the factory by Dr. Bernard Watney.

The porcelains ascribed to Samuel Gilbody are of the bone ash type, and include thinly potted tea bowls decorated in underglaze blue, coffee cups painted in enamel colours; some with red/brown monochrome, coffee pots of elegant shape with distinctive knops and scroll handles, teapots with 'crabstock' style handles and spouts, and mugs with well-painted enamel decoration.

A mug in the Victoria & Albert Museum is decorated with an early black printed version of the 'Arms of the Society of Bucks', which is in the manner of

Coffee pot attributed to the factory of Phillip Christian of Liverpool, c.1765-78, printed with a pastoral scene in rather dense black, typical of Sadler & Green printing of this period. Notice the down turned 'comma' terminal on the handle and the moulded decoration on the spout, both of which help in the identification of wares from this factory. H.21.8cm

Courtesy Colonial Williamsburg Foundation

Liverpool teapot painted in underglaze blue with added enamel colours. Philip Christian, c.1772. H.11cm.

Courtesy Simon Spero

This teapot shape is always associated with Liverpool. The example shown is moulded with a design of palm trees and decorated with enamels. Attributed to Seth Pennington, c.1778. H. 16.5cm.

the engraver Jeremiah Evans, who worked for Sadler & Green, and has a rare form of handle which can be matched to wasters found on the site. Further Gilbody mugs are known, one depicting Frederick the Great in Armour, signed 'Sadler Liverpool Enl. & Evans Sct'. These mugs mainly have flat bases, although on occasions they do have foot rings. Wasters of a Derby-like figure were found, and further figures have been identified by Dr. Bernard Watney, including Minerva, a Turkish woman, and a set of The Seasons. These porcelains are exceedingly rare.

WILLIAM REID & CO. We know that William Reid and his partners, John Baddeley, Daniel McNeale and William Yates, were managing a factory on Brownlow Hill from about 1755 until they became bankrupt in 1761. The type of wares made there at the time are described in an advertisement for the sale

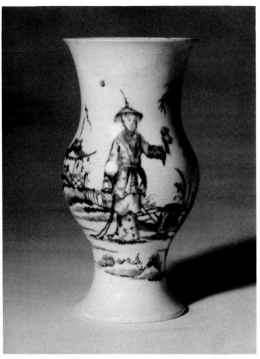

Pear-shaped bottle attributed to Phillip Christian of Liverpool, c.1765-78. The underglaze blue border with added gilding is a feature often found on wares of this factory. The flowers are painted in enamel colours. H. 22cm.   Courtesy City Museum & Art Gallery, Stoke-on-Trent

Liverpool vase from the factory of Seth Pennington, painted in underglaze blue, c.1780. H. 15cm.
Formerly Gilbert Bradley Collection

of bankrupt stock, which appeared in the *Liverpool Advertiser* on 4th December, 1761, 'Notice of Sale of Bankrupt Stock. Buildings and Colour Mill etc. Best blue and white cups and saucers @ 3s per set. 2nd Best blue and white cups and saucers @ 2s. per set. Enamelled coffee cups from 6s to 2s per dozen, and all sorts of china cheap in proportion'.

The group of wares formerly believed to have been made at this factory, have now been reallocated to the factory at Limehouse in London as mentioned above. Unfortunately there have been no excavations possible on the site of

Teapot transfer printed in underglaze blue attributed to Seth Pennington of Liverpool, c.1778-1805.
H.16cm.
Courtesy City Museum & Art Gallery, Stoke-on-Trent

Rare Liverpool porcelain bowl, painted in underglaze blue and enamel colours with 'The Stag Hunt'
pattern, from Samuel Gilbody's factory, c.1758. D. 16cm. Courtesy Roderick Jellicoe Antiques

Liverpool 'sparrow-beak' cream jug painted in underglaze blue and red enamel. Seth Pennington,
c.1785. H.8.2cm.
Allan Weaver Collection

Bowl printed in underglaze blue in the 'Fisherman' or 'Pleasure Boat' pattern, from Liverpool, one of the Pennington factories, c.1780-5. D. 15.5cm. Private Collection

Bowl similar to the previous example printed in underglaze blue, in the 'Fisherman' or 'Pleasure Boat' pattern, from Liverpool, one of the Pennington factories, c.1780-5. D. 16cm. Private Collection

Coffee can painted in underglaze blue with a Chinese lady standing in a garden; a Chinese boy is on the reverse. A can is always straight-sided and does not normally have a matching saucer. Liverpool, from one of the Pennington factories, c.1780. H. 6.5cm. Private Collection

Cream jug with 'biting snake' handle, and shell and dolphin moulding on the lip, decorated with a transfer in underglaze blue. Liverpool, probably from the factory of Seth Pennington, c.1780-90. L. 12cm. Private Collection

William Reid's factory, so therefore we cannot attribute any wares to this concern with any certainty, at this time.

RICHARD CHAFFERS & CO. occupied a factory on Shaw's Brow next door to the factory of Samuel Gilbody, whom we have already discussed. Chaffers was in partnership with Philip Christian from about 1746, at which time they were making tin glazed earthenware. In 1755 an agreement was signed with Robert Podmore, who had been employed at the Worcester factory, in which he agreed to instruct them in the manufacture of porcelain. The company also leased a mine at Predannock in Cornwall, to enable them to obtain soap-rock, such as was used in the manufacture of Worcester porcelain. Their first shipment of soap-rock was in 1756, and by the end of the year the first advertisement for Chaffers porcelain was published; it has been suggested that this first porcelain may have been of the bone ash type, shortly to be followed by porcelain containing soapstone. Various table wares have been attributed to this factory, also vases and miniature wares, many in the style of Worcester. The bases of mugs and coffee cans are generally flat and unglazed, although there are exceptions. Plain rolled or strap handles are mainly found, together with rarer grooved handles, which are shallower than those used at Worcester. On-glaze printing in red or black was sometimes added to the wares by John Sadler. It has been suggested that figures may also have been made at the factory, one possibility being the bust of George II which can be seen in the Schreiber Collection at the Victoria & Albert Museum.

PHILIP CHRISTIAN continued to run the factory together with Richard

Tea bowl and saucer printed in underglaze blue showing a pair of quails. Seth Pennington, Liverpool, c.1790. Saucer D. 13cm.
Private Collection

Chaffers' widow after Chaffers died in 1765, but in 1769 he bought her share of the factory and continued production with his son until 1778. The wares produced at this time were all of soapstone porcelain and continued the styles of Chaffers; they were thinly potted, but did not have the deep blue glaze tinting which is found on the earlier wares. On coffee cans Christian favoured plain rolled or grooved handles and unlike Chaffers rarely used the strap handle; foot rings were undercut and the handles on mugs and coffee pots often have a distinctive 'comma' terminal. On-glaze black printed wares are usually found to be darker on Christian's porcelain than on that of Chaffers, this was probably due to the fact that Sadler & Green by this time were improving the density of their black printing. In the 1770s Christian introduced underglaze printing in blue, a technique not used by either Chaffers or Gilbody. His mask jugs were similar in style to those produced at Worcester, but the masks have an unmistakably youthful appearance. A very distinctive teapot with moulded and painted leaves and palm trees was also introduced by Christian.

Towards the end of the Christian occupancy his wares seemed to deteriorate, perhaps because of the need to serve a lower priced market, and by 1776 he had sold the lease of the soap-rock mine in Cornwall, and in September 1778 the factory was taken over by Seth Pennington and John Part.

SETH PENNINGTON AND JOHN PART continued at the factory on Shaw's Brow from 1778 producing wares in a similar style to the previous owners, probably having bought the moulds with the factory, their porcelain however was all of the bone ash type. Seth Pennington introduced further versions of Worcester & Caughley designs, such as the 'Fisherman' or 'Pleasure Boat' which can sometimes be seen in conjunction with the Christian style mask jug and the down-turned 'comma' terminal to the moulded handle. Coffee cups appear to be smaller, having simple rolled handles and taller foot rings. It seems that Seth Pennington was catering for a cheaper market. The partnership with John Part was dissolved in 1799 and Seth Pennington continued with different partners until the factory finally closed c.1805.

There were limited excavations possible on the Shaw's Brow site, which helped with the identification of this group of wares.

JAMES PENNINGTON was one of Seth's two older brothers, who had at one time been a partner of Richard Chaffers & Co.; we know from an insurance policy that this partnership was dissolved in 1763, at which time he is thought to have commenced potting at Brownlow Hill, a factory which had belonged to William Reid prior to his bankruptcy in 1761. In an insurance policy of 1763 the works were described as 'used for a China Manufactory in the tenure of James Pennington & Co.' In about 1767 James seems to have moved to the Park Lane Pothouse, where we know he remained until at least 1773.

Unfortunately there have been no excavations on either of these sites to enable his wares to be identified, but specialists in Liverpool porcelain suggest that he probably made a soapstone porcelain at Brownlow Hill, changing to bone ash on moving to Park Lane.

Pounce pot attributed to Pennington of Liverpool, probably Seth. The top is pierced — a pounce pot was used as a container for a fine powder used to prevent ink spreading on unsized paper. Inscribed in underglaze blue 'James Lyon 1791' and with a floral sprig on reverse. H. 7.5cm.

Courtesy Phillips, London

Cup of hybrid hard-paste porcelain decorated with underglaze blue transfer prints. These are of a type matching wasters found on the Liverpool site of Thomas Wolfe & Co. who were making porcelain from c.1796-1800. H. 6.2cm.

Private Collection

JOHN PENNINGTON was another of the Pennington brothers and also a master potter, who with his wife Jane seems to have been manufacturing at Copperas Hill from about 1771. In January 1779 they moved to a new site at Islington (which had been named Folly Lane), and in June 1779 he announced in the Liverpool and Chester newspapers that he was making 'Elegant, cheap and serviceable china ware, which are, for brilliancy of colour, equal to any made in Great Britain'. He was also prepared to decorate wares to order, with devices, coats of arms, etc. John died in 1786 and his widow continued to run the factory until 1794, when it passed into the hands of Thomas Wolfe & Co.

Some excavations were carried out on the Islington site by Professor Alan Smith in 1968. Among the wasters found of the later Thomas Wolfe type, a few pieces were found of the earlier John Pennington factory, which included glazed pieces showing a cell border, a floral pattern and part of the 'cannon-ball' pattern. These were all similar to the type of wares produced by Seth Pennington, and are not easily divided. One unglazed waster was found, however, which has been matched to an unusual mask jug. The mask with its distinctive 'Red Indian' type of head-dress is of a different form from that used by Christian & Seth Pennington, and the jug has a handle with an upturned 'comma' terminal.

THOMAS WOLFE & CO. took over the Islington factory from Jane Pennington in about 1794. He was in partnership with the London china dealer, so-called

'China Man', Miles Mason, and John Lucock, a potter. They produced a hybrid hard-paste porcelain similar to that of New Hall, decorated in many cases with underglaze blue prints with versions of the Pagoda/Willow type, and also wares with polychrome decoration. Many examples of tea wares were found to have foot rims stained brown, in imitation of the Chinese. The partnership was dissolved and the works closed in 1800. Rare examples of porcelain marked Wolfe & Hamilton are known to have been made in Stoke-on-Trent where Wolfe continued to pot in partnership with Robert Hamilton and later William Arrowsmith until 1810 when this partnership was dissolved, after which it appears that Thomas Wolfe continued to produce wares until his death in 1818.

ZACHARIAH BARNES was another rather elusive Liverpool potter who was in partnership with James Cotter. They were probably working in the Haymarket Pottery from about 1783 and Barnes was listed in the *Liverpool Directory* as having a china manufactory until 1796. There was also a newspaper advertisement in 1783 for 'English China of fine quality with variety of patterns at the lowest prices', issued by Barnes & Cotter of the Haymarket Pottery. There are some rare pieces of bone ash type of porcelain found with the rare mark 'HP' in underglaze blue, the initials either separate or in monogram form. This mark, which has been found on tea wares decorated with on-glaze enamels, could stand for the Haymarket Pottery, but as yet it has not been possible for excavations to be carried out on the Haymarket site to enable us to recognise the wares of this factory with any certainty.

THE HERCULANEUM POTTERY is the last of the Liverpool manufacturers to be discussed and was a comparative latecomer to the scene. The factory was situated in Toxteth Park on the outskirts of the city, away from the main pottery sites. Samuel Worthington was an astute business man, who in 1796 brought a group of forty Staffordshire potters and their families up the Mersey & Trent Canal to settle and work in his new factory. The name given to this concern was Herculaneum, the classical name following the fashion set by Wedgwood when he named his factory Etruria. The pottery soon achieved success, and became greatly involved with the overseas trade, not only selling and exporting their own wares, but also acting as agents for other Staffordshire potters, such as Josiah Spode. The factory reached its peak in 1806 when shareholders brought in a large investment and by means of a commitee, managed the factory. The overseas trade, however, was diminishing by 1816, and the shareholders, looking for a more profitable investment, sold the factory in 1833 to Ambrose Lace, who in turned leased it to two potters, Thomas Case and James Mort. When Thomas Case retired in 1836, the factory continued under James Mort and John Simpson whose trade continued until 1840 when the factory finally closed.

The Herculaneum factory produced a great variety of wares in earthenware and from about 1800 until about 1833 two types of porcelain were made, a bone china and a harder body similar to that of New Hall. Useful wares of all kinds

Tea bowl and saucer of hybrid hard-paste porcelain decorated with underglaze blue transfer prints. Attributed to Thomas Wolfe & Co., Liverpool, c.1796-1800. D. (saucer) 13cm.

Gift of R. and D. Haggar
Courtesy City Museum & Art
Gallery, Stoke-on-Trent

Cream jug, shape known as 'High Chelsea Ewer', decorated in polychrome enamels and bearing a rare mark, 'H P' in underglaze blue. Possibly from the factory of Zachariah Barnes at the Haymarket Pottery, Liverpool, c.1783-96. H.7.7cm.

Courtesy City Museum & Art
Gallery, Stoke-on-Trent

were produced, decorated with underglaze blue printing, on-glaze black printing and bat printing, for which they employed their own engravers. Well-known modellers and painters were engaged, including William Lovatt, John Edwards and William Dixon. Special prestigious pieces were sometimes made, some painted in the style of such famous artists as George Morland. The inspiration for these impressive wares is thought to have come from the influence of William Roscoe (1753-1831), who was a well-known patron of the arts in Liverpool at the time. These outstanding, but rare pieces sometimes warranted a special mark of a liver bird within a wreath, whereas their useful wares, if marked, just have the word HERCULANEUM impressed.

Group of wares. in underglaze blue, showing a Chinaman seated in a garden painted in a primitive manner. So far the attribution of these wares is uncertain, they are bone porcelain of c.1770, probably made in Liverpool. H. (cream jug) 8cm.   Private Collection

JOHN SADLER and his partner Guy Green ran an important printing business in Liverpool from 1749 to 1799. They were not ceramic manufacturers, but were engaged in applying enamel prints from copperplates to at least eight independent potters' wares. In 1756 they swore a joint affidavit that within six hours they applied prints to twelve hundred delftware tiles and boasted of their superiority to the hand painted type. This claim was certified as true, by two Liverpool potters, Thomas Shaw and Samuel Gilbody. Sadler retired in 1770 after which Green ran the business until 1799.

FURTHER READING:
Godden, G.A., *Encyclopaedia of British Porcelain Manufacturers,* Barrie & Jenkins, 1988.
Hillis, Maurice, 'The Liverpool Porcelains', *Northern Ceramic Society Occasional Paper,* No. 1, 1985; 'The Liverpool Porcelain of John & Jane Pennington c.1771-94', *Journal of the Northern Ceramic Society,* Vol. 6, 1987; 'Diversity Discovered (Gilbody & Wolfe)', *Antique Dealer and Collectors Guide,* August, 1988; 'The Liverpool Mainstream (Chaffers & Christian)', *Antique Dealer and Collectors Guide,* April, 1989; 'Later Liverpool (The Penningtons)', *Antique Dealer and Collectors Guide,* Nov. 1989.
Smith, Prof. Alan, *Liverpool Herculaneum Pottery,* Barrie & Jenkins, 1970; 'Samuel Gilbody — Some recent Finds at Liverpool', *English Ceramic Circle Transactions,* Vol. 7, Part 2, 1969; 'Thomas Wolfe, Miles Mason and John Lucock at the Islington China Manufactory, Upper Islington, Liverpool', *English Ceramic Circle Transactions,* Vol. 8, Part 2, 1972.

DERBY

c.1748-1848

Our knowledge of the Huguenot Andrew Planché, credited with establishing the first porcelain factory in Derby, is a little vague. He lived with his father in Soho, London, and in 1740 was apprenticed to a goldsmith. He may well have learnt the secrets of the making of porcelain in London, prior to moving to Derby in about 1747 or 1748 and there are just three documentary cream jugs with varying incised marks, 'Derby', 'D' and 'D/1750'. At about this same time a series of unmarked figures were also produced, they are of a lightweight chalky material, made by the slip-casting method, with a distinctive margin around the base devoid of glaze, referred to as 'the dry-edge group'. The exact site of the factory is unknown, but a newspaper report in 1753 writes of the 'China Works near Mary Bridge'.

Prior to becoming a partner in the major Derby porcelain concern in 1756, William Duesbury was occupied as an 'Enameller' in London and in his account books of 1751/2 he enters several porcelain figures attributed to

There seems little doubt that a potter by the name of Andrew Planché was working at 'the China Works near Mary Bridge' from c.1750, before the major Derby factory established by William Duesbury in 1756. The figures illustrated are of the Planché period and known as the 'dry-edge' group, due to the removal of the thick glassy glaze from the lower edges of the base. This Shepherdess and her Bagpiper companion appear to have been taken from Meissen originals and were also made at Bow. Sometimes they are enamelled in colour, which would have been applied by William Duesbury when working as an enameller in London. H. 17.5cm.

Courtesy Simon Spero Antiques

122

Small soft-paste porcelain figure of a charging bull, painted with enamel colours. Attributed to the factory of Andrew Planché, c.1750-5, it has the typical 'dry-edge' where the glaze has been removed from the edge of the base. H. 6cm.

Courtesy Royal Crown Derby Museum

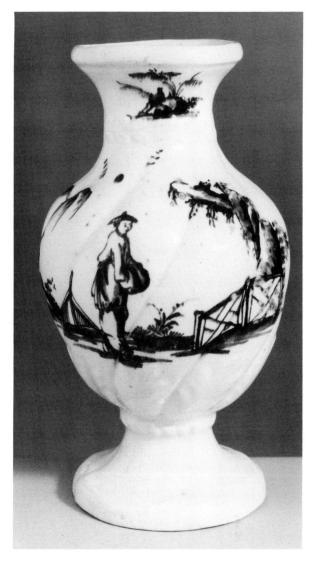

A Derby vase of unusual form, moulded in relief with spiral gadrooning and leaves, painted in underglaze blue, c.1760-5. On the reverse a Chinese fisherman seated under a tree. Unmarked. H. 14.5cm. Courtesy Simon Spero Antiques

Planché, including 'Darbeyshire sesons'; '2 pr. of Dansers Darby figars'; and '1 pr. Large Darbey Figars'.

This same site near St. Mary's Bridge appears to have been occupied for a short while by 'Mr. Heath & Company' prior to moving into a new factory. Although an agreement of January 1, 1756, named John Heath, William Duesbury and Andrew Planché, as co-partners in establishing a new china works in Nottingham Road, this agreement was never signed and William Duesbury obviously felt that he had sufficient knowledge of the manufacture to continue without the aid of Planché, which he did very successfully for many years. John Heath, the banker, who had financed the original project became bankrupt in 1779 and the manufacture was continued by Duesbury until his death in 1786, when he was succeeded by his son, of the same name. William Duesbury II increased the size of the works, which became known as 'The Old China Manufactory'.

In 1795 William Duesbury II took Michael Kean, an Irish miniature painter, into partnership, who after Duesbury's death in 1795, married his widow, the factory continuing as the Duesbury & Kean concern until 1809, when the entire

A rare soft-paste porcelain mug, made by William Duesbury, Derby, to celebrate the crowning of George III and Queen Charlotte in 1761. The cupid above Queen Charlotte's head carries a banner which reads 'Crown'd Sept 22nd 1761'; other decoration on the same mug shows George III being crowned by an angel and Britannia with outstretched hand to Hibernia or Minerva, all transfer printed in black, including a small anchor and 'DERBY', the rebus of Richard Holdship, the engraver. H. 13cm.   Courtesy Royal Crown Derby Museum

Porcelain figure of a leopard, painted in enamel colours made at the Derby factory of William Duesbury and Co., c.1760. The distinctive 'patch marks' caused during the firing of the glaze appear on Derby figures from as early as 1760. L. 8.5cm.

Courtesy Brian Haughton Antiques

124

Derby soft-paste porcelain feeding cup, decorated with underglaze blue transfer prints of carnations, which have again lost their detail due to the extensive running of the glaze, c.1775. Very few Derby transfer prints have been identified and the technique does not appear to have been adopted until after the arrival at the factory of Richard Holdship, one of the original Worcester partners, c.1763. L. 17.7cm.
Formerly in the Gilbert Bradley Collection

Derby soft-paste porcelain chestnut bowl, with pierced cover, and stand, decorated in the typical Derby 'inky' underglaze blue, the interior of the bowl is painted with the same scene as on the stand, c.1762. The bowl has the typical Derby patches showing on base. D. (stand) 20.5cm.
Formerly in the Gilbert Bradley Collection

Porcelain figure of Shakespeare, modelled after the statue of the bard by the sculptor Peter Scheemakers after a design by William Kent, which is in Poets' Corner, Westminster Abbey. Made by William Duesbury & Co. at Derby, showing Derby patch marks under base, c.1765. H. 31cm.

Courtesy Royal Crown Derby Museum

Porcelain figure of Diana the Huntress, decorated in enamel colours and gilt with a typical Derby rococo base of c.1765. Made at Derby by William Duesbury & Co. H. 31.3cm.

Courtesy Royal Crown Derby Museum

Early Derby porcelain coffee cup of quatrefoil form and 'wishbone' handle, painted in enamel colours by the so-called 'cotton-stalk' painter, who is recognised by the thread like stems to the flowers, the rim is painted with a brownish red enamel, unmarked. H. 6cm.

Private Collection

Two Derby figures of a dancing girl, painted in varying enamel colours, one rarely sees identical painting on the figures of this period. Adapted from the early wares of the Planché period and dating c.1758-60; a companion figure is a Scotsman playing bagpipes. H. 15.5cm.

Albert Amor Ltd

factory and the London warehouse was put up for sale as a going concern and was taken over by Robert Bloor, the company clerk, in 1811. Bloor had great difficulty in raising the necessary £5,000, which probably brought about his mental breakdown in 1828, but the factory continued under his descendants until 1848, when it finally closed.

The early Derby figures attributed to Planché and often decorated by Duesbury are decidedly more pleasing than those produced from 1756 at the new factory, when Duesbury endeavoured to justify his claim of establishing 'A Second Dresden' factory by applying a decidedly blue tinted glaze in order to give the colder appearance of the hard-paste porcelain of Meissen (Dresden).

Derby wares were rarely marked prior to about 1770, but their method of preventing pieces fusing into the saggar during the firing of the glaze is a good, but not infallible guide. Many of the figures and useful wares were stood upon

Pair of soft-paste porcelain figures of dancing children, dressed as Turks. Decorated in enamel colours and showing 'patch marks' on base. Made by William Duesbury and Co. at Derby, c.1760. H. 21.1cm.
Courtesy Royal Crown Derby Museum

small pads of clay, leaving three or more small round dark patches on the base, referred to as 'Derby patch-marks'. It must be remembered that this Derby manufacture was started as the rococo style became fashionable and so the high scrolled bases are not such a guide to dating as those of Chelsea or Bow.

In 1770 Duesbury purchased the Chelsea concern and ran both factories until 1784, a period referred to today as Chelsea/Derby, it being impossible to separate the wares produced at each factory, except by the applied marks. The gold anchor alone is unreliable, as a bowl in the Victoria & Albert Museum painted with the arms of the Coopers Company is dated 1779, but still bears the simple gold anchor of Chelsea, which should have been abandoned in 1770 in favour of the 'D' and anchor in monogram form.

In their 'first public sale of the last year's produce' in 1771, the 'Chelsea and Derby Porcelain Manufactories' offered for the first time figures and groups left in the unglazed 'biscuit' as popularised by Sèvres and Tournay. These figures, mostly in the then popular neo-classical styles, were more costly to buy than those glazed and enamelled, due to the fact that they had to be in mint condition, whereas minor defects and blemishes could always be repaired in the glaze firing or obscured with enamel colours. This is one of the rare occasions when the artist Angelica Kauffmann can be related to ceramics; engravings of her paintings were frequently used by the Derby modeller, Pierre Stephan, to create many attractive biscuit or enamelled groups. Angelica Kauffmann herself never painted porcelain.

Early Derby coffee pot, painted in underglaze blue with Chinese figures, c.1760-2. There were few Derby wares painted in this colour until after the arrival from Worcester of Richard Holdship, but coffee pots with this shape and decoration appeared to have been a popular model. H. 24cm.

Courtesy Simon Spero Antiques

Derby soft-paste porcelain vase, c.1765. The broken underglaze blue ground suggests the cobalt was applied by the sponging technique, the C-scroll cartouches are painted in underglaze blue with European landscapes and butterflies, repeated on the reverse. H. 12.5cm.

Formerly in the Gilbert Bradley Collection

Large soft-paste porcelain Derby leaf dish, decorated in the Chinese fashion with a powder blue ground with circular and fan shaped reserves painted with flowers and buildings, the blue ground has 'flown' into some of the reserves, probably due to overfiring, c.1768. L. 10.4cm.

Formerly in the Gilbert Bradley Collection

Derby porcelain wine taster, with small moulded handle and sixteen lobes on the exterior, painted in underglaze blue, c.1768. D. 6.3cm.

Private Collection

129

Derby porcelain group painted in enamel colours and gilt, known as 'Isabella, Gallant and Jester', taken from the Commedia dell'Arte *series, a similar figure known as 'The indiscreet Harlequin', taken from Meissen, shows Harlequin peeking at Columbine's ankles, whilst she is otherwise engaged with her lover. Made by William Duesbury & Co., c.1765. H. 30cm.*

Courtesy Royal Crown Derby Museum

Early Derby porcelain coffee pot and cover. Note the form of handle, painted in enamel colours by the so-called 'dishevelled bird painter', an apt description coined by the late W.B. Honey. Made about 1760 and once in the Brayshaw Gilhespy Collection. D. 23.5cm.

Courtesy Royal Crown Derby Museum

A rare Derby centrepiece, comprising four kneeling Blackamoor figures each holding a dish in the form of a shell, with a further shell on top of the moulded pillar, painted in enamel colours and gilt. Showing the typical Derby 'patch marks' under base. Made by William Duesbury & Co., c.1765. H. 29.4cm. R.H. Williamson Bequest, Tullie House, Carlisle

Derby porcelain figure of Justice, painted in enamel colours and gilt. Made by William Duesbury & Co., c.1770. A figure of Justice features in the list produced by John Haslem in The Old Derby China Factory, *published in London, by George Bell in 1876 and it was originally priced at 15 shillings. H. 32.2cm. (which is much higher than that in Haslem's list)* Courtesy Bearnes, Torquay

Many Derby figures in the 1770-84 period were inspired by Meissen models, including the 'grotesque Punches' or dwarfs; only those carrying advertising material on their tall hats should be referred to as 'Mansion House' dwarfs.

The neo-classical style is better suited to earthenware, such as Wedgwood's creamware, but in the Chelsea/Derby period some tablewares were produced decorated with classical urns, the running honeysuckle and other classical features, in an attempt to keep up with the current fashion.

The decorators employed at Derby, some of whom transferred from Chelsea at the time of the 'Take-over' are very well documented and include such names as Richard Askew, who left Chelsea for Derby in 1772, where he continued to paint muscular cupids; Zachariah Boreman, who worked at Chelsea until just

A porcelain group of figures dancing, painted in enamel colours and gilt, modelled after a Meissen original by J.J. Kaendler. Made at Derby by William Duesbury & Co., c.1775. H. 16.8cm.

Courtesy Bearnes, Torquay

Two caddy spoons, most probably Derby, painted in blue enamel, c.1785. L. 10cm. The larger Chinese type spoon is decorated in underglaze blue and is marked with the crescent of the Worcester factory, c.1775. L. 13.5cm.

Private Collection

133

A large Derby figure of Jupiter, painted in enamel colours and gilt and showing many firing faults (fire cracks). The colour of the cloak is again well described by W.B. Honey as 'dirty turquoise', a colour that Derby appeared to have difficulty in firing during their early years. Unmarked, made during the William Duesbury & Co. period, c.1770. The author recently saw a similar figure wearing a necklace, which had been applied during recent years, to hide the fact that the head had been broken off and repaired. H. 45cm.
Courtesy Royal Crown Derby Museum

Derby porcelain plate painted in enamels and gilt, c.1785 by William Billingsley. From a service once in the possession of the Duke of Newcastle, the pattern is number 80 and the gilder's number '2' is that of Joseph Stables, who worked at the factory for a long period, sometimes as manager. Mark, crown, crossed batons and 'D' in puce

Courtesy Royal Crown Derby Museum

Derby porcelain soup plate from a service formerly in the possession of the Duke of Northumberland, decorated with paintings of roses by William Billingsley, c.1790 for Duesbury & Co. The mark of crown, crossed batons and 'D' in puce, together with the mark of the gilder, Thomas Soar, number 1. D. 22.5cm.

Courtesy Royal Crown Derby Museum

A Chelsea-Derby figure of Minerva, the Goddess of Wisdom; she is the Roman counterpart of Athene, said to be a daughter of Zeus. At her feet the wise owl is perched on a pile of books and as she was also a warrior, she holds a shield upon which the head of the Gorgon Medusa is moulded. Unmarked, c.1775. H. 27cm.

Courtesy Bearnes, Torquay

prior to the closure in 1784, when he continued working at the Nottingham Road Factory in Derby and began to paint his much admired landscapes of local beauty spots until 1787, when he returned to London and worked for an independent decorator until his death in 1810. Edward Withers, the flower painter, moved from Chelsea in 1770, later returning for a while to work in London, but returned to Derby in 1789 at the low wage of 3s 6d per day. This was almost certainly due to the fact that his work was far inferior to the most talented of all flower painters, William Billingsley. He was apprenticed to William Duesbury in 1774 for a period of five years at a wage of five shillings a week for the entire period. Billingsley's much admired technique was his use of his brush to wipe away the colour to obtain his highlights, a unique method at that time which achieved pleasing naturalistic effects.

A finely thrown porcelain egg cup, decorated in enamel colours with the cornflower pattern, rimmed with gilt. The three small patch marks on base suggest Derby as the most likely factory. H. 4.8cm. Private Collection

Derby coffee can and saucer, painted in enamel colours and gilt with crest and initials thought to be those of the Coleridge family. The mark of crown, crossed batons and D are in purple, c.1785. D. (saucer) 13cm. Private Collection

There seems little doubt that the finest landscape and marine paintings to be seen on Derby porcelain around the turn of the century are by the hand of George Robertson. The talented painters employed at Derby are too numerous to mention here and the reader is referred to the recommended books which discuss them and their work in detail.

After having agreed to purchase the entire Derby works in 1811, Robert Bloor immediately endeavoured to raise money by organising a thirty-day auction sale at the factory, including 'five thousand sets of white china', probably old undecorated stock he was prepared to dispose of 'without the least

Coffee cup and stand, Derby porcelain painted by the very accomplished painter, George Complin, c.1790, when he must have been quite elderly since he is known to have painted Battersea enamels (1753-6) and he was later at the Chelsea factory. Today Complin's work makes record prices in the salerooms. In Derby Porcelain *by John Twitchett, he points out the diminutive size of the birds in comparison with the fruit in Complin's paintings. Pattern number 259. H. 6.4cm.*

Courtesy Royal Crown Derby Museum

The celebrated 'Prentice Plate', which was painted by William Billingsley for the purpose of showing the apprentices his manner of painting the famous roses at Derby. Made by William Duesbury & Co., c.1790-6. Marks, pattern number '138', gilder's number '10' and crown, crossed batons and 'D' in puce. D. 22.3cm.

Courtesy John Haslem Bequest, City Museum & Art Gallery, Derby

Large campana-shaped vase, known as the 'Arkwright' vase, painted in enamel colours with rural scenes attributed to the hand of Robert Brewer, who became a Derby painter in 1797, where he remained until about 1848, when he probably went with his wife to Worcester, where according to Graves' Dictionary of Artists *Mrs Brewer was painting between 1848-1853, with six exhibits at the Royal Academy. Mark, crown, crossed-batons and 'D' in red enamel, dating to about 1815. H. 41cm.*

R.H. Williamson Bequest, Tullie House, Carlisle

One of a pair of chocolate cups in soft-paste porcelain, painted in enamel colours with a profusion of flowers on a gilt ground, attributed to the hand of William Billingsley, when at the Derby factory, c.1795. Courtesy Royal Crown Derby Museum

A fine soft-paste porcelain teapot, decorated with enamel colours and gilt, with Derbyshire views attributed to the painter 'Jockey' Hill and the popular French sprig and star ground. Marked with crown, crossed batons and 'D' with descriptions in blue enamel. Made in the Duesbury & Kean period, 1795-1800. H. 16.5cm. The Derby painter William Hill came to Derby from Chelsea, c.1795, as a replacement for the retiring painter, Zachariah Boreman, his nickname 'Jockey' was due to his riding to and from the factory on a pony

Courtesy Royal Crown
Derby Museum

reserve'. During the 1811-48 period, referred to as the Bloor period, some very fine painters and modellers were employed, including the skilled William or 'Quaker' Pegg, who worked at Derby as a flower painter from 1790 to 1801, then left on religious grounds to become a stocking maker, but returned in 1813 to produce further fine floral work until 1820. This painter should not be confused with a younger William Pegg, who was not related to 'Quaker', but was apprenticed at Derby in about 1810, and was thought to have joined William Billingsley at Nantgarw in South Wales for a short period in 1819, before working for H. & R. Daniel at Stoke.

Soft-paste porcelain bough pot of bombe shape, painted in enamel colours with a view of Breadsall Farm by Jockey Hill. Made at Derby in the Duesbury & Kean period, c.1795. Title and the mark of crown, crossed batons and 'D' in blue enamel, a mark commonly used c.1782-1806
Courtesy Royal Crown
Derby Museum

Porcelain dish with a dark blue border decorated by the gilder Samuel Keys with hunting horns and the crest of the Duke of Rutland. The centre medallion painted with a hunting scene is attributed to Robert Brewer. Made by Duesbury & Kean, Derby, c.1800. Mark, Crown, crossed batons and 'D' with the gilder's number 6 all in puce. D. 25cm.
Courtesy Royal Crown
Derby Museum

FURTHER READING:

Bradley, H.G., *Ceramics of Derbyshire 1750-78*, 1978.

Gilhespy, F.B., *Crown Derby Porcelain*, Lewis, Leigh-on-Sea, 1951.

Twitchett, J., *Derby Porcelain*, Barrie & Jenkins, 1980.

Murdoch, John and Twitchett, John, *Painters and the Derby China Works*, Trefoil Publications Ltd, 1987.

Derby porcelain dessert dish, painted in enamel colours and gilt. The decorator was probably William (Quaker) Pegg during his first period at the factory, 1796-1801. The mark on the reverse, Lilium Bulbiferum/Orange Lily and crown, crossed batons and D over 197, all in script in blue enamel. L. 24cm.

Private Collection

Fine shell shaped dessert dish, painted with enamel colours by William Pegg, the Quaker, at Derby, c.1813-15. Mark, crown, crossed batons and D and name of botanical specimen in the red of the Robert Bloor period. D. 23.3cm.

Courtesy Royal Crown
Derby Museum

A fine Derby porcelain plate,
painted in the manner of
Thomas Steel, who decorated
numerous dessert services with
fruit arrangements on marble
plinths, and was working at
the Nottingham Road Works
from 1815. Mark of the early
Bloor period of crown, crossed
batons and D, in red enamel,
c.1820. Painted number '36'
Private Collection

A rare Derby porcelain swan,
painted in enamel colours, a
type which at one time were
thought to have been made only
at the Lowestoft factory,
c.1770-5. Three typical Derby
patch marks on base. Three
sizes of swans appear in the
Derby price list, priced at
10d, 1.0s, & s1.3d.
H. 8cm.   Private Collection

LOWESTOFT

1757-1799

Although not in chronological order it is convenient now to discuss the porcelains produced at the Lowestoft factory, which often have so much in common with those made at Bow. There is no documentary evidence as to the start of production at this comparatively small undertaking on the coast of Suffolk in East Anglia, but 1757 is regarded as an acceptable date, continuing until the closure in 1799.

The new collector will often find it difficult to differentiate between the Lowestoft wares decorated in underglaze blue and those of Bow, as the paste of both are almost identical, each often containing as much as forty-five per cent of calcined animal bone and neither bear any recognised factory marks. Fortunately the completely erroneous term 'Chinese Lowestoft' is now rarely heard and there is really little excuse for confusing the hard-paste Chinese porcelain decorated in enamel colours, with the bone porcelain of Lowestoft similarly decorated in Chinese taste.

Lowestoft tea bowl and saucer, painted in underglaze blue with the so-called Mansfield pattern, c.1775-80. This name was given by the Worcester factory to their 20th century version, which was printed, after their earlier painted design which they were using from c.1757. Bow, Liverpool, Derby and Caughley also used this pattern. D. (saucer) 12.2cm.   Private Collection

A range of Lowestoft dishes and fragments, all decorated in underglaze blue, left to right: fragment of a dish found on factory site, unmarked. Leaf shaped dish, once thought to be Bow, together with fragment from site with identical pattern. Unmarked dish, with large insect in centre, below a leaf shaped dish with stalk handle, mark, '5' on base (L. 16cm), and a moulded leaf dish, with mark '5' inside foot rim, all dating c.1757-80

Courtesy The Norfolk Museums Services, Norwich Castle Museum

Lowestoft cream boat, moulded with overlapping shells, painted in underglaze blue, c.1760-5. H. 6.4cm.   Allan Weaver Collection

Lowestoft cream jug with pear shaped body, sparrow beak lip and scroll handle with thumb-rest, painted in underglaze blue, c.1768. H. 6cm.   Allan Weaver Collection

Lowestoft jug painted in enamel colours and gilt, the moulded leaf decoration picked out in green and gilt. The painting is attributed to the so-called 'tulip painter' and dates c.1775. H. 25.5cm.
Courtesy The Norfolk Museums Services, Norwich Castle Museum

A rare Lowestoft mug, painted in underglaze blue and inscribed 'A Trifle from Lowestoft', possibly the work of Robert Allen, c.1780. See next caption for full information on the bathing machine. H. 14cm.
Courtesy Phillips, London

A rare Lowestoft porcelain flask, painted in enamel colours, possibly the work of Robert Allen, c.1780, reminding us that as early as the second half of the 18th century Lowestoft was a popular seaside resort 'of genteel and fashionable company'. Sea bathing was considered to be highly beneficial to one's health and bathing machines of the type illustrated were first introduced in 1768. H. 15.5cm.
Courtesy The Norfolk Museums Services, Norwich Castle Museum

A very rare Lowestoft veilleuse, a food or pap warmer. The detachable food container, with handles, is suspended over a small oil lamp, the knob on the lid shaped to hold a candle, c.1765-70. Decorated with painting in underglaze blue, with painter's mark '5' on inner foot rim. H. 25.3cm.
Courtesy The Norfolk Museums Services, Norwich Castle Museum

There were five original partners, the best known name being that of Robert Browne, after whom a rather dull pattern in underglaze blue is named, which looks a little like a Worcester pattern, but lacks the red enamel and gilding. There are so many similarities between the early wares of Lowestoft and those of Bow, that the tradition of Robert Browne himself obtaining employment at the London factory in order to learn their secrets, may be well founded.

Prior to about 1768 only wares decorated in underglaze blue were produced, but unlike other contemporary English factories who were catering for a wider market, Lowestoft produced a charming range of wares, often obviously made to order with local views, names and dates of the owners and perhaps the most humble and the most interesting, were the small circular birth tablets, inscribed in underglaze blue or enamel colours with the name and date of the birth of a child, possibly the most pathetic being that inscribed on the front 'MARTHA/LIFFIN/BORN/AUGUST 17/1794' and on the reverse 'MARY/LIFFIN/Died/MAY4/1795', the mother was a member of the Redgrave family, several of whom were employed as decorators at the Lowestoft factory. The earliest birth tablet recorded is dated 1761, but is thought to have been made in about 1765 or later, whereas the majority of these examples, which can be seen in the Norwich Castle Museum, date towards the end of the life of the factory in 1799.

This typical Lowestoft handle is seen less frequently on teapots, which usually have a simple Oriental type loop. The decoration in underglaze blue is painted in a reserve within shallow moulded decoration, which includes four cartouche (two on body, two on lid) with '1761', 'I H', 'I' and 'H' in relief numbers and lettering. Mark, '5' on inner foot rim, dated 1761. The initials 'I.H' may refer to the modeller James Hughes. H. 12.6cm.

Courtesy The Norfolk Museums Services, Norwich Castle Museum

The Lowestoft porcelain bowl with everted rim on the left is painted with a Chinese river scene, but no painter's mark, c.1765. D. 25.4cm. The smaller bowl on the right is also painted in underglaze blue with a chained swan on the inside and a Chinese scene, a warship and rowing boat on the outside. The painter's mark is '5', written twice on the inside of the foot rim and on the base 'M.P/ 1765'. D. 21.3cm.

Courtesy The Norfolk Museums Services, Norwich Castle Museum

A rare Lowestoft cornucopia, painted with a Chinese garden scene in underglaze blue, c.1765-70. There are two holes on the back for suspension and the painter's number '3'. H. 22cm.
Courtesy The Norfolk Museums Services, Norwich Castle Museum

Three teapots of Lowestoft porcelain painted in underglaze blue. The miniature pot on the left is marked with an illegible painter's number on the inside foot rim, c.1764. H. 5.4cm. The centre teapot painted in underglaze blue, bears the painter's number '3' on the inside foot rim, c.1765. H. 13.3cm. The miniature pot on the right, painted with a Chinese river scene in underglaze blue, has the painter's number '5' on the inside of the foot rim, c.1760-4. H. 8.8cm.
Courtesy The Norfolk Museums Services, Norwich Castle Museum

Although Lowestoft did not use any recognised factory mark of their own, the practice of the underglaze blue decorator applying his 'tally' mark in the form of a number, usually on the inside wall of the foot rim, between about 1758 and 1775 is almost unique, numbers '3' and '5' are the most common but numbers as high as '17' have been recorded.

From their beginnings Lowestoft produced a very wide range of wares, most of which have been clearly identified by the numerous wasters found on the site in the early excavations in 1902, 1903 and again as late as 1967. These included coffee pots, teapots, numerous coffee cups, tea bowls and teacups, spoon trays, scallop-shaped and leaf-shaped dishes, sauce boats, a large variety of mugs and even spittoons, some of simple circular form, thrown on the wheel and others with relief decoration made from moulds. Although the factory would appear to

Lowestoft porcelain dish of octagonal form, painted with a Chinese river scene in underglaze blue. The oval foot rim is very unevenly applied. Unmarked, c.1765-70. L. 34.1cm.
Courtesy The Norfolk Museums Services, Norwich Castle Museum

A rare Lowestoft porcelain cup and cover, commonly referred to as a custard cup, painted in underglaze blue in a style of painting associated with the Redgrave family, of whom six are known to have worked at the factory. The flower knob and leaf are a crude imitation of Worcester, c.1785-90. H. 8.9cm.
Courtesy The Norfolk Museums Services, Norwich Castle Museum

Two Lowestoft porcelain mugs, painted in enamel colours. The mug on the left shows a typical Lowestoft handle, c.1770-5. H. 14.3cm. The mug on the right is also painted in enamel colours and is inscribed: 'JOSEPH.BARKER/TROSTON./1775.'
The verse reads: 'Know all the Good that Individuals find/ Of God and Nature, meant to meer Mankind./Reasons whole Pleasures, all the Joys of Sense,/Lie in three Words, Health, Peace; and Competence./ But health Consists with Temperance alone/ And Peace O Virtue; Peace is all thy Own.' Dating to 1775. H. 14.7cm.
Courtesy The Norfolk Museums Services
Norwich Castle Museum

Two Lowestoft porcelain jugs, that on the left is attributed to the painter Robert Allen and inscribed above the windmill 'JERM^H WARNER' and on the reverse 'Success to the miller,/ Likewise to his wife./May they live happy,/ All the dys of their life.', c.1780-90. H. 19.2cm. The lidded jug on the right is painted in black enamel and gilt, with an unidentified building very much in the style of the painting seen on some German faïence, c.1780-90. H. 22.4cm.

Courtesy The Norfolk Museums Services, Norwich Castle Museum

Lowestoft porcelain plate painted in underglaze blue, brick red enamel and gilt with a Chinese garden scene, including two perky birds, c.1780-90. Note the three evenly spaced blemishes in the glaze on the rim, caused by the supporting pegs during the glost firing, D. 20.3cm.

Courtesy The Norfolk Museums Services, Norwich Castle Museum

151

Excavations from the site of the Lowestoft factory have produced shards which have enabled several groups of animal figures to be recognised as having been made at this Norfolk factory, rather than Longton Hall or Bow. The cream jug in the form of a cow is decorated with sponged manganese, with eyes outlined in underglaze blue, c.1770-80. H. 9.1cm. The small standing pug of solid porcelain, of the same date, is also sparsely decorated with manganese, with underglaze blue eyes and collar; a slightly larger, but similar model was made at Bow. H. 5cm. The seated pug, decorated in the same colours might well have to be chemically analysed to prove Lowestoft rather than Longton Hall, c.1770-80. H. 8.5cm.

Courtesy The Norfolk Museums Services, Norwich Castle Museum

Late Lowestoft teapot, painted in enamel colours with a style of decoration associated with the painter Thomas Curtis, which was often imitated on late Chinese export wares, c.1780-90. H. 15.8cm.

Courtesy The Norfolk Museum Services, Norwich Castle Museum

Large Lowestoft porcelain bowl, painted in enamel colours with two large and two small panels of rural scenes. Due to frequent 'spooning' of the contents, the inscription on the interior is much rubbed and reads 'John and Eliz./(. . . . ant)/ Success to the Jolly Farmer, 1774'. No positive reading of the surname has been possible. D. 24.3cm.

Courtesy The Norfolk Museums Services, Norwich Castle Museum

Rare Lowestoft porcelain butter dish, with moulded decoration framing reserves, picked out with green enamel, c.1770-5. The scenes in pink enamel within the reserves might well have been suggested by those on Meissen. L. 12.5cm.

Courtesy The Norfolk Museums Services, Norwich Castle Museum

A rare documentary Lowestoft mug, painted in colours with the armorial arms of the Trinity House Brethren, two lighthouses, fish houses and ships at sea, probably painted by Robert Allen. Once the property of Mr. Davey, the lighthouse superintendent. The form of the lighthouse dates the piece to post-1778. H. 11.4cm. Courtesy The Norfolk Museums Services, Norwich Castle Museum

Lowestoft tea bowl and saucer, painted in enamel colours with typical Chinese style design, c.1780-5. D. (saucer) 12cm.
Private Collection

have been catering primarily for local trade, the demand for their wares was sufficient to justify a London warehouse from as early as 1763.

From about 1768 two further forms of decoration were used, underglaze blue transfer printing and overglaze enamel colours. Perhaps the most desired acquisition of any Lowestoft porcelain collector is an item decorated in colour by the so-called 'Tulip Painter' whose groups of flowers usually include a full-blown tulip; the name of the decorator is as yet unknown, but date from about 1770-80.

It was during the last ten years of the factory that the well known class of 'A Trifle from Lowestoft' were produced, these 'presents from the seaside' were

Two Lowestoft cream jugs, painted in enamel colours, with typical pear shape, sparrow beak lip and scroll handle, c.1775-85. H. 8.5cm.   Private Collection

usually in the form of mugs, the later examples were usually decorated in sparse enamel colours, whilst the most interesting; such as a large mug in underglaze blue depicting a contemporary bathing machine on wheels, probably dates to the late 1770s.

The attribution of a wide range of figures to Lowestoft is at times dangerous, unless confirmed by the numerous wasters and moulds found on the factory site. They include male and female musicians on high Bow-like bases and a variety of small animals, including swans, cats, sheep, rams and dogs, which are very heavy for their size; the bases are covered with glaze and the small hole in the base appears to have been reamed out, giving a screw-hole effect.

Lowestoft loving cup painted in underglaze blue with plants and birds. Painter's mark '3' on base near foot rim, c.1757-60. H. 9.4cm.

Courtesy The Norfolk Museums Services, Norwich Castle Museum

Left: Lowestoft porcelain plate of Chinese saucer shape, painted in underglaze blue. Painter's mark '3' on inside of foot rim. Dating c.1757-60. D. 18.5cm. The similarly shaped dish on the right is painted in underglaze blue which has 'run' in the firing. The painter's mark '3' painted on the inside of foot rim, c.1760-5. D. 18.4-18.7cm. (due to warping).

Courtesy The Norfolk Museums Services, Norwich Castle Museum

Various reasons have been suggested as to why the Lowestoft production came to a halt in 1799. The Napoleonic Wars might well have made exports too difficult, and certainly by this time the well-established factories in Staffordshire and elsewhere were producing fine earthenwares and porcelains, catering for all classes of society, but the still charming, but nevertheless humble, wares of Lowestoft were no longer competitive.

FURTHER READING:

Godden, G.A., *Lowestoft Porcelains*, Antique Collectors' Club, Woodbridge, 1985.

Smith, Sheenah, *Lowestoft Porcelain in Norwich Castle Museum, Vol. 1. Blue and White. Vol. II. Polychrome,* Norwich Museum Services, 1975 and 1986.

PLYMOUTH AND BRISTOL

c.1768-1781

The hard-paste porcelains produced from 1768 by William Cookworthy at Plymouth are so rarely offered on the market that it is only by visits to certain museums that the would-be collectors can train their eyes to recognise these important, but often dull and faulty, examples of the first porcelains to be produced in England from materials first used by Chinese potters from at least the ninth century AD. Prior to becoming involved with the manufacture of porcelain, Richard Champion, who was eventually to take over the Bristol hard-paste factory after its transfer from Plymouth in 1770, wrote in 1765 to his brother-in-law, Caleb Lloyd, of 'a new work just established. Porcelain is composed of two materials, Clay and Stone. This new work is from a Clay and Stone discovered in Cornwall, which answers the description of the Chinese'. It is thought today that William Cookworthy was experimenting with these materials at Bristol in 1765, but due to 'their not being able to burn the ware without Smoaking', he gave up. These early experiments are discussed in detail in the paper read to the English Ceramic Circle in 1973 and raises the question as to whether those wares and figures, very discoloured by the smoke from the coal fired kiln, are in fact the experimental pieces, or did they actually sell such faulty wares after the opening of William Cookworthy's factory at Plymouth in 1768?

William Cookworthy was born in Kingsbridge, Devon, in 1705; at the age of fourteen years he was apprenticed to a London chemist, after which he returned

Pair of Bristol hard-paste porcelain figures with bocage, decorated in enamel colours, c.1768-70. Note the Plymouth figures usually have rococo bases, whilst those made slightly later at Bristol are most frequently on rock like bases. H. 25.5cm.

Courtesy Bearnes, Torquay

157

Plymouth hard-paste porcelain mug, painted in enamel colours after the Worcester Kylin pattern, c.1768-70. Mark, the so-called 2/4 sign, the alchemical sign for tin, probably symbolic of the county of Cornwall. H. 12cm.
Courtesy Allan Weaver Collection

to Plymouth, Devon, where he set up as a wholesale chemist and druggist. In 1768, after obtaining a lease from Thomas Pitt, later Lord Camelford, on whose property he had located the essential china clay and china stone, he obtained a patent giving him the sole right to produce a hard-paste porcelain from these materials in this country until 1782. Cookworthy was obviously very optimistic in employing over fifty hands and produced a wide range of table wares, decorative vases and figures for just over two years before moving his manufactory in 1770 to Castle Green, Bristol, where he probably found more experienced potters could be hired.

The firing of these wares necessitated a kiln temperature of about 1400°C and in their early days even their small useful wares, such as sauce boats or creamers, were very heavily potted in an endeavour to prevent warping. Rococo styles had enjoyed many years popularity and it is the early articles made at Plymouth which still favoured this fashion, which was soon to yield to the new vogue of the neo-classical.

Chinese porcelain was still at this time readily available at modest prices, but the wares produced at Plymouth in competition, were rarely a match, probably due to the difficulty of controlling the kiln temperature and in consequence the

Plymouth hard-paste porcelain sauce boat, decorated in underglaze blue and red enamel, c.1768-70. Unmarked. L. 16cm.
Courtesy Allan Weaver Collection

Bristol hard-paste porcelain cup and saucer, painted in enamel colours, c.1775. Mark in blue, of the so-called 2/4 sign, the alchemical sign for tin. D. (saucer) 14cm.
Courtesy Allan Weaver Collection

159

Bristol hard-paste porcelain plate, decorated in underglaze blue with a transfer printed bouquet, cell and foliage pattern around well and flower sprays on rim. Made at Richard Champion's factory, c.1775. D. 20.5cm.

Formerly Gilbert Bradley Collection

Two Bristol hard-paste porcelain sauce boats, painted in enamel colours, c.1775. The sauceboat on the left is marked with crossed swords in blue enamel. L. (of both) 15cm.

Courtesy Bearnes, Torquay

usually sparsely applied underglaze blue often fired to a greyish black. One distinguishing feature so often seen on these wares which were thrown on the wheel, is shallow spiral 'wreathing' or ridges, said to be due to the poor plasticity of the paste, a fault which was obviously not apparent prior to firing, as this could have been rectified by turning on the wheel whilst still 'cheese-hard'.

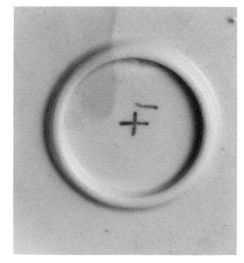

Bristol hard-paste porcelain dish, painted with floral swags in enamel colours and gilt, c.1775. Mark, as illustrated, in underglaze blue. D. 20cm.
Allan Weaver Collection

Bristol hard-paste porclain bowl, painted with enamel flowers, c.1775. Mark, B in blue enamel, as illustrated. D. 14.5cm.
Allan Weaver Collection

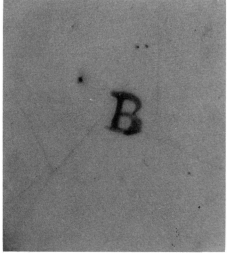

Whilst there was little Cookworthy could do to hide the smoke stained glaze on much of his blue and white, such faulty figures were often made to appear more acceptable by the lavish use of bright enamel colours. Although there does not appear to be any record of just how Cookworthy acquired some of the materials used at the Longton Hall factory after its closure in 1760, there are several groups and figures which he appears to have produced from the earlier

Small covered cup, hard-paste porcelain with gilt decoration, c.1775. Mark, + in blue enamel. Commonly called a custard cup, but this shape in the records of the Sèvres factory is said to be for meat juice. H. 7cm.   Allan Weaver Collection

Tea bowl and saucer, hard-paste porcelain with enamel decoration. Made at Bristol, c.1775. Mark, on cup and saucer 1. in gilt. D. (saucer) 15.5cm.

Allan Weaver Collection

Longton moulds, some of which had to be made more fashionable by the addition of the then popular bocage, generally in the form of a shrub or small tree as a background.

Many of the figures made at Plymouth and Bristol were a little too large and statuesque and frequently some of the enamel colours tended to flake off the hard felspathic glaze. These figures rarely bear a factory mark, such as the so-called '2-4' mark, the alchemist's sign for tin, relating to the mineral being found in Cornwall, and often seen on the useful wares, or the small enamel cross, together with a workman's tally mark, which was adopted as a mark on the Bristol wares. Some of the figures and highly decorative pieces were at times impressed with the 'repairer's' mark, 'T' or 'T°', now thought to identify the assembly work of a John Toulouse, rather than Mr. Tebo, as previously suggested. The earlier Plymouth figures are usually precariously perched on a

Pair of hard-paste porcelain figures of a hurdy-gurdy player and a girl dancing, the triangle she should be holding is missing. These figures were probably modelled by Pierre Stephan, who at the time was working at the Derby factory; painted in enamel colours, c.1775. A figure of the hurdy-gurdy player in the Schreiber Collection, Victoria & Albert Museum, is impressed with the mark of the repairer 'T'. H. 17.5cm.   R.H. Williamson Bequest, Tullie House, Carlisle

rococo scrolled base, whilst those made at Bristol favoured the increasingly popular neo-classical rock mounds.

By the time of the move to Bristol many of the difficulties of production had been overcome, although the occasional wreathing, tears in the body and fire-cracks, due to the shrinkage when the clay is of varying thickness, are frequently to be seen.

After the move to Bristol in 1770, the company was seemingly under the direction of Richard Champion, one of the original partners at Plymouth and by 1774 the full patent rights had been transferred to him. Eager to protect the patent, Champion applied for a renewal to extend the term beyond 1782. This application was vigorously opposed by other Staffordshire potters, under the leadership of Josiah Wedgwood, resulting in the patent for the manufacture of the hard-paste porcelain being extended to 1796, but from 1775 any potter was permitted to use china clay and china stone in other ceramic bodies.

By 1778 Richard Champion was on the verge of bankruptcy, but apparently given financial aid by friends, he was able to continue with a limited production until 1781. It was then his ambition to set up a large company, involving many potters already working on their own account, but due primarily to the high cost he was still contracted to pay for his necessary clays, his scheme was not taken up and he was again opposed by the powerful Josiah Wedgwood. Champion eventually disposed of a factory he was able to establish at Tunstall to a group of Staffordshire potters, which after a move to Shelton Hall, became known as New Hall, where production of porcelain of varying types continued until 1835. Champion now forsook the ceramic industry and became Deputy Paymaster to the Forces in London, prior to emigrating to South Carolina, America, in 1784.

FURTHER READING:
MacKenna, F. Severne, *Cookworthy's Plymouth & Bristol Porcelain,* F. Lewis, 1946; *Champion's Bristol Porcelain,* F. Lewis, 1947; 'William Cookworthy and the Plymouth Factory, an Updating', *English Ceramic Circle Transactions,* Vol. II, Part 2, 1982.
Charleston, R.J. (Editor), *English Porcelain 1745-1850,* Benn, 1965.
Mallet, John, 'Cookworthy's First Bristol Factory of 1765', *English Ceramic Circle Transactions,* Vol. 9, Part 2, 1974.

CAUGHLEY

1772-1799

Thomas Turner had formerly been employed at the Worcester porcelain manufactory, where he learnt the art of engraving designs on copper plates, for the production of paper transfers which were used to apply the decoration on so many ceramic wares. In 1772 he left Worcester and commenced building the Royal Salopian Porcelain manufactory, more commonly known today as Caughley (pronounced Calf-ley), in partnership with Ambrose Gallimore, who had been producing pottery on the same site since 1754. The factory was ideally situated, about two miles south of Broseley in Shropshire, where deposits of clay suitable for the making of saggars was readily available, coal for firing the ovens also virtually on the site and not too far from the River Severn, and the canals for the transportation of both the finished wares and the bringing in of the necessary raw materials to produce a fine soapstone porcelain, the ingredients of which were almost identical to those in use at the Worcester concern.

The earliest reference to the actual production of marketable wares appeared in the *Birmingham Gazette* of 3rd July, 1775, when Robert Hancock, the well-

Caughley soapstone porcelain teapot, printed with the 'Bell-toy' pattern in underglaze blue, an early Caughley print, later used at Coalport, but not at Worcester, c.1775-80. H. 13.5cm.
Courtesy The Victoria and Albert Museum

Dessert dish, hand painted in underglaze blue and gilt. The centre scene of the ruined building is probably taken from the book of engravings The Virtuosi's Museum, *containing select views in England, Scotland and Ireland by Paul Sandby, R.A., printed in London for G. Kearsley in 1778. Made at Caughley by Thomas Turner, c.1780. D. 17.5cm.* Private Collection

Miniature tea bowl and saucer, printed with the popular 'Fisherman' pattern in underglaze blue, 'wasters' of this type were found on the Caughley factory site. Unmarked, c.1780-90. D. (saucer) 8cm.   Private Collection

A mask headed spout jug of baluster shape, printed in underglaze blue with the Caughley version of the 'Fisherman', 'Cormorant' or 'Pleasure Boat' design; an almost identical pattern was used at the Worcester factory during the same period. Made at Thomas Turner's Caughley factory, c.1780-90. Unmarked. H. 17.8cm.   Private Collection

known engraver of the Worcester factory, announced he had 'disposed of his share in the Worcester work' and was in a position to supply blue and white porcelain from the Salopian China Warehouse at Bridgnorth.

Following the excavations on both the Worcester and Caughley sites (as discussed under 'Worcester', when it was proven that Caughley should not be blamed for so many inferior blue and white wares), Caughley porcelain has become less plentiful and generally is of a very good quality, both in body and

A paper 'pull' from a copperplate of the popular 'Fisherman' pattern known originally as the 'Pleasure Boat'. This pattern was used at both Worcester and Caughley, and also at other minor factories in varying materials. The two major variations between Caughley and Worcester are that in the Caughley version illustrated they have caught a short, fat fish and the other fisherman appears to have a 'bite', whilst on a Worcester version the fish is longer and thinner and the figure above has a slack line. Note the 'T.T.' (Thomas Turner) and the 'S' (Salopian) are in reverse, but when used would print correctly.

Lobed dish, decorated with underglaze blue transfer print with the Caughley version of the 'Fisherman' pattern. Made by Thomas Turner at Caughley, c.1785-95. Mark, 'Salopian', the old name for Shropshire, impressed. Private Collection

Caughley soapstone porcelain inkpot and cover, the cover being in the form of a well, c.1785. The scattered flowers and cell pattern borders are in painted and printed underglaze blue, there are four holes for holding the pens. D. 9.5cm. Formerly in the Gilbert Bradley Collection

Bucket form Caughley flower pot of soapstone porcelain, here all the decoration has been applied in underglaze blue with transfer prints, c.1780. Mark, in underglaze blue of 'C', not to be confused with the Worcester crescent. D. 12cm. Formerly in the Gilbert Bradley Collection

Three rare examples of Caughley soapstone porcelain, decorated in underglaze blue, a pounce pot or sander, used for drying ink prior to the introduction of blotting paper, a flask and an asparagus server, all made c.1780-90. H. (pounce pot) 8.5cm.

Courtesy Phillips, London

A range of rare Caughley miniature wares, painted in underglaze blue with the 'Island' pattern, a small design which appears to have only been used on miniature pieces, c.1780-90. Wasters of this type were found on the factory site. H. (tureen) 5.5cm.

Courtesy Simon Spero Antiques

decoration. At least seventy-five per cent of the large variety of table and other useful wares made at Caughley were decorated with either painted or printed underglaze blue, and often, unlike Worcester, with added names and dates of the person for whom the piece had been made, such as the large jug in the Victoria & Albert Museum, which depicts the famous iron bridge over the River Severn, at the town of Ironbridge, which is inscribed 'Han[h]. Hacket, Dec[r].25 1793'. Caughley also produced many attractive miniatures, or 'toy' pieces, eagerly sought by collectors today, wares which are still often described as travellers' samples, a completely erroneous suggestion.

Group of Caughley 'toy' or miniature wares of soapstone porcelain, painted in underglaze blue, c.1785-90. These small useful wares were at one time wrongly thought to have been made as travellers' samples, but they are frequently listed among the various objects for sale and the fact that they were most probably intended to be used by children might well account for their comparative rarity as complete services. H. (teapot) 7.6cm. Courtesy The Victoria & Albert Museum

Caughley coffee cup and saucer, decorated with the 'Dresden' flower pattern in underglaze blue, with gilt decoration added by the Chamberlains at their decorating shop in Worcester, c.1790. The saucer shows an early use of a sunken well in the centre to locate the cup. The gilt dentil rim decoration is typical of an 'outside decorator'. D. (saucer) 13.5cm. Private Collection

Whilst many Caughley wares were formerly hard to separate from those of Worcester, Turner produced a wide range of pieces of an entirely different style. He was particularly inspired by the late eighteenth century French wares, such as those of Tournai, with moulded basketwork borders and the scattered flower sprays as used on Chantilly porcelains, of which there are four main varieties.

Some of the more lavishly decorated Caughley is the result of Turner selling

*Jug of moulded cabbage leaf form with mask spout.
Transfer printed with floral pattern, a rare print.
Inscribed 'Edwd Jeffreys Salop'. Unmarked, made
at Thomas Turner's factory at Caughley, c.1785.
H. 23.5cm.*   Private Collection

*Cabbage leaf moulded jug, transfer printed in
underglaze blue with the pattern referred to as the
'Conversation Pattern'. Made at Thomas Turner's
Caughley factory, c.1785. Mark, a cross in
underglaze blue. H. 23cm.*   Private Collection

Rare punt-shaped dessert dish, hand painted in underglaze blue with the 'Weir Pattern'. Painter's mark inside foot rim. Made at Thomas Turner's factory at Caughley, c.1785-90. This pattern is sometimes wrongly attributed to Derby, but known examples bear the impressed 'Salopian' mark and were exhibited at the Caughley Bi-Centenary Exhibition in Shrewsbury Art Gallery in 1972. L. 31cm.   Private Collection

Three soapstone porcelain salts or 'pudding caps', hand painted in underglaze blue. Made by Thomas Turner at Caughley, c.1785. The centrepiece is inverted to show the 'S' mark for 'Salopian'. D. 5.7cm.   Private Collection

wares 'in the white' to James Giles, the London decorator, who may well have been responsible for some of the added gilt and enamel decoration in their early years, but the majority of these 'outside decorated' pieces were the work of Robert Chamberlain and his son Humphrey, who had left Worcester by 1788 and had established their own workshops where they decorated Caughley porcelain, some of which was to order for Thomas Turner and some which they

Cabaret set, comprising tray, teapot, creamer, sucrier and lid and two cups and saucers. Made at Thomas Turner's factory at Caughley, c.1775. Hand painted in underglaze blue and gilt. The tray is marked with the word 'Salopian' impressed, the remaining pieces bear a letter 'S' in underglaze blue and gilder's mark '27' in gilt
Courtesy Venner's Antiques

decorated and sold on their own account. By 1791 the Chamberlains had started to manufacture their own porcelain.

From 1795 Thomas Turner was purchasing china clay, obviously for use in the production of a hard-paste porcelain, which he did make from 1796 to 1799, but it was of a poor quality, from which he produced among other things a series of military jugs, of the type to be seen in the Lady Charlotte Schreiber Collection in the Victoria & Albert Museum. This jug is of his new body and inscribed 'Brimstree Loyal Legion' referring to a local Territorial-type military unit which had been formed under the authority of Parliament at the time of the threatened Napoleonic invasion, when we were at war with France. Thomas Turner, who was very active in local affairs, was awarded a commission to become a Captain early in 1799; he probably had the jugs made at his factory prior to 12th October, 1799, when he sold his works to John Rose & Co. of Coalport. There is now little doubt as to who made these jugs, for the copperplates used to make the transfer prints were not among those which Rose acquired at the time of the 'take-over', but they are now in the collection of the British Museum, having been acquired indirectly from the Turner family and

Sparrow beak cream jug, hand painted in underglaze blue with an Imperial Mandarin Boy. Made by Thomas Turner at Caughley from soapstone porcelain, c.1780-5. Mark, hand-painted 'C' for Caughley. H. 9.4cm.
Private Collection

bear the initials 'T.T.' for Thomas Turner. It is a little more difficult to attribute certain wares to makers on the evidence of the fragments found on the Caughley site, where in some instances only the slight differences in the quality of the porcelain can be used as a guide as to whether they were made by Turner prior to 1799 or by John Rose, who continued to produce similar wares at both Caughley and his new Coalport factory until 1814, when production at Caughley ceased. At present many of these puzzle pieces are still described as Caughley/Coalport.

FURTHER READING:
Godden, G.A., *Caughley & Worcester Porcelains 1775-1800,* Herbert Jenkins, 1969.
Shrewsbury Art Gallery, *Caughley Porcelains. A Bi-Centenary Exhibition,* 1972.
Edmundson, Roger, 'Shropshire Porcelains: The End of Caughley and the Beginnings of Coalport', *Antique Collecting,* Vol. 25, No. 2, June, 1990; *Salopian Rivalry, Antique Dealer and Collectors Guide,* November, 1990.
Roberts, Gaye Blake, 'Sources of Decoration on an unrecorded Caughley Dessert Service', *English Ceramic Circle Transactions,* Vol. 10, Part 1, 1976.

BADDELEY-LITTLER

c.1777-1785

Due to the patient research of Mr. John Murray, a member of the Morley College Ceramic Circle, together with Mr. Geoffrey Godden, it has been suggested that Ralph Baddeley, either in partnership with Hugh Booth, or alone, with the help of William Littler as his manager, made a type of soft-paste porcelain. After analysis the porcelain was found to have almost the same ingredients as that used at the Longton Hall factory, where William Littler had worked from about 1750-60, prior to his venture at West Pans in Scotland from about 1764-77.

The allocation of this group of porcelains is linked to a documentary tea canister, exhibited in the City Museum & Art Gallery, Stoke-on-Trent, which has a label applied at some time in the early nineteenth century by Enoch Wood,

Documentary porcelain tea caddy, painted in enamel colours and attributed to the so-called Baddeley-Littler period, when William Littler had returned from West Pans in Scotland and was probably employed by Ralph Baddeley and his partner Thomas Fletcher. Many other tea wares are now attributed to this production on what must be considered rather vague evidence. Made c.1780-84 and previously in the Enoch Wood Collection. H. 13cm.
Courtesy City Museum & Art Gallery, Stoke-on-Trent

Tea bowl and saucer, of a similar frit porcelain to that of Longton Hall, painted in enamel colours. Now attributed to the Baddeley-Littler group, Shelton, Staffordshire, c,1777-85. D. (saucer) 12cm. Private Collection

Teapot of soft-paste porcelain, painted in enamel colours with a pink scale border. Made at Shelton, Staffordshire, by Baddeley/Littler, c.1780. Unmarked. H. 15.5cm. Courtesy Mr. and Mrs. P. Miller

the well-known potter, who at one time owned this important piece. The now fragmentary label attached to the canister records that it was given to him by a William Fletcher in 1809, who recalled knowing it to have been made at an earlier date by William Littler, but just when, is difficult to ascertain, although Simeon Shaw writes in his *History of the Staffordshire Potteries,* published in 1829, of the fact that William Littler was manager for Baddeley, prior to his death in 1784, at the age of sixty years.

Further view, showing the side decoration, of the important porcelain tea caddy also shown in colour, which has a fragmentary label attached in the handwriting of Enoch Wood, in which he says the piece was given to him by William Fletcher, who said the caddy was made by William Littler, c.1780-85. H.13cm.

Courtesy City Museum & Art Gallery, Stoke-on-Trent

The paste of the so-called Baddeley/Littler group is rather glassy and contains a high percentage of lead oxide, as does that of the earlier Longton Hall, it shows a greenish white translucency. The glaze is inclined to discolour, especially towards the foot rims, where speckling sometimes occurs. Poor quality underglaze blue painting or printing is occasionally seen in this group, but overglaze enamels are more common, including a bright deep blue, red and a rather loud pink used to paint either naturalistic flowers or popular chinoiserie patterns. Monochrome painting was at times used, as were overglaze transfer prints, in purple, pink, black or brown. These prints are usually accompanied by a distinctive painted border in a feather-like design. No gilding has as yet been seen on this class, but white enamel was used as an occasional addition to the border decoration, which is of course a feature seen on some of· the porcelains associated with William Littler.

Tea wares appear to have been the main items produced, apart from small table wares, tankards and masked jugs of a form obviously inspired by either Worcester or Caughley. No factory marks have been seen on the wares of this group and the identification at present relies solely upon the similarity in every way to the documentary tea canister.

The name Baddeley/Littler has been given to this interesting group of porcelains by Geoffrey Godden as a tribute to William Littler's last involvement with the manufacture of porcelain, and today, collectors, dealers and auction houses appear to have accepted this very distinctive class as originating in Staffordshire, despite the lack of sure evidence.

FURTHER READING:

Godden, G.A., *Staffordshire Porcelain*, Chapter 3, Granada Publishing, 1983.
Murray, John, 'Storm in a Tea-caddy', a paper read to Morley College Ceramic Circle, November, 1978.

NEW HALL

c.1782-1835

For many years almost all English hybrid hard-paste wares thought to have been made about 1780 to 1820 were considered by most collectors and dealers to be New Hall, especially when of silver form and decorated with flower sprays, reminiscent of sprigged muslin, baskets, ribbons, chinoiserie scenes, sparse gilding, or even underglaze blue transfer prints. Today it is recognised that many other Staffordshire manufacturers were from about 1796 producing wares of the New Hall type. It was during the early post-war years that the late Dr. T.A. Sprague, who was a frequent visitor to the Ceramic Department of the Victoria & Albert Museum and a pioneer into research on the New Hall factory, was always prepared to identify wares he considered New Hall, but was unable to make any firm decisions as to where the many look-alikes were produced and today most collectors are still similarly baffled.

Shelton Hall, Staffordshire, had been a potworks for many years before being occupied by a group of partners, including Peter Warburton, Samuel Hollins, William Clowes and others who were interested in producing wares from a hard-paste porcelain. Some later withdrew, leaving those named to engage John Daniel as their manager to produce the wide range of hard-paste porcelains made under the patent they had acquired from Richard Champion, of the

A New Hall hard-paste porcelain coffee cup and saucer with underglaze blue transfer prints of the willow pattern type of decoration with added gilding, note clip handle on cup, c.1782-7. D. (saucer) 13cm.
Allan Weaver Collection

Rare hard-paste porcelain punch pot painted in enamel colours, unmarked, but attributed to New Hall, this item is seemingly unique and so at the time of writing the attribution cannot be considered positive, c.1781-1800. H. 20cm.   Allan Weaver Collection

A New Hall hard-paste porcelain bowl painted in sepia by Fidelle Duvivier, c.1782-87, a so-called slop bowl of a tea service. The painting would appear to be from life as no source material has been found; his portrayal of windmills and smoking ovens suggests a Continental influence. D. 15cm.
                    Allan Weaver Collection

A New Hall hard-paste plate painted by Fidelle Duvivier with a hoopoe bird, a species recorded as having been seen in England in the 1760s, made c.1782-7. The number '5' written on the reverse in a reddish brown is thought to refer to the underglaze blue and gold decoration. D.21.5cm.
Allan Weaver Collection

Tea bowl, coffee cup and saucer of hard-paste porcelain, decorated in colour with pattern number 20, c.1782-7. This early pattern was a very popular and colourful one and was used on a wide variety of table wares, including teapots, coffee pots, jugs and both the high and low 'Chelsea' shape ewers. D. (saucer) 13cm.
Allan Weaver Collection

Small New Hall creamer, of hard-paste porcelain with typical 'clip' handle, decorated with pattern number 20. This form is appropriately called 'Robin shape' and dates c.1782-7. H. 6.5cm.
Allan Weaver Collection

New Hall hard-paste porcelain teapot stand, decorated with an underglaze blue transfer print, lined in gilt, c.1782-7. Recognised by collectors by the would-be bamboo fence looking like a row of drain pipes. W. 20cm.
Allan Weaver Collection

former Bristol porcelain factory. The partners traded initially as Hollins Warburton & Co.

Whilst the materials were basically the same as those used by the Chinese potters, their firing differed; the first 'Biscuit firing' was to a high temperature of 1,300-1,400° C, any underglaze blue decoration was then applied before applying the glaze and firing to approximately 900°C, resulting in a thicker glaze, which contained a high proportion of lead and consequently did not fit the body so well as that on Oriental porcelains.

The early wares of New Hall, made prior to 1796, when the patent purchased from Richard Champion expired, are rather more distinctive in form and decoration than those made from the last years of the century, when their many rivals were able to use an almost identical formula to produce so many similar silver shaped table wares.

It is fortunate for the collector that from about 1790 New Hall adopted a series of pattern numbers, which were applied to the major pieces of tea services, seemingly rarely on the matching cups, tea bowls and saucers or on a variety of other miscellaneous wares, such as dessert dishes, posset pots, chocolate cups and muffin dishes. No original pattern books have been found, but in his excellent book on New Hall, David Holgate has listed the known patterns under their numbers with a photograph and a description of the pattern where it has been possible. The numbers range from a rare number 3 to number 3639 before the closure of the factory in 1835.

It was not until the New Hall partners abandoned their hard grey paste in

New Hall hard-paste porcelain creamer with corrugated moulding, decorated with enamel colours in pattern 22, which was used on a variety of table wares, c.1782-7. H. 10cm.

Allan Weaver Collection

New Hall tea bowl, saucer and coffee can of hard-paste porcelain decorated in enamel colours with pattern 421, c.1790-1805. The same pattern is sometimes painted in a different palette and given pattern number 431. Painter's mark V. D. (saucer) 14cm.

Allan Weaver Collection

favour of bone china in about 1813-15 that a recognised factory mark was adopted in the form of the transfer printed name 'New Hall' within two concentric circles, but this mark was by no means regularly used, and may well have been abandoned by about 1825. The very rare mark of a crowned rampant lion printed in underglaze blue, which for many years has been accepted as a New Hall mark, is at present subject to further research, with opinions varying between well-informed specialists in Staffordshire porcelains of the New Hall period, suggesting that this lion mark was used during a partnership between John Turner and Louis Victor Gerverot, or alternatively, was it used during the early experiments being carried out at Keeling's premises at Tunstall by Richard Champion and John Turner?

Teapot in hard-paste porcelain painted in enamel colours with pattern number 20. The shape of the handle is one that is more commonly seen on large mugs and jugs. Made at the New Hall factory, Shelton, Staffordshire, c.1785. H. 16cm.

Courtesy City Museum & Art Gallery, Stoke-on-Trent

Dish, cup and saucer of New Hall hard-paste porcelain, decorated with gold bat printing, surrounded with gilt decoration on a underglaze blue ground, c.1810. The dish is marked 'Warburtons Patent' under a crown in red enamel, with script N.888 pattern number. Note the ring shaped cup handle, a popular New Hall form. D. (dish) 20.5cm. Allan Weaver Collection

Rare mark in red enamel on New Hall dish above. Peter Warburton, who was the son of Jacob Warburton, one of the founder partners of the New Hall factory, patented his process for printing in gold in 1810

Allan Weaver Collection

New Hall cup and saucer of bone china, decorated with pattern No.1159, comprising tinted bat prints within an underglaze blue border which is decorated with gilding and three reserves also decorated with tinted bat prints, c.1812-20. Note the oval shaped ring handle. D. (saucer) 14cm.
Allan Weaver Collection

New Hall bone china dessert dish moulded in relief and decorated with tinted bat print of fruit on a basket in underglaze blue and gilt, c.1822-35. Pattern no. 1478. L. 23cm.
Allan Weaver Collection

New Hall tea bowl and saucer of hard-paste porcelain, c.1782-93. Decorated with pattern number 170, consisting of underglaze blue scrolls and gold. D. (saucer) 13cm.

Allan Weaver Collection

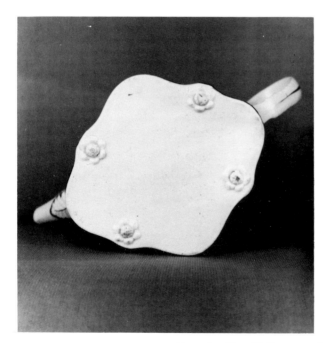

Base of a New Hall teapot, showing the unusual feature of four small moulded applied rosettes. The purpose of these 'feet' is hard to suggest as teapots of this type were usually supplied with a matching porcelain stand, c.1782-7. Allan Weaver Collection

New Hall hard-paste porcelain jug painted in colours, with an iron red line and green, magenta and blue florets, c.1790-1805. Pattern number 839. L. 14cm. Allan Weaver Collection

A rare New Hall jug of bone china, made for the American market. On one side is painted the American ship of war, The Independence *and on the other a steamship which is most probably* Fulton the First. *In 1814 Robert Fulton was authorised by the U.S. Government to build a steamship of war. Similar prints were used by other manufacturers catering for the American export market. Name and address of New York retailer on base. H. 18.5cm.*

Courtesy Phillips, London

As with so many Staffordshire factories in operation in the late eighteenth to early nineteenth centuries, it is only rarely possible to name the painters responsible for the decoration, but the one important name associated with New Hall is that of the Huguenot, Fidelle Duvivier, who had previously worked at the Derby concern. Rare signed examples in either monochrome or a full polychrome palette show a very distinctive style: his busy shipping or country scenes owing a great deal to some of the minor German porcelain factories or the French painters of *genre* subjects. Whilst Duvivier appears to have been engaged as a decorator at New Hall from about 1781 to 1790, although probably only part-time, there are some fine examples of what appears to be his work on New Hall wares made during the first decade of the nineteenth century.

Following the publication of David Holgate's earlier book, *New Hall and Its Imitators* (Faber & Faber, 1971) many examples of hybrid hard-paste porcelain, once thought to be New Hall, are still today classified as factories X, Y or Z.

Many dedicated ceramic researchers, such as Philip Miller and Geoffrey Godden, are endeavouring to attribute, with some degree of certainty, these New Hall type wares. A large class of teawares which appear to have been made between 1785 and 1815 can well be confused with New Hall by the collector, but at present, four well-known potters are on the 'short list': Turner of Lane End, Hugh Booth, Ralph Baddeley and Keeling. Further silver shaped teapots are today classified as Group Y, this class is rarer than those of X, a fairly short-lived factory which produced a very limited range of recognisable wares.

New Hall trio of coffee can, teacup and saucer of hard-paste porcelain, decorated with pale blue bat prints, with gilt border and lining, 1800-12. D. (saucer) 14cm.   Allan Weaver Collection

New Hall sucrier and cover of hard-paste porcelain, decorated with an underglaze blue transfer print and gilt, the pattern of which is often referred to as 'the lurching Pagoda'. There would have been a matching teapot and jug with the remainder of the tea service. Note the pine shaped knob, a popular form, c.1782-90. H. 13.5cm.   Allan Weaver Collection

Teapot of hybrid hard-paste porcelain, c.1800, of the type previously always attributed to the New Hall factory, but this form with spiral fluting and the unusual 'clip' type handle with applied enamel 'dot' is at present considered to be from factory 'X', one of the factories which made New Hall type wares, but to date the researchers in this field have not been able to make any certain attribution regarding the potter responsible. H. 15.7cm.

City Museum & Art Gallery, Stoke-on-Trent

New Hall bone china plate, painted in underglaze blue in dark and light tones, with added gilding, c.1814-31. D. 21.5cm. Allan Weaver Collection

Covered chocolate cup, porcelain decorated with bat printing, washed over in translucent colours, after the series of engravings designed by Adam Buck, the painter of society portraits. Many of 'The Mother and Child' designs are inspired by Buck's work, rather than direct copies. Made at New Hall, c.1815-20. H. 7cm. Courtesy City Museum & Art Gallery, Stoke-on-Trent

Two New Hall coffee cans of hard-paste porcelain, that on the left is painted in enamel colours with pattern 1040, c.1810. The coffee can on the right is decorated with a black bat print of about the same date. H. (of both) 6cm. Allan Weaver Collection

New Hall plate of bone china, with wickerwork moulded decoration painted with pink roses and green leaves, c.1825-30. Pattern no. 1915. D. 21.5cm. Allan Weaver Collection

London shaped jug in New Hall bone china, this version of the so-called 'window pattern' is 425, transfer printed and washed in with translucent colours, c.1830. Mark, 'New Hall' in two concentric rings. L. 15.5cm.

Allan Weaver Collection

Factory Z, the last group of these three factories, produced similar wares to those of New Hall, from a hybrid hard-paste and also in bone china. Opinions again differ among the researchers as to the manufacturer, one suggestion being James Neale of the Church Works, Hanley, who was previously in partnership with Robert Wilson, the other being that they were made by a member of the Ridgway family, known to be manufacturing both porcelain and earthenware at Shelton from about 1805 until 1815.

FURTHER READING:
Stringer, G.E., *New Hall Porcelain*, Art Trade Press, 1949.
Holgate, David, *New Hall*, Faber & Faber, 1987; (Ed. G. Godden), *Staffordshire Porcelain*, Chapter 5, Granada Publishing, 1983.

Chapter 2
British Porcelain Factories,
late 18th - early 19th Centuries

JOHN TURNER & SONS
c.1786-1806

The reader should note the name of John, not to be confused with Thomas Turner, who was proprietor of the Caughley factory in Shropshire from about 1772 to 1799.

John Turner was producing earthenware at Lane End, Staffordshire, from 1759, but it was nearer 1786, when together with his two sons, William and John, he ventured into the field of porcelain, following his short-lived partnership with the original New Hall partners.

John Turner died in 1787, so it is the two sons we have to consider as continuing with the development of porcelains, for which in 1800 they took out a patent, resulting in a variety of tablewares, bearing the mark 'TURNER'S PATENT' written in red enamel. Although porcelain wares with this mark, or that of 'TURNER' impressed, are rare, their form and moulded features are often used as guides to identifying unmarked pieces as the work of the Turner brothers, for example most writers on the subject point out the importance of the very well moulded knob in the shape of a strawberry, which is found on many stoneware and porcelain tewares.

From 1803 the Turner brothers took William Glover and Charles Simpson into partnership for the manufacture of porcelain and earthenware, but in the

Rare porcelain mug, painted in greyish monochrome with chinoiserie scene below a green scale pattern rim decoration, showing traces of gilding. This is the only recorded example bearing the name 'TURNER' impressed, attributed to John Turner of Lane End, Longton, Staffordshire, c.1785. H. 9.8cm.
Courtesy City Museum & Art Gallery, Stoke-on-Trent

Dish of a porcellaneous experimental material, painted with the Royal Arms in enamel colours. Made by J. & W. Turner, Lane End, Staffordshire, painted mark of 'Turner's Patent'. W. 27cm.
Courtesy City Museum & Art Gallery, Stoke-on-Trent

following year John Turner retired and the company continued until 1806 when both brothers were declared bankrupt.

The certain identification of porcelains as having been made by the Turner family is at present subject to much discussion and there are several differences of opinion among the researchers, all due primarily to the fact that around this time there were so many Staffordshire potters experimenting with new ceramic bodies, that it is difficult to separate them.

A class of comparatively rare porcelain at present under discussion is that bearing the mark of a lion rampant crowned, painted in underglaze blue, a very Germanic form of mark. This mark has for many years been accepted as one used on early New Hall, but in the *Journal of the Northern Ceramic Society,* Vol 6, 1987, Roger Pomfret makes out a very good case in suggesting that the 'lion marked' wares may well be the work of the French arcanist, Louis-Victor Gerverot, who enjoyed a very short partnership with John Turner, shortly before Turner's death in 1787. Two very important pieces discussed in the article are both inscribed 'Lane End July 1787', the French word *juin* being used in one instance in addition, within a painting signed 'Duvivier pxt'. The majority of the wares marked with the rampant lion are decorated with underglaze blue prints, of which only three variations are as yet recorded.

Unlike the mark used at the German factory of Frankenthal from about 1756, the Gerverot(?) lion is crowned and printed, not painted. A further opinion is that expressed by Geoffrey Godden who suggests that this mark refers to 'the local Lord Talbot, Earl of Shrewsbury', who used the crest device at this period in the 1780s.

FURTHER READING:
Hillier, B., *The Turners of Lane End,* Cory, Adams & Mackay, London, 1965.

NEALE & CO
c.1778-1792

James Neale was originally a London agent or 'chinaman', who purchased wares directly from Humphrey Palmer, a potter who was in business in Hanley. When Palmer got into financial difficulties in 1778, Neale took over his establishment with all hands, including Robert Wilson as manager. The pottery at first was producing a fine earthenware only, but at sometime during the late 1780s a fine porcelain was produced, which contained 25% of bone ash, but very few marked pieces have been recorded.

Tea and coffee wares were made, but no dessert, dinner services or ornamental wares have so far been noted. Wares are generally neat in design, with finely painted borders. Delicate flower painting is found, and some pieces are ascribed to the famous ceramic painters, Fidelle Duvivier and Zachariah Boreman. It is not surprising, therefore, that wares at times have been wrongly attributed to the better known Derby factory, especially as they also have in common a simple ring knob to the lids of teapots and sugar bowls and a similarity of design in the spiral and leaf mouldings used on some pieces.

In 1786 James Neale took Robert Wilson into partnership, when the concern became known as Neale & Wilson. In 1792 Robert Wilson became the sole proprietor, to be followed after his death in 1801, by his brother David, who continued to trade as David Wilson & Sons until he died in 1816. The sons were

Rare example of a porcelain mug, with the impressed mark of 'Neale & Co.' of Hanley, Staffordshire, decorated with engine turning and sparse enamel decoration, c.1785. H. 10.8cm.
Courtesy City Museum & Art Gallery, Stoke-on-Trent

Rare bone china teapot of an early form, decorated in green and pink enamels and gilt. Unmarked, but attributed to James Neale & Co. of Hanley, c.1800. H. 16.2cm.
Courtesy Mr. & Mrs. P. Miller

A rare teapot made at Hanley by James Neale & Co., c.1800, decorated with pink and blue enamels and gilt. Mark, a painted 'B' on foot rim. The moulded leaf decoration is commonly seen on Derby wares. H. 17.1cm.
Courtesy Mr. & Mrs. P. Miller

unsuccessful and became bankrupt in 1817. Although David Wilson and Sons were listed as china manufacturers, no marked wares have so far been recorded.

The marks used are impressed Neale & Co., or even rarer Neale & Wilson; pattern numbers have not been noted, but tally marks have sometimes been seen.

FURTHER READING:
Edwards, Diana, *Neale Pottery & Porcelain,* Barrie & Jenkins, London, 1987.
Godden, G.A., *Encyclopaedia of British Porcelain Manufacturers,* Barrie & Jenkins, London, 1988; *Staffordshire Porcelain,* Chapter 4, Granada Publishing Ltd, 1983.

FLIGHT & HIS PARTNERS (WORCESTER)

1783-1840

Following the retirement of Dr. Wall from the Worcester factory in 1774, William Davis, one of the original partners, continued to run the concern until 1783, when it was purchased by Thomas Flight. Flight was already well acquainted with the Worcester Porcelain factory prior to becoming the owner, as he had for many years been the manager of their London shop, but being the manager of a retail store and running a manufactory making the wares, called for skills which he and his two sons, Joseph and John, were lacking. Within a very short period their position was made even more difficult, when Robert Chamberlain and his son, Humphrey, left Flight's employ to start their own rival business nearby. Today the period from 1774 to 1793 is referred to as the Davis/Flight period.

Whilst continuing to produce a wide range of wares similar to those made at the Worcester Porcelain Company prior to his takeover, many of his pieces decorated with underglaze blue prints were of a very poor quality. In the late 1940s and 1950s it was quite common for the keen Worcester collectors to allocate these inferior wares to the Caughley factory of Thomas Turner in Shropshire, sometimes suggesting that Caughley porcelain was deliberately marked with an underglaze blue 'C' which resembled the hatched crescent of the Worcester

Part tea service in porcelain, painted in brown enamel and gilt. Made at Worcester during the Flight & Barr partnership, c.1792-1804. Mark, an incised 'B'. D. (saucer dish) 19.8cm.
Courtesy Bearnes, Torquay

A group of Worcester wares all painted with shells on various coloured grounds. The earliest is the sucrier with a green ground, c.1783-92, the trio on a grey marbled ground and the coffee can and saucer on yellow ground are both Flight & Barr, c.1792-1804. The square dish with gilt ground and that with crest, on a grey marbled ground, are both Barr, Flight & Barr, c.1804-13; the round plate has a sky blue ground, the two-handled cup, cover and stand is pink, both are of the final Flight, Barr & Barr period, c.1813-40, when the company merged with Chamberlain. D. (square dish) 21.5cm.
Courtesy Phillips, London

Jug and stemmed cup in porcelain painted in enamel colours and gilt, both made at Worcester during the Barr, Flight & Barr period, c.1804-13. The jug has the initials of the painter Samuel Smith, dated 1807. Mark, incised 'B' and red script mark as used on selected wares H 17cm. The cup, also attributed to the same painter is unmarked. H. 12.5cm.
Courtesy Phillips, London

Porcelain dessert plate, made by Barr, Flight & Barr, Worcester, with painted enamel decoration on a ivory ground in reserves within an underglaze blue ground. The central armorial crest is of Worcester College, Oxford, the motto reading 'DEO. REGI. VICINO'. Mark, 'BFB' under crown impressed and printed circular factory mark with Royal Crest and fleur-de-lis, c.1807-13. D. 25.3cm.
Courtesy Andrew Hartley Fine Arts, Ilkley

factory and that the so-called 'disguised Chinese numerals' from 1-9 were definitely Caughley marks. When in the 1960s, excavations became possible on the former sites of both factories, the thousands of wasters found proved that these suggestions were untrue; numerous fragments were found at Worcester with the numeral mark, none were found at Caughley, and the 'C' for Caughley is a distinct capital letter with a serif, and not a bit like the crescent. In consequence today it is recognised that these often very inferior blue and white wares were made at Worcester during the Davis/Flight period, c.1785 and are comparatively common, whilst those of Thomas Turner's factory at Caughley are of quite high quality and not so plentiful.

Apart from the large production of useful wares decorated in underglaze blue prints, many more attractive styles of decoration were used, usually consisting of sparsely applied underglaze blue patterns to which gilding was added.

It was during the Davis/Flight period that so many transfer prints were used, which require close inspection to decide whether they were being used by Flight or Turner. This is particularly the case with the Fisherman or Pleasure Boat pattern, although in contrast more elaborate decoration, such as scale blue and enamel painting of the Dr. Wall period was still being used, probably to order to enlarge earlier services or replace breakages, as proven by Henry Sandon when excavating on the Warmstry House site.

Coffee can and saucer in porcelain made by Flight, Barr & Barr, Worcester. Decorated in colours and gilt in bold Japan style. Mark, FBB under crown, impressed. D. (saucer) 14.5cm.

Courtesy Andrew Hartley Fine Arts, Ilkley

Plate, saucer, tea and coffee cup of Flight, Barr & Barr, Worcester porcelain, painted with enamel colours and gilt, the feathers are a rare style of decoration, c.1813-20 and are much sought after by collectors

Courtesy Phillips, London

It was during the Davis/Flight period that the Royal Lily pattern was introduced, known as the Blue Lily until chosen by George III when ordering a service in 1788, this pattern remained popular over many years. One of the favourite forms during the Flight period were useful wares with spiral fluting, the popular floral knob was also continued, sometimes on moulded wares with reeded decoration, often painted with scattered underglaze blue flowers, similar

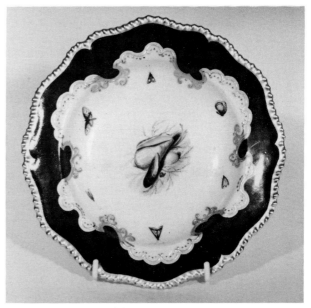

Flight, Barr & Barr porcelain dish painted in enamel colours and gilt, with an apple green ground. The shell painting is attributed to Samuel Smith, dating to about 1820. Mark, 'FBB' under a crown impressed and the full circular printed mark including the Royal coat of arms and fleur-de-lis. D. 21cm. Courtesy Andrew Hartley Fine Arts, Ilkley

Flight, Barr & Barr porcelain dish painted with enamel colours and gilt on an underglaze blue ground, the painting of shells, seaweed and butterflies; is in the manner of J. Barker. Made at Worcester, c.1813-40. D. 19.5cm. Courtesy Andrew Hartley Fine Arts, Ilkley

One of a pair of porcelain dishes, decorated in gilt with a centre vignette of exotic birds in enamel colours by Charles Stinton. Made at Worcester by Flight, Barr & Barr, c.1820. Mark, F.B.B. impressed under a crown. L. 30cm. Courtesy City Museum & Art Gallery, Stoke-on-Trent

Porcelain basket on four paw feet, painted in enamel colours and gilt with 'The Fishermans daughter' within a light green ground. Made at Worcester, c.1813-40. Standard printed mark and F B B under crown, impressed for Flight, Barr & Barr of Worcester. D. 25cm.

Courtesy Bearnes, Torquay

A Worcester porcelain dish made by Flight, Barr & Barr, painted in enamel colours and gilt with a view of the 'Straits of Menai from Anglesea', painted on a white ground within a pale blue border, c.1825. Mark, FBB under crown impressed. W. 29.5cm.

Courtesy Bearnes, Torquay

to those on the late eighteenth century porcelains of Chantilly, often called 'gilly' flowers. During the Dr. Wall period the translucency of the porcelain was often cited as a guide, as most Worcester porcelains up to about 1775 showed a pleasing green in varying shades, depending on the thickness of the potting, but from the start of the Flight concern this feature is no longer indicative, and a wide variety of hues are to be seen, usually of different tones of orange.

Following the death of Thomas Flight's son John, the remaining brother Joseph took Martin Barr as a partner and the firm became known as Flight & Barr, a partnership which continued until 1804, but few new patterns were introduced. The popular Kylin and Royal Lily were continued, together with various Japan styles, flowers, feathers, shells and landscapes, all of which were of a very high quality and were retailed from Worcester direct, London, and elsewhere in the country through major china dealers. The mark during this period was Flight & Barr under a crown, impressed, 'F. & B.' or just incised 'B' or 'Bx'.

Porcelain pedestal jar and cover, painted with flowers in enamel colours in reserves on a green ground. Made at Worcester during the Flight, Barr & Barr partnership, c.1813-40. Impressed mark of FBB under crown. H. 21.5cm.
Courtesy Bearnes, Torquay

A pair of Worcester porcelain sauce tureens, made by Flight, Barr & Barr, c.1825. Painted in bright enamel colours and gilt with a deep blue ground. H. 22.5cm.
Courtesy Bearnes, Torquay

About 1804 there was a further change of partners, when the son of Martin Barr, also named Martin, joined the firm, now to be known as Barr, Flight & Barr using the mark of B F B under a crown impressed. By this time fluted and reeded shapes had become outdated, the smoother finish now allowed ornate enamelling and gilding or in contrast the soft bat prints.

On the death in 1813 of the earlier partner, Martin Barr, yet another son, George Barr, becme a partner. Joseph Flight appears to have become the senior partner, giving us the partnership of Flight, Barr & Barr, which was to survive

Worcester porcelain dessert plate, with enamel flowers painted in the ivory reserves on an underglaze blue ground, which is further decorated with raised gilding and white jewelling, the flower painting is attributed to Henry Stinton; c.1825. Mark, in red with crown and 'ROYAL PORCELAIN WORKS, FLIGHT, BARR & BARR, WORCESTER AND COVENTRY STREET, LONDON'. D. 25.3cm. Courtesy Andrew Hartley Fine Arts, Ilkley

until 1840. By this time, in common with other porcelain manufacturers, they began to suffer increasing competition from the growing number of Staffordshire firms who were making very high quality tablewares. Following the death of Joseph Flight in 1838, the two remaining Barr brothers, Martin and George, amalgamated with the thriving Chamberlain company, selling the manufactory, all stock, both finished and unfinished, implements and utensils to Chamberlain & Co. for the total sum of £13,000.

Dr. Wall's original factory was sold and the Chamberlain factory was to continue under that name until 1852, when it was taken over by Kerr & Binns, until 1862, from which time the famous Royal Worcester Porcelain Company came into being, continuing to the present day on the same site, together with the Dyson Perrins Museum, which houses the fine collection of Worcester wares, with examples from the mid-eighteenth century.

FURTHER READING:
Sandon, Henry, *Flight & Barr Worcester Porcelain 1783-1840,* Antique Collectors' Club, Woodbridge, 1978.

CHAMBERLAIN'S WORCESTER
1788-1852

The name of Dr. Wall is always associated with the wares of the early Worcester factory during their most successful years, but following his death in 1776 the factory went through a bad period, during which time they were to encounter a good deal of competition from neighbouring concerns.

We are told by R.W. Binns in his 1865 volume, *A Century of Potting in the City of Worcester,* that 'Mr. Robert Chamberlain (*b.*1737. *d.*1798), who was the first apprentice of the Porcelain Company, left the factory after its purchase by Mr. Flight in 1783, and commenced business as a decorator, at premises in King Street, St. Peter's, close to the present works', Binns failed to tell us that Chamberlain also took with him some of the talented painters and gilders from their previous employer, Thomas Flight.

When Chamberlain first started this new business he was solely concerned

Chamberlain's Worcester porcelain dish painted in enamel colours and gilt with the 'Kylin' or 'Dragons in Compartments' pattern. Script painted mark 'Chamberlains Worcester 75' in orange L. 33cm. The kylin (ch'i lin), is best described as the Chinese mythological unicorn, a combination of ch'i *male and* lin *female, regarded as an emblem of perfect Good*
Courtesy Andrew Hartley Fine Arts, Ilkley

Chamberlain seemingly made a speciality of dessert services painted with various Aesop's Fables *from as early as 1794, for this purpose Chamberlain had purchased two volumes of* The Fables of Aesop, *with a life of the author, which were printed and published by John Stockdale of Piccadilly, London, in 1795. The fable of the hare and the tortoise on this dessert dish was probably painted by George Davis, c.1795. The rim decoration is gilt on underglaze blue, the fable in brown monochrome. D. 21.8cm.*
Courtesy Bearnes, Torquay

Elaborate ice pail with cover and liner, decorated with enamel colours and gilding. Made by Chamberlains of Worcester, probably the work of George Davis, c.1786-1810. Mark, 'Chamberlains Worcester' in red script. H. 36.3cm.
R.H. Williamson Bequest, Tullie House, Carlisle

Part tea service of Worcester porcelain, made by Chamberlains c.1810, painted in colours and gilt with Japan pattern. Mark, on inside of teapot cover, 'Chamberlain Worcester Warranted N.240'. D. (dish) 19.7cm.
Courtesy Andrew Hartley Fine Arts, Ilkley

Chamberlain's Worcester dessert dish, painted with armorial arms in gilt. The form of mark which includes the term 'Regent China' and the Bond Street address printed in red enamel indicates a date c.1811-20. L. 29.5cm.   Private Collection

with adding decoration to wares made elsewhere, we know that he acquired most of his 'blanks' from Thomas Turner's factory at Caughley, all soapstone porcelain, some entirely in the white, and other pieces which were already partially decorated with underglaze blue. Some of these wares were to have enamel and gilt decoration added to the order of Thomas Turner to help stock his London warehouse, and some for the Chamberlains to decorate and dispose of in their own shop.

Robert Chamberlain married in about 1755 and his first son, Humphrey, eventually joined his father as a decorator for the Worcester/Flight factory. It seems that later they gave them cause for concern for it was recorded in 1789 that they were worried because 'Chamberlain and his Son had taken our old house and intended setting up a Retail Shop', leaving them without any skilled personnel capable of enamelling and gilding their wares, until they engaged a Mrs. Hampton. Records indicate that the Chamberlains were probably working for themselves as early as 1788, by which time they were already

*Chamberlain's Worcester
teapot, stand and covered sugar
bowl, decorated in colour with
armorial crest of bull's head
within coronet and a gilt
'seaweed' ground. The 'New
Oval Shape' is of c.1810; a
similar teapot illustrated by
Phillip Miller is marked
'Chamberlain's Worcester
Warranted' and 'N410' in
script inside cover.
L. 15.9cm.*
Courtesy Bearnes, Torquay

*Finely decorated inkstand
painted in enamel colours and
gilt on a dark blue ground.
Unmarked, but probably the
painting of Walter
Chamberlain, c.1810-20,
with Neptune in the front
panel and landscapes in the
two side panels. L. 19cm.*
Courtesy Bearnes, Torquay

*Chamberlain's Worcester
teapot and stand, sugar bowl
and cover and milk jug of the
'New Oval Shape', decorated
with gilt marbling on an
orange ground.
'Chamberlains/Worcester'
painted in script, c.1810.
L. 15.9cm.*
Courtesy Bearnes, Torquay

purchasing Caughley wares from Turner. Further accounts also suggest that the Chamberlains were selling decorated wares direct by this time, prior to opening their own shop in 1789.

There was constant friction between the Chamberlains and Thomas Turner regarding the Caughley wares sent for decoration. Those which they were sent to decorate and market for themselves were apparently old stock, or unpopular shapes for which there was little demand, which was obviously a good incentive for the Chamberlains to consider producing their own porcelain, which they were eventually doing by at least the end of 1791, although initially without any great success. They were having extreme difficulties in fulfilling orders in 1793, despite still buying additional wares from Caughley, to which they were adding their own decoration and which they were having difficulting paying for. One can well understand that Turner was not prepared to make things too easy for a new rival manufacturer in the field.

By about 1794 the Chamberlains had seemingly overcome the initial problems and were producing the fine wares with which we associate the factory, wares even admired by the Prince of Orange, from Hampton Court, who ordered a fifty-nine piece dessert service 'all blue and gold with different figures'.

A Chamberlain's Worcester porcelain cup and saucer with gilt flowered rim, the castle painted in colours within a lavender ground, the castle inscribed 'SHERBOURN', c.1815. Both cup and saucer marked in red on base, 'The Seat of Lord Macclesfield, Oxfordshire, Chamberlain's Worcester'. D. (saucer) 14cm. Courtesy Andrew Hartley Fine Arts, Ilkley

A pair of fine Chamberlain's porcelain sauce tureens and covers, from a tea, coffee and breakfast service ordered by Sir James Yeo in 1815. The service was a very ornate pattern, number 298, to which was added to order the armorial crest, mottoes and orders of Sir James; regrettably the large order was not completed until after he had died on his way home from Jamaica at the early age of thirty-six. H. 19.5cm.

Courtesy Bearnes, Torquay

Three bone china vases, painted in enamel colours and gilt. Made at the Chamberlain factory, Worcester, c.1815. The painting attributed to Humphrey Chamberlain is of scenes from Shakespeare's Henry V, Henry VI *and* Henry VIII. *Mark, Chamberlain/Worcester in script*

Courtesy Phillips, London

The founder Robert Chamberlain had died in 1798, but by the turn of the century his son, Humphrey, was producing wares far superior to those of the Flight & Barr concern. This warranted the patronage of such notabilities as Lord Nelson in 1802, and the Prince of Wales in 1807, from which time they were styled 'Porcelain Manufacturers to His Royal Highness the Prince of Wales', later changed to 'Prince Regent', after which a new and expensive porcelain, known as 'Regent China' was introduced in 1811.

Business was now obviously so good that in 1813 they opened a London shop at 63 Piccadilly, moving to 155 Bond Street in 1816, addresses which are often included in their marks and are a help in accurate dating. This thriving situation continued until 1840, when they were merged with Flight, Barr & Barr, under the name of Chamberlain & Co. Eventually the factory passed into the hands of the grandson, Walter, who continued with various partners until he too retired in 1851, the year of the 1851 Exhibition, where their exhibits did not arouse any great interest. This left W.H. Kerr as the remaining partner,

Chamberlain's Worcester mug, with a hand painted view of Worcester in coloured enamels on a green ground. The name 'Sussanah' has been applied in gilt at the base, but is now barely legible. Mark, 'WORCESTER/CATHEDRAL' & 'CHAMBERLAIN'S/WORCESTER', c.1847-52. H. 10.5cm.
Private Collection

Pair of porcelain wall plaques, painted in enamel colours and gilt. Made by Chamberlain at Worcester and painted with views of Dover Castle and Malvern Abbey, in a manner attributed to Enoch Doe, who was formerly employed at Chamberlain's factory and afterwards started his own decorating business with Rogers in High Street, Worcester, c.1820, continuing until 1835. W. 20.5cm.
Courtesy Phillips, London

who in 1852 took R.W. Binns into a partnership that was to last for ten years as Kerr & Binns.

Certainly by 1795 the Chamberlains were no longer relying on the supply of Thomas Turner's Caughley wares to supplement their own, which were now of a very high quality, including large moulded jugs, spiral fluted tea sets, marked

Worcester cache-pot and stand, painted in enamel colours and gilt. Mark, 'Chamberlains Worcester' in red script, c.1820-30. H. 18.2cm.   R.H. Williamson Bequest, Tullie House, Carlisle

Two Chamberlain's Worcester porcelain plates, with gadrooned border; the decoration is painted in enamel colours and gilt with a green ground. The mark of Chamberlain's is impressed, dating to c.1850. D. 22.5cm.
Courtesy Bearnes, Torquay

Chamberlains/Worcester, in script, and tea sets which were at one time thought to have been made at New Hall. Between 1795 and 1800 further tea sets and dessert services were being produced which were decorated with their versions of the earlier Worcester 'Royal Lily' and 'Dragon in Compartments' (sometimes called Kylin after the Chinese mythological beast) patterns. Some very beautiful dessert services painted with various *Aesop's Fables* attributed to the hand of George Davis are among their finest productions.

Wares of this very high quality were produced by Humphrey and Robert Chamberlain until about 1820, from which time many Staffordshire concerns were also making very competitive bone china at lower prices, a situation which continued until the takeover by Kerr & Binns.

FURTHER READING:
Godden, G.A., *Chamberlain-Worcester Porcelain 1788-1852,* Barrie & Jenkins, 1982.

MINTON

1793-1842

Thomas Minton, who was born in Shropshire in about 1766, was probably first involved with the ceramic world as an apprentice to Thomas Turner to learn the art of engraving copperplates, which were used on Turner's Caughley porcelain decorated with underglaze blue prints, such as the well-known Willow Pattern, which he is credited with engraving.

By the late 1780s Minton was working in London, where at the age of twenty-four he married Sarah Webb, and later became the father of ten children. He may well have continued his craft in London, and he was almost certainly in partnership with his brother, Arthur, a successful London dealer in pottery and porcelain, until about 1789 when he returned to Stoke, where in 1793 he purchased land on which to build his own ceramic factory which was in operation from 1796. By that time he had two partners, Joseph Poulson, who had previously been a manager for Spode, and Thomas Pownall, a Liverpool merchant. Their first productions were of earthenware, almost certainly printed in underglaze blue, and it was probably nearer 1800 before Minton was firmly established in a separate china works, leaving Poulson to concentrate on the

Early bone china teapot, decorated with blue enamel and gilt, pattern number 'N.62'. Made by Thomas Minton at Stoke, c.1805. Typical 'Old Oval' shape, made with a heart shaped pouring guard. H. 16.2cm.
Courtesy Mr. & Mrs. P. Miller

Many factories other than Derby were influenced in their designs by the important Oriental wares, and the Japanese and Chinese manner of painting to be seen on screens, pictures, silks and fans, was also used to decorate English useful wares, such as this cup and saucer as early as c.1810
Courtesy Minton Museum, Royal Doulton Ltd

A bone china Minton dish, c.1810, painted with a botanical study of Falgora candelaria, *which is named on the reverse. Such painting was not particularly popular at the Minton factory until after 1870, when two of their painters, William Mussill and Richard Pilsbury, specialised in painting botanical specimens*
Courtesy Minton Museum, Royal Doulton Ltd

The shell patterns on this bone china plate were applied by bat printing, c.1812. The tedious process of bat printing was used by Minton from as early as 1805 for about ten years, when the production of bone china was to cease for a period of about a further ten years until 1824, from when the use of bat printing was again introduced. It was particularly popular during the 1860s-'70s, continuing into the early 20th century
Courtesy Minton Museum, Royal Doulton Ltd

Group of bone china tablewares of the period 1805-10, showing Imari, Derby, Regency and landscape patterns. H. (teapot) 16cm.
Courtesy Minton Museum, Royal Doulton Ltd

Group of bone china tablewares of the period 1805-10, showing gilding and the influence of contemporary French porcelain. Leaf pattern cup and saucer, no.85
Courtesy Minton Museum, Royal Doulton Ltd

Bone china cup, cover and saucer of the period 1805-10, decorated with the Chinese Sports pattern no. 539. H. (cup and cover) 12.5cm.
Courtesy Minton Museum, Royal Doulton Ltd

Minton bone china cabinet cup and saucer, c.1875. Butterflies were a favourite form of cup handle from the 1830s and detailed features are often used to help identify unmarked wares

Courtesy Minton Museum, Royal Doulton Ltd

Minton bone china group of a Guitar Player and Harpist, painted in enamel colours and gilt, probably modelled after a German original of about the same period, c.1835. H. c.18cm.

Courtesy Victoria & Albert Museum

earthenwares, probably until he died in 1808, with Pownall remaining a partner until his death in 1814.

Minton's earliest bone china wares are hard to separate from those of his contemporaries, such as Coalport, Spode, Derby, etc. but much help is gained from the few records which are kept in the Minton Museum, Stoke, some of which date from as early as 1796. Few pieces were marked and then only with pattern numbers. The Minton production obviously flourished, for within

Pair of Minton bone china candlesticks, c.1835-6, painted in enamel colours and gilt, these same figures can also be found on footed bases. The female figure features in the Minton design drawing as 192, 'Single Figure Candlestick'. H. 22.2cm. Courtesy Phillips, London

Typical Minton candlestick, c.1837, in bone china, decorated with enamel colours, which invariably include a rich turquoise blue. Fashioned very much in the style of the figures being made at Meissen at that time. Referred to in Minton design drawing as 'Single Figure Candlestick 192'. H. 22.2cm. Courtesy Minton Museum, Royal Doulton Ltd

twenty years their pattern numbers had reached at least 948, and whilst they did not blatantly copy the marks of Sèvres or Meissen, from 1805 they were using a somewhat similar mark to that of early Sèvres (the crossed 'L' cypher) but including the letter 'M' for Minton on these wares which were shaped and decorated in the popular styles of the French factory until 1816. The reader is cautioned that plates with six indentations at regular intervals around the rim, were produced at Minton's and not solely at Coalport, as has formerly been suggested.

The production of porcelain was discontinued between about 1816 and 1824, when the china works were again taken over for the making of a very superior form of bone china, which they used for the manufacture of tea services, dessert services, and a wide range of figures and decorative wares, all of a very high quality. These wares were still unmarked except for the pattern numbers.

In 1817 Thomas Minton had taken two of his sons into partnership, Thomas Webb and Herbert, but the former left the business in 1823 and following the death of the founder in 1836, the works were continued by Herbert, who took John Boyle into a partnership which lasted until 1842, when it was dissolved following labour troubles in the factory and personal differences. The wares made during this seven year period were again only rarely marked, other than

Bone china 'Globe' pot-pourri, listed as Minton's ornamental shape number 19, decorated with relief floral decoration in enamel colours and painted with a view of Carisbrooke Castle, Isle of Wight, with floral painting on reverse, c.1835. About this time Minton were employing over fifty-five hands as 'flowerers'. H. 18.5cm. Courtesy Minton Museum, Royal Doulton Ltd

with the pattern number and an occasional tally mark, used to identify a painter's work for payment.

In 1845 Minton took Michael Daintry Hollins and Colin Campbell, both relatives, into partnership and so the factory continued into the Victorian period (discussed in a later chapter); the production continues to this day as part of Royal Doulton Ltd.

FURTHER READING:
Godden, G.A., *Minton Pottery and Porcelain of the First Period,* London, 1968.
Atterbury, Paul, and Batkin, Maureen, *The Dictionary of Minton,* Antique Collectors' Club, 1990.

DAVENPORT

1794-1887

Once again we are discussing only the porcelain wares produced by an outstanding factory which during their many years of establishment, made just about every type of popular ceramic ware, and also glass.

The founder, John Davenport (b.1765) was first introduced to the pottery world when he was engaged by Thomas Wolfe in 1785, he was first employed in Dublin and then in Liverpool where he became a partner in 1788 until 1794, when the partnership was dissolved. Davenport continued the business of both manufacturing and selling earthenware and glass in Liverpool and in addition purchased his first Staffordshire works in Longport, where from about 1800 he commenced the production of useful wares from a hybrid hard-paste.

Terry Lockett, Chairman of the Northern Ceramic Society, who has been responsible for most of the valuable research into the firm of Davenport, tells us that these early hard-paste wares were only rarely marked with the impressed name of Davenport. The production of this material continued until about 1808, by which time they were also producing the more popular bone china. The factory obviously continued to flourish and by 1840 Davenport & Co. of Longport, Staffordshire were retailing from 82 Fleet Street and had warehouses

Davenport porcelain stand for a basket, painted with a chinoiserie scene in enamel colours and gilt, c.1800-15. Mark, 'Longport' written in red enamel their earliest known porcelain mark. L. 28cm.
Courtesy City Museum & Art Gallery, Stoke-on-Trent

Davenport bulb pot of hybrid hard-paste porcelain, painted with fruit in enamel colours in the manner of Thomas Steel, c.1807-12. H. 12.7cm. Private Collection

Davenport bone china sugar box and cover of characteristic shape, painted in enamel colours, c.1810. L. 20.3cm.   Courtesy Lockett Collection

A Davenport bone china creamer of the 'New Oval' shape, painted in enamel colours and gilt, c.1810-15. Note form of handle. H. 11cm.   Private Collection

Davenport bone china dessert plate, painted with a bird in natural colours, c.1810 and bearing the early porcelain mark of 'Longport' painted in red. D. 24.7cm.   Private Collection

Davenport bone china sugar box and cream jug, decorated in gold, c.1810-15. Mark, DAVENPORT/LONGPORT printed in red and pattern number 327 in gold. L. (box) 20.3cm. Private Collection

Tureen and cover, porcelain painted in enamel colours and gilt with 'Chinese Temple' pattern. Made by Davenport, c.1810. The choice of The Prince of Wales in 1806. L. 45.5cm.
Courtesy City Museum & Art Gallery, Stoke-on-Trent

Two examples of Davenport porcelain, with white relief decoration on a pale blue ground (the stand of the cachepot is wrongly inverted), c.1815-25. Mark, a printed ribbon inscribed DAVENPORT, encircling an anchor. H. 8.3cm.
Private Collection

217

Davenport bulb pot of hybrid hard-paste porcelain, painted in gilt, c.1810. Marked with impressed name and anchor. H. 15.2cm.
Private Collection

Plate of bone china with relief moulded rim, picked out in gilt, around three bouquets painted in enamel colours. Made at Longport, c.1810-20. Mark, printed strap, inscribed DAVENPORT encircling an anchor in sparsely printed red enamel. D. 21cm. Private Collection

Davenport plate, painted in enamel colours and gilt with a botanical plant, 'Bladder Podded Alyssum', c.1820. Mark, a lightly drawn anchor with ribbon inscribed 'DAVENPORT'. D. 24.2cm.
Private Collection

in Liverpool, Lübeck and Hamburg and had become manufacturers to William IV and Queen Adelaide.

The new collector may well be confused with the word 'Longport', which is their location in Staffordshire, but was often used as their mark.

Due to the great similarity of early Davenport wares to those of several contemporary competitors and the scarcity of marked pieces, certain identification of the hybrid hard-paste porcelain wares is extremely difficult, but we know that they were of such a high quality that in 1806 the Prince of Wales gave a large order following a royal visit to the factory.

Davenport Etruscan shaped teacup and saucer of bone china, painted with enamel colours and gilt, c.1820-5. D. (saucer) 15.2cm. Private Collection

Porcelain vegetable dish and cover from a service made for George IV, painted with enamels and gilt, with a blue ground, c.1820. Pattern number 242. 'Davenport' printed mark. L. 28.5cm. Private Collection

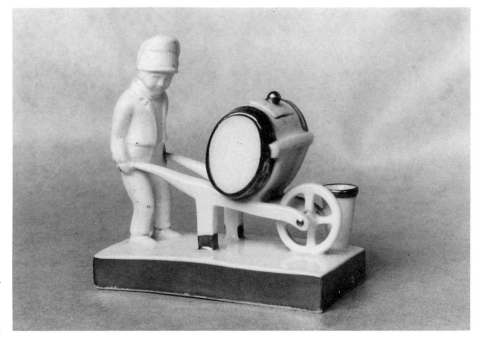

Rare Davenport novel ink-well of porcelain in Continental style, c.1830. Printed mark of DAVENPORT on ribbon encircling an anchor. H. 9.5cm. Private Collection

Three pieces of Davenport bone china, all decorated with enamel colours and gilt; the frill vase, c.1870-80, is marked with DAVENPORT/LONGPORT/STAFFORDSHIRE under a crown in red; the miniature inkstand and cover in the form of a teapot, c.1825-35, is marked with an anchor under a ribbon inscribed DAVENPORT, printed in red; whilst the pastille burner and cover, with the same mark, is c.1820-30. H. 12.7, 5.2, 12.7cm.   Private Collection

Davenport coffee can and saucer of bone china, decorated with an underglaze blue ground, with reserves showing classical figures in white on a red ground, c.1830-5. Marked with strap inscribed DAVENPORT/LONGPORT/STAFFORDSHIRE with crown, enclosing MANUFACTURERS TO THEIR MAJESTIES, printed in puce. D. (saucer) 13cm.

Courtesy City Museum & Art Gallery, Stoke-on-Trent

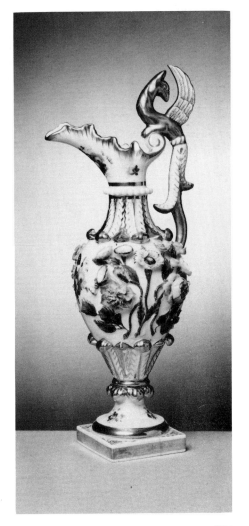

Davenport ewer, decorated with encrusted flowers and enamelled in colours and gilt, c.1830-5. Marked with an anchor under a ribbon inscribed DAVENPORT, printed in red. H. 29.2cm.   Private Collection

Three Davenport porcelain plates, painted in enamel colours and gilt. Left to right: the border moulded with gilt flower-heads and leaves on a ecru ground, pattern number 315, suggesting a date c.1830-40. Printed mark in puce. D. 24cm. The leaf and flower decoration in gilt on the centre plate has a turquoise ground, c.1850-5. Pattern number 1152 painted in red. Printed mark in underglaze blue. D. 23.5cm. Plate with central panel of tulips painted in pink, yellow and green with pale yellow border, c.1845-50. Pattern number 607. Printed mark in underglaze blue. D. 24cm.   Courtesy Henry Spencer & Sons, Retford

Finely painted coffee can and saucer, decorated with enamel colours and gilt. Made by Davenport, c.1830-7. D. (saucer) 12cm.
Courtesy City Museum & Art Gallery Stoke-on-Trent

Davenport Etruscan shaped teacup and saucer of bone china, painted with enamel colours and gilt, c.1820-5. D. (saucer) 15.2cm. Davenport bone china trio painted with enamel colours and gilt, c.1849-52. D. (saucer) 14.5cm. Davenport bone china teacup and saucer, painted in enamel colours and gilt, c.1855. D. (saucer) 14cm.
Courtesy Lockett Collection

Plate painted with a portrait of George III, in fine enamel colours, probably by an outside decorator, c.1825. Mark, lightly printed anchor with ribbon inscribed 'DAVENPORT'. D. 25.4cm.

Private Collection

The rare marks sometimes to be found on the early bone china, seemingly favoured the word 'Longport' or Davenport/Longton in red script, but most of the attributions have to be made by accurately matching with marked pieces. After about 1815 marking was more consistent and the high quality was maintained, surpassing the wares of their English contemporaries and resulting in their being patronised by both George IV and William IV, both of whom ordered services for their coronation banquets, a few pieces of which can still be found in both royal and private collections.

Large Davenport porcelain vase, painted with flowers in enamel colours, c.1875. H. 37.5cm. Private Collection

Two Davenport plates, painted in enamel colours and gilt, with a lilac ground colour border. The name of the view 'Scarborough' is inscribed in red and the late standard mark, DAVENPORT/ LONGPORT/STAFFORDSHIRE under a crown printed in red. D. 24cm. The plate on the right, with green ground colour border has the view 'Peak Teneriffe' inscribed in red and has the same mark, both c.1870-80. D. 23.5cm.
Courtesy Henry Spencer & Sons, Retford

The pair of Davenport plates are decorated in enamel colours and gilt with an apple green ground colour border. The views inscribed in red are, 'Bolton Abbey, Yorkshire' and 'View on the River Taner', the mark DAVENPORT on a ribbon above an anchor, in underglaze blue, c.1855. The central plate in enamel colours and gilt has a bleu lapis ground colour border and the view is identified as 'Loch Earn' in red. Signed by the painter R. Ablott. Standard Davenport mark for c.1865-70 in red enamel   Courtesy Henry Spencer & Sons, Retford

Two Davenport bone china plates, painted in enamel colours, c.1881-7. Mark, DAVENPORT impressed. D. 22.8cm.
Courtesy City Museum & Art Gallery, Stoke-on-Trent

As yet no Davenport pattern books have come to light, but it is known that by the 1880s their pattern numbers had reached to at least 6,000, mostly found on tea wares and other table wares.

The pottery remained in the hands of members of the Davenport family until 1887. The story of this important factory and the vast output can only be touched upon here and the reader is referred to the excellent writings of Terry Lockett, as listed under further reading.

FURTHER READING:

Lockett, T.A., *Davenport Pottery & Porcelain 1794-1887*, David & Charles, Newton Abbott, 1972. (Ed. G.A. Godden), *Staffordshire Porcelain*, Chapter 10, Granada Publishing, 1983.
Lockett T.A., and Godden, G.A., *Davenport China, Earthenware & Glass 1794-1887*, Barrie & Jenkins, 1989.

COALPORT

(John Rose & Co. c.1795-1837) & Anstice, Horton & Rose: 1800-1814

Following the completion of his apprenticeship with Thomas Turner at Caughley, John Rose, with the financial backing of Edward Blakeway, a wealthy local man, established a pottery for the production of soapstone porcelain at the Calcut China Manufactory at nearby Jackfield in about 1793, where by the following year he was making some well designed tea wares, some of which were from a type of transitional hybrid body, bordering on to a hard-paste. By 1796, when Rose, Blakeway & Co. moved to their new factory at Coalport, they were producing a good quality hard-paste, fashioned in many instances after those of Flight & Barr of Worcester, the material was much superior to that of his former employer, Thomas Turner. His wares were very well received, justifying the opening of a London retail warehouse in 1797. It was in 1799 that John Rose & Co. took over the Royal Salopian Porcelain Manufactory of Turner and continued to operate both factories up to about 1814. Although all the wares made at Caughley and Coalport were sold under the name of Coalport, they were favourably compared with the porcelains of Worcester and attracted many well-to-do patrons including the Prince and Princess of Orange.

Dinner services decorated with underglaze blue transfer prints of chinoiserie scenes, in imitation of the blue painted Chinese export wares were especially popular, helped by the fact that the East India Company had ceased to import the Oriental wares themselves and the only Chinese porcelain available in quantity was that imported as Private Trade. At this same time attractive dinner and dessert services were being produced by John Rose in European shapes with enamel and gilt decoration, such services fetching as much as fifty guineas for a dessert service and one hundred and seventy for a full table service.

John Rose did have some local competition from the adjacent factory of Messrs. Anstice, Horton & Rose, the latter being a brother of John Rose, a production operating from 1800-1814. Initially the partnership consisted of William Reynolds, William Horton and Thomas Rose, who took over the pottery of Bradley & Co. for their production of porcelain. It was in 1803 that William Reynolds died and his place in the partnership was taken over by his cousin Robert Anstice, the company continuing for a further eleven years, when the partnership was dissolved, with John Rose taking over the factory in 1814 and operating it together with his new factory and finally closing the Caughley works.

The wares made by this short-lived rival factory were not marked and were of a hybrid hard-paste porcelain which, without attention to minor differences in the moulding of shapes and the applied decoration, are very hard to separate from those of John Rose, and it is surprising that in their fourteen years of production it is estimated that pattern numbers reached to over 1400.

*This very rare plate can be clearly identified in the foreground of the watercolour in the Victoria &
Albert Museum, showing the interior of Thomas Baxter Senior's decorating studio in Goldsmith
Street, Gough Square, London, where most of their enamel and gilt decoration was added to 'blanks'
purchased from the Coalport factory. The sketches made by Thomas Baxter, Junior, following his
visit to Merton, the home of Lord Nelson and Emma Hamilton, resulted in this unique plate
showing Emma dressed as Britannia, unveiling the bust of Nelson, c.1810-13, now exhibited in
the Victoria & Albert Museum. D. c.21cm.* Courtesy Phillips, London

It was probably due to failure in their banking business that the partnership
of Edward Blakeway, John Rose & Robert Winter was declared bankrupt in
1803, necessitating both the Caughley and Coalport factories, with their full
contents, being put up for sale. The concern was purchased by two business
men Cuthbert Johnson and William Clarke. They retained John Rose to
continue to administer their investment, and the name John Rose & Co.
continued in use, but the wares were from then on of a fine white, soft-paste
porcelain, which from about 1820 sometimes bore a printed mark, drawing
attention to the fact that the company had been awarded a Society of Arts Gold
Medal for the introduction of a leadless glaze, which was a lot healthier for the
workers.

Their main production at this period was of tea, dessert and dinner services,
sometimes with shallow rococo moulding on the rims, fashioned after Sèvres
and later copied at Swansea, Nantgarw, Derby and Davenport, together with
beautiful flower painting. Under John Rose the factory continued to flourish
and had by 1820 acquired the porcelain factories at both Swansea and

Coalport shape bone china plate with six rim indentations, purchased by Thomas Baxter, Sen., 'in the white' to have the enamel and gilt decorated added in his London studio at No. 1 Goldsmith Street, Gough Square, c.1810-14. D. 21cm.
Private Collection

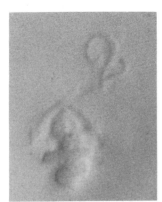

A lavishly decorated Coalport plate, with particularly delicate gilding applied to the border. Marked with an impressed top-heavy '2', and also with a fouled anchor. The figure '2' is not found before about 1810, and this plate appears to be c.1820.
Private Collection

Nantgarw, mainly for their equipment and not as working concerns, or even possibly to prevent their purchase by a rival.

It was quite early in the century that the factory was sometimes referred to as Coalbrookdale, a word which was at times used as a hand-written mark, but today the word is mostly used in association with their heavily encrusted flower decorated wares made from about 1820.

The marks found on much of Coalport from about 1820 to 1840 can be confusing as they usually name the London retailer, who preferred his merchandise not to be marked with the name of the manufacturer. After 1842 the familiar 'diamond' mark of the Patent Office was applied, indicating that the design, either shape or decoration has been patented and thus protected for a period of three years against 'piracy'. From published tables (such as in the author's books on ceramic marks), the actual date and 'parcel' number can be

A Coalport porcelain trio in 'Japan' style, c.1812-15. Pattern number 387. The shape of the cups is known as the London shape. It was quite usual during the 18th and the beginning of the 19th century to provide only one saucer to accompany two cups, one for tea and the other for coffee, when supplying a service. D. (saucer) 14cm. Private Collection

deciphered and the name of the manufacture arrived at. This system is good until 1884, after which many pieces just have a registered number, which as yet cannot be interpreted other than through the Patent Office (see chapter on Registered Designs).

The pattern numbers used at Coalport up to the end of the nineteenth century are often of more use in deciding that an object is not Coalport, for the number up to that time never exceeds 1,000, this number was reached in about 1812 and we start again at 1, but now as a fraction under 2, which continues until 1,000 is once more reached in about 1833, when the fraction changed to 3, by about 1860 the fraction 8 was in use, after which no further records appear to exist, although we do know that by the end of the nineteenth century, this system had been replaced with a number together with a letter indicating the type of ware.

The excavations on the Caughley site clearly identified a popular form of plate with six regularly spaced indentations around the rim, they are of a type that was obviously among those sold in the white glazed state to outside decorators, including Thomas Baxter in London, Thomas Pardoe at Bristol and other decorators and retailers, these wares are often signed and dated between about 1800 and 1810. The form of plate noted was also made by some other porcelain manufacturers.

This practice of selling undecorated wares to outside decorators is well illustrated in the well-known watercolour painting shown in the Ceramic galleries of the Victoria & Albert Museum, which is the work of Thomas Baxter, junior. in 1810, illustrating his father's London studio. Many Coalport wares can be easily identified on the workbench, but most important is a notice pinned to the wall, which clearly reads 'New Price List. Coalport White China'. A plate obviously placed in the foreground of the picture is painted with Britannia unveiling a bust of Admiral Nelson; this same plate was sold as recently as 1982 at Phillips auction house for £11,000. There seems little doubt that the majority of the white wares used by Baxter were purchased from John Rose, which enables one to assume that any wares signed by Baxter are a good guide to the unmarked wares used at the factory for their own decoration.

FURTHER READING:

Godden, G.A., *Coalport & Coalbrookdale Porcelains,* Herbert Jenkins, 1970.
Edmundson, Roger S., 'The End of Caughley & Beginnings of Coalport', *Antique Dealer & Collectors Guide,* June, 1990.

PINXTON
1796-1813

It had always been the ambition of William Billingsley to produce his own porcelain and the opportunity came when he approached John Coke, a landowner, living on his father's estate at Brookhill Hall on the outskirts of Pinxton, some fifteen miles from Derby.

Billingsley seemingly gave John Coke a very optimistic view of the prospects of a new china works in that area, resulting in the building of a factory in 1795, financed by John Coke, with the first production starting in the following year. It was anticipated that within three years of operation the profits would be such as to pay John Coke the interest on his investment and then to provide profits for the two partners, but unhappily there were little profits and the partnership was terminated in 1799. Billingsley moved with his family to nearby Mansfield in Nottinghamshire, where he decorated a wide variety of porcelain bought in the white from other sources, including hard-paste from Paris.

It is very difficult at times to separate the limited range of wares produced at Pinxton from those of the Derby factory, remembering that Billingsley was previously apprenticed there in 1774, and similarities do occur. Pinxton almost certainly had a very high proportion of wasters and even some of the finer decorated examples, which are sometimes attributable to the hand of the

Teapot of soft-paste porcelain, made at Pinxton, Derbyshire, by William Billingsley, c.1798. Decorated with green enamel and gilt. Unmarked. H. 15.2cm. Courtesy Mr. & Mrs. P. Miller

Cache-pot and stand in soft-paste porcelain, painted with enamel colours, the pot has a drainage hole in the base and fits on to a separate stand. Made at 'The New Pinxton China Factory', Derbyshire, c.1798, during the period when William Billingsley was in partnership with John Coke (1796-9). H. 16.5cm. Courtesy City Museum & Art Gallery, Stoke-on-Trent

Pair of porcelain bough pots of 'D' shape, with perforated lids, painted in enamel colours and gilt, c.1799-1801. Probably decorated at Mansfield by William Billingsley, when he was working as an independent decorator of wares he purchased from elsewhere 'in the white'. The views, as written on base, are 'Preston Hall, Scotland' and 'New Battle House in Scotland'. D. 19cm.

Courtesy Phillips, London

master, have a tendency to be misshapen. They can often be identified on the evidence of the forms of handles, etc., which match the wasters found on the site and the occasional marks, such as 'Pinxton' in full, or a letter 'P' together with a pattern number. Opinions vary as to the maximum pattern number recorded differing from about 367 to about 600.

After the departure of Billingsley, John Coke continued alone, possibly only decorating wares in stock until 1801, when he entered a new partnership with Henry Bankes, a Lincoln attorney, but this agreement was terminated in 1803 and the factory was put in the charge of John Cutts, a Derby trained painter, who leased the concern from 1806 until 1813, when Pinxton finally closed. Cutts then went to work for Josiah Wedgwood at Etruria, where he was employed as a decorator on their production of bone china.

Following the departure of Billingsley, the warm toned, thinly potted, soft-paste porcelain was replaced with a more stable, greyer toned body, often with neo-classical inspired handles, so ill-suited to the material of porcelain.

FURTHER READING:
Exley, C.L., *The Pinxton China Factory,* Mr. & Mrs. Coke-Steel, Sutton-on-the-Hill, 1963; *A History of the Torksey & Mansfield China Factories* (re. William Billingsley), G.R.G. Exley, Lincoln, 1970.

JOSIAH SPODE

1796-1833 (continued as Copeland & Garrett.)

The story of how Josiah Spode's father died in 1739, and was buried in a pauper's grave, when his son was only six years old, is well known. Josiah started his career the following year, and in 1749, at the age of sixteen, he was apprenticed to the now famous potter, Thomas Whieldon, for a period of five years, after which he was employed by William Banks. This same year, at the age of twenty-one, Josiah Spode was married and Josiah Spode II was born the following year. By 1770 he had returned to William Banks's pottery, now as the owner, but spreading the purchase price over a period of six years.

Spode's pottery flourished beyond all expectations in Stoke, and at the age of twenty-three, his son Josiah II had established a retail shop in London, to market their wares. Josiah Spode I died in 1797 and in 1805, William Copeland, a former member of their staff, was taken into partnership together with William, son of Josiah Spode II. By 1812 the company was known as Spode & Copeland.

In 1833 William Taylor Copeland became sole proprietor of the concern, taking Thomas Garrett, who was formerly the chief clerk of their London

Spode teapot of the 'old oval' shape, painted in colours and gilt with pattern number 287, painted in red together with the name 'SPODE', c.1801. H. 15.2cm.

R.H. Williamson Bequest, Tullie House, Carlisle

Spode two-handled bone china vase, painted in enamel colours and gilt with pattern number 967, which was introduced c.1804, but continued in production over many years. H. 19cm.

Courtesy Bearnes, Torquay

A selection of items from a Spode dinner service (of 125 pieces), all of porcelain with the exception of eight large dish covers, which are of pottery. The whole painted with brightly coloured enamel flowers within a 'wicker weave' embossed border, painted in light blue enamel with gilt lining. Pattern No. 1182, c.1810. H. (ice pails) 18.4cm. Courtesy Bearne's, Torquay

Pair of violet baskets, painted in enamel colours and gilt with Spode's most popular pattern No. 1166, which was introduced c.1806, but kept in production for a long period. L. 10.7cm. Courtesy Bearnes, Torquay

business, into a partnership which continued until 1847 from when the firm became known as W.T. Copeland.

Prior to the end of the eighteenth century the factory was producing nearly every type of ceramic ware common to Staffordshire at that time, with the exception of porcelain which is our concern.

The invention of bone china following the expiration of Cookworthy and Champion's patent in 1796, which had been enjoyed by New Hall since 1781, is still a subject about which various ceramic authorities differ. Did Josiah Spode I actually invent bone china prior to his death in 1797 or did he greatly improve upon it? At the time of writing the latter premise is accepted by the majority.

Today, Robert Copeland, a direct descendant and specialist on the factory and the wares produced, favours the suggestion that porcelain containing a high

Spode jar and cover of the 'Beaded New Shape', c.1815, painted in enamel colours and gilt with Spode's most famous pattern, no. 1166, as marked on base. H. 22.7cm.

Courtesy Andrew Hartley Fine Arts, Ilkley

Basket with pierced lid, for flowers or pot-pourri, painted with flowers in enamel colours on a gilt ground, pattern no. 711. Made by Spode, c.1805-10. Marked 'SPODE'. H. 11.8cm.

R.H. Williamson Bequest, Tullie House, Carlisle

Bone china trio in 'Two Temples' pattern, c.1810-33. These wares are typical of those made to take the place of Chinese porcelain, the import of which was discontinued in bulk, in the late 18th century. Printed mark, 'SPODE' in underglaze blue. D. (saucer) 13.5cm.   Private Collection

Fine pair of Spode cabinet cups with stands, c.1810, painted with enamel flowers on a gilt ground, butterfly finials were popular with several manufacturers. Mark, 'Spode 711' in puce.

Courtesy Andrew Hartley Fine Arts, Ilkley

Part tea service of Spode's 'New Oval Shape' painted with enamel colours and gilt on an underglaze blue ground, c.1810. Pattern no. 715 (in gold) which is influenced by the Japanese Kakiemon style rather than the so-called Imari. W. (teapot) 26.7cm.

Courtesy Andrew Hartley Fine Arts, Ilkley

Spode pot-pourri bowpot, c.1810, painted with enamel colours and gilt on a dark blue ground, with pattern no. 1166. This shape is listed as a Patera in the 1820 Spode Shape Book. Mark, in red 'Spode 1166'. H. 19.7cm.

Courtesy Andrew Hartley Fine Arts, Ilkley

Spode porcelain plate, painted in colour with Oriental scene, c.1810-20. Marked 'SPODE'. D. 25cm.
R.H. Williamson Bequest, Tullie House, Carlisle

Spode porcelain plate, painted with Oriental scene, c.1810-20. Marked, 'SPODE'. D. 25cm.
R.H. Williamson Bequest, Tullie House, Carlisle

Porcelain ice pail, with liner and cover, painted with flowers and fruit in enamel colours and gilding, c.1815-21. This form was very popular and made at several English factories; the dessert was packed in a basin shaped liner over ice, with further ice held in the lid which is pan shaped. Mark, 'Spode', painted in red enamel. H. 29.9cm.
R.H. Williamson Bequest, Tullie House, Carlisle

percentage of bone was being produced as early as 1796, under the name of 'Stoke China'; 'bone china' is a term introduced over more recent years. Spode's bone china is a near perfect ceramic body, the pure white colour and extreme translucency of which is comparable to that of soft-paste Sèvres. It was a very stable body, which enabled large dinner services to be made without the likelihood of distortion in the firing.

From the early years of the nineteenth century until 1822, a great deal of the superb decoration seen on Spode wares was applied by the decorating

JOSIAH SPODE

Three pieces from a Spode dessert service in porcelain painted in enamel colours with botanical specimens, the titles of which are painted on the reverse in lilac enamel, c.1815. Mark, 'Spode'. L. (dish) 21.5cm.
Courtesy Phillips, London

Selection of wares from a Spode porcelain tea service, painted in underglaze blue and enamel colours with 'Japan' pattern no. 2375. The cup is the Spode version of the 'London' shape, c.1820-5. This pattern was continued and the waste bowl was made nearer the middle of the century by Copeland
Courtesy Phillips, London

Four porcelain taper sticks of various factories, all painted with enamel colours and gilt, c.1815-20. Left to right: Spode, pattern no. 1388, with panels of bright green, Chamberlain's Worcester mark in red. D. 10cm. Spode, in their famous 1166 pattern, from an unknown factory, but possibly London decorated
Courtesy Phillips, London

238

Plate in porcelain, painted in enamel colours with the arms of the East India Company, similar to a 1,300 piece service made for the Canton factory of the company, but which may well be part of a second service made for the captain of The London, *the vessel which is thought to have delivered the initial order. Marked Spode, c.1824-5. D. 25.5cm.*

R.H. Williamson Bequest, Tullie House, Carlisle

establishment of Henry Daniel, whose later factory of H. & R. Daniel is dealt with in a separate entry.

The marking of Spode porcelain was very inconsistent; most had the word 'SPODE' written in enamel, sometimes with a pattern number, sometimes just the number and in a service only a few items were usually so marked.

By comparison with some contemporary wares Spode's services and decorative wares might well be considered a little too heavily decorated, with their bright enamel colours and burnished gilding, often with 'chased' decoration. Spode's wares decorated by Daniels from about 1805, were probably the first to be decorated with 'silver lustre', derived from platinum.

The large variety of porcelain wares produced by Spode can only be covered in a book entirely devoted to their products. Their reproduction of oriental, so-called 'Imari', botanical and armorial wares, made to special order, are all outstanding, a standard which was to be maintained into the Copeland & Garrett period of 1833-47.

FURTHER READING:
Copeland, R., *The Marks of Spode,* Spode Ltd, 1983.
Copeland, W.T., *Spode-Copeland 1765-1965,* Catalogue of 1966 Exhibition, Spode Ltd, 1966.
Whiter, L., *Spode,* Barrie & Jenkins, London, 1970.

W(***)

c.1798-1810

Among our mystery factories we have a group of wares using the strange mark W(***) impressed, the 'W' in the form of two Vs overlapping. These puzzle pieces are of a hard grey porcelain and are rather thickly potted. They are a very rare group indeed, but a few marked pieces are known, among these is a group of tea wares, which includes one marked piece only, the teapot stand. These pieces are decorated with landscapes painted in sepia, and embellished with gilding. The handles of both the teapot and cups are of a distinctive squared shape, which could lead by comparison to the identification of further unmarked pieces. A vase of neo-classical shape, incompletely decorated with cupids supporting a cornucopia, also a flower container decorated with painted landscapes and gold and platinum lustre have been recorded. Seemingly however, the most prolific of their productions, certainly the most found to be marked, are very fine bulb pots; of these the most interesting is on show in the Derby Museum, as not only does it show the W(***) mark, but it is also inscribed 'Billingsley, Mansfield, Nottingham'. It is known that after the dissolution of his partnership with John Coke at Pinxton in Derbyshire in 1799, Billingsley opened a decorating workshop in Mansfield, where he continued until 1802, so we are able to date this piece reliably, between these dates. At this time Billingsley found it necessary to buy undecorated wares from any available source, including Chamberlain of Worcester, and our W(***) factory.

*Group of teawares in a hybrid hard-paste porcelain, decorated with landscapes painted in sepia enamel and added gilding, c.1800-5. The mark is impressed (W***). This mark cannot be attributed to any particular potter. H. (teapot) 16.5cm.*

Courtesy City Museum & Art Gallery, Stoke-on-Trent

A bulb pot (with flat back) of hybrid hard-paste porcelain, decorated in enamel colours and gilding, with an unidentified landscape, c.1860. Made by an unknown factory and marked with W (***) impressed. W. 19cm. Courtesy City Museum & Art Gallery, Stoke-on-Trent

There have been several suggestions for the identification of this group. For many years they were thought to have come from the pottery of Enoch Wood of Burslem; Thomas Wolfe of Stoke was also considered, also Warburton of Cobridge was suggested by Miss Diana Darlington. Mr Godden in *Staffordshire Porcelain,* makes a very good case for calling the wares the work of the Whiteheads, in Hanley from *c.*1777 to *c.*1810, but unfortunately we still have no definite evidence that they were making porcelain.

Our mystery factory was largely engaged in making cream coloured earthenwares, basalt ware, green glazed and printed pottery. A jug printed in overglaze black prints, on loan to the Hampshire Farm Museum, Manor Farm, Botley, bears an interesting mark of W(***), in addition to four impressed marks of 'W.S', in this case the W is in normal caps.

FURTHER READING:
Godden, G.A., *Staffordshire Porcelain,* Appendix VI, Granada Publishing, 1983; *Encyclopaedia of British Porcelain,* Barrie & Jenkins, 1988.
Darlington, Diana, *Northern Ceramic Society Journal,* Vol. 4, 1980-1.
Hillis, Maurice, *Northern Ceramic Society Newsletter,* No. 42, June, 1981.

Teapot and stand in porcelain, of fluted form, painted in colours and gilt. One of the nine early teapot shapes made by Miles Mason at Fenton, Staffordshire, c.1800-15. H. 16.5cm.

Gift of R. & D. Haggar. The City Museum & Art Gallery, Stoke-on-Trent

MILES MASON & SONS
1802-1830

Miles Mason was a successful 'Chinaman' (a retailer of pottery and porcelain) who had a flourishing business with premises in Fenchurch Street, London, which he had acquired through his marriage into the family of Richard Farrar, who was already an established retailer. When in 1791 the East India Company ceased importing Chinese porcelain in bulk, Miles Mason was compelled to look elsewhere for his supplies. To help fill this need and continue his lucrative business, he went into partnership with Thomas Wolfe and John Lucock (or Luckock) at the Islington China Works, Liverpool, for the production of wares in close imitation of the Chinese imported wares. He was obviously keen to expand, because he also went into a further partnership with George Wolfe (Thomas Wolfe's brother) to make earthenware at Lane Delph, in Staffordshire, and there is also a suggestion that he entered into partnership with James Green and Limpus, ceramic wholesalers in Upper Thames Street, London, which gave him a further trade outlet.

The Islington China Works, in Liverpool, was closed on 7th June, 1800 and a month later the pottery concern at Lane Delph also ceased operation. After the ending of these two partnerships Miles Mason manufactured porcelain and stone china from about 1802 at a small pottery in Market Street, Fenton, Staffordshire, which became known as the Victoria Works and by 1804 he claimed to be making china of 'superior qualities to Indian Nankin China', and offering to make replacements for broken pieces. This factory proved to be too small for his thriving business and about 1807 he moved to the Minerva Works, where he continued until he retired in 1813. He was by this time making the popular bone china.

The wares produced at the Islington China Works, Liverpool, are described in the chapter on Liverpool porclains. The wares at Fenton naturally followed the styles made at the Liverpool concern and were launched under the name

Miles Mason porcelain bowl and cover, decorated with bat prints in black enamel and gilt decoration, made at Lane Delph, Staffordshire, c.1805

M. Martin Bequest, City Museum & Art Gallery, Stoke-on-Trent

Dessert plate, porcelain with relief moulded decoration, sparsely decorated with enamel colours. Made by C.J. Mason at Lane Delph, Fenton, Staffordshire c.1813-18. D. 21cm.

Gift of R. & D. Haggar, City Museum & Art Gallery, Stoke-on-Trent

'British Nankin', copying the Chinese porcelains once more. Between 1800 and 1815 the firm was producing approximately seventy-five designs a year. The New Hall type of patterns of flower sprays and baskets were also continued, these having low pattern numbers ranging from 2 to 153 and beyond. Their wide range of decorations included Japan patterns, transfer overglaze bat printing in black, grey, sepia, purple-brown and other colours, which were sometimes further tinted with enamel colours. Rich flower decoration and painted landscapes are also to be seen, although it is not known how much of this decoration was the work of 'outside decorators'. Miles Mason rarely marked his wares except on blue printed china and stone china. Two marks were used, M. MASON impressed and a printed blue pseudo-Chinese seal with/or without the name MILES above and MASON below, the latter restricted to underglaze blue wares. The impressed mark is found on the back of plates and dishes and at times on the foot rims of teapots, sugar boxes and other small table wares.

After the retirement of their father in 1813, two of Miles Mason's three sons, George Miles and Charles James, continued the business until 1830, when the former retired. Their productions were primarily concerned with the very popular Mason's Patent Ironstone China, although bone china was also produced on a small scale, but being unmarked is difficult to attribute with any degree of certainty.

FURTHER READING:

Godden, G.A., *Godden's Guide to Mason's China and the Ironstone Wares,* Antique Collectors' Club, Woodbridge, 1980, Revised edn., 1991; *Encyclopaedia of British Porcelain,* Barrie & Jenkins, London, 1988.

Haggar, R., & Adams, E., *Mason's Porcelain and Ironstone 1796-1853,* Faber & Faber, London, 1977.

GRAINGER

c.1805-1899 (Continued by the Worcester Royal Porcelain Company Ltd until 1902)

A further Worcester factory whose wares are sought today are those of the Royal China Works of Messrs. Grainger & Co, a firm in production for almost the entire nineteenth century. Thomas Grainger was apprenticed to his uncle, Robert Chamberlain, before starting his own factory in 1800 taking John Wood, a Chamberlain painter 'of considerable skill and eminence' as a partner. Grainger and Wood, like Robert Chamberlain, were probably restricted to decorating blanks which they purchased from other factories until about 1805, by which time the company had established a good business. Their early wares

Teapot of hybrid hard-paste porcelain, decorated with underglaze blue and gilt, flowers reserved in white. Made by Grainger & Co., c.1810. Mark, 'Grainger & Co. Worcester Warranted 816' in script inside lid. H. 15.2cm.

Courtesy Mr. & Mrs. P. Miller

Bone china teapot, decorated in Japanese taste with underglaze blue, enamel colours and gilt, pattern number '1267'. Made by Messrs. Grainger & Co. Worcester, c.1815-20. H. 16.2cm.

Courtesy Mr. & Mrs. P. Miller

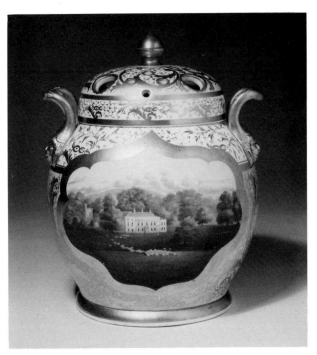

Porcelain mug, painted with enamel colours and gilt, c.1812-20. The scene is 'N.W. of Worcester', showing river, bridge, Cathedral and churches, a popular view with various Worcester factories. This example is marked in orange script with title and 'Grainger Lee & Co. Worcester'. H. 13.2cm. Courtesy Andrew Hartley Fine Arts, Ilkley

Pot-pourri of bone china painted in enamel colours and gilt. Made by Grainger, Lee & Co., Worcester, c.1815-25. Decorated with named views of Langdon Hall and Mamhead, both in Devonshire. H. 25.5cm. Courtesy Phillips, London

Bone china coffee can, printed in blue with a poor quality version of the so-called Broseley Dragon. The mark of Grainger Lee & Cº/Worcester is also printed in blue, c.1825-37. H. 6cm. Private Collection

Worcester porcelain framed plaque, painted in enamel colours with a view of Worcester from the north-west, with frame in gilt. Made by Grainger, Lee & Co., a partnership which extended from 1812 to 1839. Mark, Grainger, Lee & Co./Worcester. L. 27.5cm. Courtesy Phillips, London

Three pieces from a Grainger dessert service, c.1840-50, each piece bearing a named view, including Beddgelert, Melrose Abbey, Belvoir Castle, Black Rock Castle, Cork and Ben Lomond. D. (plate) c.24cm.

Courtesy Phillips, London

Three pieces from a Worcester dessert service, made by George Grainger, c.1850. Decorated in enamel colours and gilt on a turquoise ground. Mark, G.G.W. impressed. This factory was merged with the major Worcester factory in 1889, but continued to produce wares bearing their own mark until 1902, when it finally closed

Courtesy Phillips, London

Pair of Grainger's Worcester vases, with serpent-like handles. They are of flattened ovoid form and decorated with white pâte-sur-pâte flowers on a blue ground, whilst on the reverse is a single bee. Handles, rim and foot in gilt. Impressed with Grainger impressed mark of c.1870-89 (G & Cº/W within a shield). H. 31cm.

Courtesy Bearnes, Torquay

Three Grainger's Worcester vases, the pair with reticulated handles in Persian style are painted with enamel colours and gilt on an ivory tinted ground. They have the date code for 1897, by which time the company had been taken over by the Royal Worcester Porcelain Company, but the original name was retained until 1902. The large vase is decorated with birds and flowers in enamel on a peach and ivory ground. Printed mark and date code for 1899. H. 34.5cm.

Courtesy Bearnes, Torquay

of hybrid hard paste porcelains showed very little originality and can well be mistaken by new collectors for those of Chamberlain, for they are rarely marked and if they are, they follow the Chamberlain practice of only marking the teapot and/or the sugar bowl inside the covers.

In about 1808 a Mr. Lee, Grainger's brother-in-law, became a partner and the firm continued as Grainger, Lee & Co. until the death of the founder in 1839, when he was succeeded by his son, George, and the firm continued under the name George Grainger & Co. This full title was used in some of the early marks, but other marks only included such initials as 'G.W.', 'G.G.W.', 'G.G. & Co.' or 'G. & Co'.

From about 1815 their wares were made from the popular bone china and only the modelling details of knobs, handles and spouts, etc., help to separate the early Chamberlain and Grainger wares. Those pieces made under the direction of George Grainger from about 1840, show much more originality in form and decoration, which was often of the Rockingham style, but usually bearing a pattern number well beyond the range of those seen on genuine Rockingham, which is unlikely to be higher than 1600. The pattern numbers used by Grainger had reached about 2000 by 1839, when a new series was started with numbers reaching about a further 2000 by the late 1840s, but to this later series was added a small cross, a system that was followed by the use of fractions until the last quarter of the century, when a 'G' for Grainger was written before the number. During their last twelve years a letter was used below the mark to tell the date of decoration, starting with 'A' for 1891 and ending with 'L' in 1902.

The Grainger firm was taken over by Royal Worcester in 1889, but they continued to run the factory until 1902, which saw the final closure of an important nineteenth century production of ceramics.

FURTHER READING:
Sandon, Henry and John, *Grainger's Worcester Porcelain,* Barrie & Jenkins, 1990.

RIDGWAY

c.1808-1858

In 1808 John Ridgway and his brother William, were given equal shares in their father Job's factory at Cauldon Place, Hanley, in Staffordshire, where they commenced to make wares of a fine quality bone china. They continued together after their father retired in about 1810, but in 1830 they separated, and William left to work at other potteries where he made mainly earthenware. The first recorded mark was 'Ridgway & Sons' impressed, *c.*1808-1813. This mark occurred when the two sons were in partnership. After 1813 a few 'Ridgway' impressed examples are found, most pieces however, pre-1830, only bear a pattern number. The production of fine bone china was continued by John, who shortly prior to 1843 was appointed 'Potter to Queen Victoria', when he adopted a printed mark incorporating the Royal Arms with J.R. or J.R. & Co. in a ribbon beneath the shield. Sometimes on smaller objects, such as cups and saucers using a printed crown alone, he also used the wording 'John Ridgway & Co., Cauldon Place, 'Potters to her Majesty'. Fortunately, five of the original pattern books have been preserved, dating from 1810 to 1844, these are now in the possession of the present day Coalport China Co., which is a member of the Wedgwood group. These pattern books are most helpful in the attribution of

Ornate Ridgway cup and saucer, moulded with white relief classical figures on a coloured ground, c.1810. D. (saucer) 14.6cm. Courtesy City Museum & Art Gallery, Stoke-on-Trent

Ridgway dish of moulded form as illustrated in their early pattern book, c.1818-20. The centre decoration showing cows is applied by bat printing, pattern no. 675. D. 20.3cm.

City Museum & Art Gallery, Stoke-on-Trent

Bone china teapot of the London Shape, painted in pale blue and gilt, with a typical domed strainer. Pattern no. '2/32'. Made by John & William Ridgway at Cauldon Place Pottery, Shelton, c.1815. H. 13.6cm.
Courtesy Mr. & Mrs. P. Miller

A richly decorated porcelain dessert service made by J. & W. Ridgway, c.1825-30, painted in enamel colours and lavish gilding. A somewhat similar service of about thirty-seven pieces would have cost in the region of £50 at the time. H. (tureen) 17cm.
Courtesy Phillips, London

pieces, when only a pattern number is found. For tea wares the pattern numbers appear in two forms, in c.1808, they are found as a fraction under the number 2, thus 2/1 continuing up to 2/9999. A new series appeared in about 1850, again in fraction form, this time under the number 5. The pattern numbers on dessert services were not fractionalised until during the 1840s when the number 9999 was reached, after which a new series under the number 6 was adopted. Ornamental wares, such as vases, were given numbers in fractions under the number 3.

In about 1856 John Ridgway & Co. became J. Ridgway, Bates & Co., continuing at the Cauldon Place works. Wares from this period bear the full name, or marks, including the initials J.R.B. & Co., this partnership was ended in 1858. In 1859 until 1861 there was a new partnership at Cauldon Place, of Messrs. Bates, Brown-Westhead & Moore, using the marks B.B.W. & M., B.B.W.M. & Co. or the name in full, but most pieces are unmarked, making positive attributions difficult.

Soup plate of bone china, decorated with enamel colours and gilding. Made by John Ridgway & Co. Hanley, c.1830-40. Mark, the Royal coat of arms printed. D. 25.5cm.

R.H. Williamson Bequest, Tullie House, Carlisle

Teacup and saucer of Ridgway bone china, painted in enamel colours and gilt with pattern no. 2/7429, on a Rivoli shape, c.1840-5. D. (saucer) 15.2cm.

Courtesy City Museum & Art Gallery, Stoke-on-Trent

We know from a government report on child labour, printed in 1833, that at that time, five hundred people were employed at the pottery, and many talented artists were engaged in the production of the fine painted pieces, some of which are believed to be the work of George Speight and Daniel Lucas, known for their landscape and figure painting. Joseph Bancroft, George Beddow, Thomas Brentnall and George Hancock are also thought to have been employed, specialising in flower painting.

Wares were also produced for the lower price range, some of which were decorated with transfer printed outlines which were filled in by unskilled hands, sometimes of children. Fine bat prints were also produced.

John Ridgway exhibited at the Great Exhibition of 1851, the catalogue of which shows the great variety and quality of the wares produced by John Ridgway at this time.

FURTHER READING:

Godden, Geoffrey A., *The Illustrated Guide to Ridgway Porcelains,* Barrie & Jenkins, 1972; **(Editor),** *Staffordshire Porcelain,* Chapter 12, Granada Publishing, 1983; *Ridgway Porcelains,* Antique Collectors' Club, Revised edn., 1985.

MACHIN & CO.
1809-1840

A further Staffordshire potter to whom wares have only been attributable over recent years is Joseph Machin, all due to the patient research of Philip Miller. Early writers on the history of Staffordshire ceramics record that Machin's was in 1843 one of the oldest and largest surviving porcelain factories in Burslem.

Prior to going into partnership with Jacob Baggaley, Joseph Machin's name appears in various trade directories as an enameller and colour maker of Nile Street, Burslem. From about 1808 Machin & Baggaley were producing bone china in addition to supplying potters' materials. The founder Joseph Machin died in 1831, when the works were taken over by his son, William, who for a short while was partnered by a Mr. Thomas (*c*.1831-3), but in 1833 William Potts, who had patented a steam driven rotary printing press, became a partner. According to local directories Machin & Potts had gone out of business by about 1837.

A limited number of wares with the printed or painted mark of MACHIN & C°./BURSLEM together with a pattern number have been used as clues for the attribution of many unmarked wares which have been previously allocated to a number of more familiar Staffordshire factories.

Philip Miller, whose immense collection of teapots has recently found a home in the Norwich Castle Museum, has now enabled the Machin enthusiasts to accurately identify at least six different shapes of teawares. Although dessert and ornamental wares, which they would undoubtedly have made during the Machin & Co. period (1818-31) have as yet to be recognised, similar wares of the Machin & Potts partnership of 1833-37 are to be seen with an elaborate printed mark of which there are several versions.

These newly identified teawares are of bone china of inconsistent quality, sometimes a good white, but sometimes seen with discoloration and crazing. The patterns so far attributed to their early days tend to follow those of such contemporary factories as New Hall and enamel colours were preferred to

Bone china teapot of octagonal form, painted in enamel colours and gilt in Japanese taste. Pattern no. 257. Made by Machin & Co., Waterloo Pottery, Burslem, c.1810. Unmarked, but some pieces of the same service are marked, 'Machin & Co.'. H. 15.2cm.
Courtesy Mr. & Mrs. P. Miller

Machin & Co. bone china teapot, decorated in blue, green and iron red enamels, pattern no. 19, c.1810. H. 17.5cm. Courtesy Mr. & Mrs. P. Miller

gilding for the decoration of rims, handles, knobs, etc. Well worthy of note are the Machin wares decorated with charming bat prints, usually seen through well applied translucent enamels and those painted in grey or puce monochrome landscapes, but such decoration alone is no sure guide to Machin wares, as several other Staffordshire factories used almost identical styles of decoration and reference must be made to the pattern numbers which appear to range from 1 to about 681, whilst those to be seen on wares of the later Machin & Potts period continue on dessert services to numbers into the 1200s.

In his article in the book recommended for further reading, Mr. Miller includes a useful list of about fifty pattern numbers, together with a short description of the decoration, marks, etc., to be found on each. He has most probably been able to make further additions to this list since his work was published in 1983.

FURTHER READING:
Philip, Miller (Ed. G. Godden), *Staffordshire Porcelain,* Chapter 13, Granada Publishing, 1983.

JOHN AND RICHARD RILEY

c.1809-1828

We know that the Riley brothers were occupying a factory in Nile Street, Burslem, at least by the year 1802 and that they had left this establishment by 1816. They were also in business by 1811, at Hill House Estate, Burslem. On the death of both the brothers, in 1828, the firm closed, as neither of them had left sons to carry on what had become a thriving business.

The first mention of this factory producing 'china', was in a directory of c.1809. The company was already well known for their earthenware products, and particularly for their underglaze blue transfer printed wares, for which by at least the closure of the factory, they had built up a large trade with America. The porcelain they produced, at least during 1818, evidently contained a substantial quantity of bone ash, according to a recipe contained in the records of the factory, held by the City Museum & Art Gallery at Hanley.

After the closure of the factory, the stock was advertised for sale in the *Staffordshire Advertiser* in 1829, and included earthenware and 'a stock of china, tea and Desert ware, plain, enamelled, and richly enamelled with burnished gold, suited either for the home or foreign trade'. In April 1831 the remaining stock was still on offer including 'a number of rich burnished gold sets of tea, dinner and dessert services...' 'The china will be offered in their respective sets'. It is obvious that the firm was well into production of porcelain of seemingly lavish decoration when the firm was closed, and yet in spite of this, the only marked porcelain wares so far discovered, are a type of fairly modest

Bone china teapot and stand, painted with enamel colours and gilt. These pieces have been attributed to the Burslem firm of John & Richard Riley, who were working c.1802-28. The painting bears a close resemblance to that seen on the jugs marked with 'RILEY/1823' in relief, which are at present the only wares which can be certainly identified

Courtesy Mr. & Mrs. P. Miller

Set of three bone china jugs, with moulded decoration and painting in enamel colours. Made by John and Richard Riley, c.1823, in Burslem, Staffordshire. Unmarked, but identical to those that sometimes are marked with the name 'RILEY' & 1823. H. 19.5cm. Private Collection

sets of jugs, relief moulded with flowers, and painted with enamels. These jugs are marked on the base with the name RILEY usually accompanied with the number 1823, moulded on the base, these numerals are accepted as a date, but we cannot find any appropriate commemorative event to justify this year.

It seems strange that marked Riley earthenware pieces are found, but so few marked porcelain wares, with the exception of these moulded jugs, which judging from the price list were a popular line, which could have been sold very cheaply and easily. A possible explanation of course, would be that the brothers had built up a good export market for their transfer printed earthenwares, but were relying on a china dealer for the marketing of their more expensive porcelain, and as was the custom, marks were discouraged to prevent the customer dealing directly with the manufacturer.

FURTHER READING:
Pomfret, Roger, 'John & Richard Riley', *Journal of Ceramic History,* Vol. 13, City Museum & Art Galleries, Stoke-on-Trent, 1988.

HILDITCH AND HILDITCH & HOPWOOD

c.1811-1867

William Hilditch & Co. is first mentioned in 1811 in a newspaper report in which a certain Mary Price is said to have divulged the secrets of the Miles Mason factory to a servant of William Hilditch & Co. It is possible that William Hilditch had been potting before this, at Lane End, in 1795. The business went through several partnerships until William Hilditch retired by 1828, the concern then being run by his three sons, Joseph, William and John. In 1833 William and John were in partnership with a William Hopwood, and by 1836 the firm was trading as Hilditch and Hopwood. The last of the Hilditch sons died in 1843, and William Hopwood carried on the business until he died in 1858, when the factory was seemingly taken over by Thomas Goodwin and William Litherland, executors of William Hopwood, who may well have been connected with the declining concern up to 1867.

Bone china plate, printed in underglaze blue by Hilditch & Sons, c.1825. Marked with H. & S. over '3' under an eagle. (See matching cup and saucer p.257.) D. c.16.5cm.

Courtesy City Museum & Art Gallery, Stoke-on-Trent

Teacup, coffee cup and saucer of bone china, painted with enamels and gilt, made by Hilditch &
Hopwood, c.1840. All three pieces are marked with a painted number 2154. D. (saucer) 15cm.
Private Collection

Teacup, coffee cup and saucer of bone china, painted in colours and gilt, c.1850, by which time
William Hopwood was operating the manufacture alone, although still trading as Hilditch &
Hopwood. Pattern number painted in gilt 2250. D. (saucer) 15cm. Private Collection

With the Hilditch porcelains, we are leaving the prestigious wares of the well-known factories, and coming down to a more homely and cheaper form of product, with the exception of the later years, when some finer pieces appeared in the Official Catalogue of the 1851 Exhibition.

Teacup and saucer, printed in underglaze blue on a bone china body, by Hilditch & Sons, c.1825. Marked with H. & S. over '3' under an eagle as shown. D. (saucer) 14cm. Private Collection

Cup and saucer in printed in underglaze blue on a bone china body. Made by Hilditch & Sons, c.1825 and marked with underglaze blue mark as shown of H. & S. D. (saucer) 14cm.
Private Collection

The Hilditch wares which are sought after by today's collector, are of a form of bone china, which seems to be rather prone to staining. A variety of table wares were made, many decorated with charming, though naïve, chinoiserie patterns with either brown, orange, red, purple or grey transfer prints, further

Part tea service, bone china, made by Hilditch & Sons, c.1825, transfer printed in brown and washed in with enamel colours. Printed marks on cups and saucers of H. & S. in wreath under a crown. D. (plate) 20.5cm.
Private Collection

Three jugs of bone china with printed and painted decoration. From left to right: Hilditch & Sons period, c.1812-32, with H. & S. mark in wreath under a crown, pattern no. 864, c.1845 and pattern no. 152, c.1835. H. (centre jug) 14cm.
Private Collection

Teapot, bone china with printed decoration in orange, with added enamel colours. Probably made by the Hilditch & Hopwood partnership, c.1835. Unmarked. H. 14cm.
Private Collection

258

Plate, printed in orange and decorated with added enamel colours. Mark, H. & H. No. 100 within circle with pyramid formed decoration. D. 24cm. Private Collection

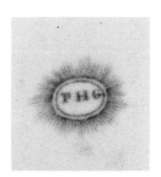

A rare marked example of the wares of Pratt, Hassall & Ger(r)ard, who were in partnership in Lane Delph, Staffordshire, c.1822-34. Cup and saucer printed in blue, could well be mistaken for Hilditch. The underglaze blue mark as shown. D. (saucer) 14cm. Private Collection

embellished with added enamels. Underglaze pale blue transfer prints in the well-known Broseley Chinese landscape pattern, thought to have been introduced by Thomas Turner, at Caughley, were made, together with other patterns in dark blue chinoiserie. Hand painted wares are also found, as well as some with applied blue sprigged decoration. Dessert services are very rare.

Marks, when found, are mainly on the pieces showing chinoiserie transfer prints, these have the letters H. & S. (Hilditch & Sons) or H. & H. (Hilditch & Hopwood).

FURTHER READING:
Helm, Peter, (Ed. G.A. Godden), *Staffordshire Porcelain*, Chapter 18, Granada, 1983.

JOSIAH WEDGWOOD

1812-1834

The newcomer to the study of English ceramics is probably surprised to learn that the great firm of Josiah Wedgwood, which started in 1759, made many ceramic bodies other than the universally recognised blue and white jasperware. We are told that Josiah I thought porcelain a very frivolous material and would probably have been very disappointed to know that his company, which ran so successfully until his death in 1795, was to find it necessary in 1812 to add the production of bone china to their many types of ware, in order to compete with a new generation of flourishing potters, who were catering for the popular demand for 'China Tea Ware'.

Josiah Wedgwood II, who was then in charge of the Etruria works, had for several years been told by Josiah Byerley, who looked after the firm's London business and their travellers, that there was now a greater demand from the ceramic retailers for the new translucent china, in preference to blue and white

The Ivy House Works in Burslem, showing the bottle ovens behind. This is where Joseph Wedgwood commenced to manufacture on his own in 1759. Taken from an old engraving

260

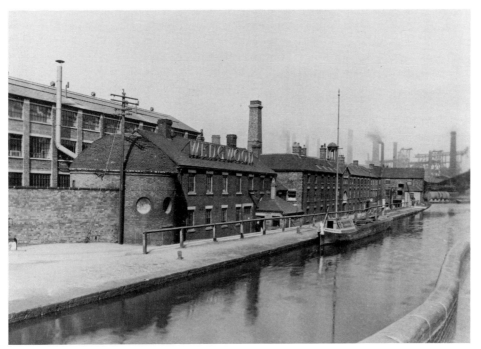

Production of ornamental wares at Josiah Wedgwood's new factory at Etruria started in 1769, the beginning of his partnership with Thomas Bentley, which lasted until Bentley's death in 1780. Sited alongside the Bridgewater Canal, linking the rivers Trent and Mersey, which was opened in 1777, the transport costs of bringing in raw materials and transporting finished wares were considerably lowered.

These works were finally abandoned in 1950, partly due to drastic subsidence caused by coal mining. The foundation of the new factory at Barlaston had been laid in 1938, with production starting in 1940, although due to the war, it was on a very limited scale, primarily for export. Today only the round house, seen in the picture, still stands

A Wedgwood 'French' shape teacup and saucer, and a coffee 'can', c.1814, shown against a page from the pattern book from which the design was taken. Pattern no. 589, known as 'Chinese Tigers' this was printed and shaded in red

Courtesy The Wedgwood Museum Trustees, Barlaston, Stoke-on-Trent

261

A group of Wedgwood tea wares in bone china, the teapot and plate painted with landscapes by John Cutts, c.1812-29. The teacup and creamer printed on glaze in green with 'Chinese Tigers', pattern number 622. Courtesy The Wedgwood Museum Trustees, Barlaston, Stoke-on-Trent

A Wedgwood compotier, in bone china, painted with pattern 784, 'New Chinese figures', by John Cutts, c.1814. 23cm. x 13cm.

Courtesy The Wedgwood Museum Trustees, Barlaston, Stoke-on-Trent

A bone china sucrier painted by John Cutts shown against a background of a page from the Wedgwood pattern book from which the design was taken, c.1814

printed earthenware, which had gone out of fashion, with the result that by 1812 Josiah II had perfected a bone china body, which was to enjoy great popularity until about 1816, when the more gaudy Regency type wares of his rivals were seemingly preferred. Nevertheless a small declining production is now known to have continued until about 1829; much later than previously thought, and Gaye Blake Roberts, Curator of the Wedgwood Museum informs us that the Wedgwood manuscripts tell us that they were still prepared to make bone china to order, probably to replace breakages or enlarge services, as late as 1834, when they produced 'China, green dragon pattern number 622' (Manuscript reference 19/17185).

These early Wedgwood china wares contained only between 21 and 25% bone ash and were covered with an almost leadless glaze. Their forms were simple and practical and included a wide range of tea wares, dessert services and the usual selection of useful and decorative items, but seemingly no dinner services. Among the most pleasing of Wedgwood's bone china are those wares

*Teaset of bone china, hand painted with landscapes by John Cutts, each piece a named view.
Showing two teacups of 'Bute' shape, and a coffee 'can'. All from the Wedgwood factory, c.1814*
Courtesy The Wedgwood Museum Trustees, Barlaston, Stoke-on-Trent

*A group of Wedgwood
teawares, known as 'Parapet'
shape, decorated with pattern
no. 470 'Gold Edge'. First
period bone china, 1812-29*
Courtesy The Wedgwood
Museum Trustees, Barlaston,
Stoke-on-Trent

A Wedgwood plate of first period bone china, made as a replacement for a Chinese export piece, which had been commissioned c.1821-2, bearing the arms of the Sneyd Family
Courtesy The Wedgwood Museum Trustees, Barlaston, Stoke-on-Trent

painted with landscapes in enamel colours by John Cutts, who arrived at the factory in 1813, after his previous employment came to a halt, with the closure of the Pinxton factory.

The archives of the Wedgwood company are so extensive, that it has been possible through pattern numbers and the corresponding pattern books, to trace with certainty many wares bearing only a pattern number, ranging from very low numbers to over one thousand, although they do not all relate to bone china. The name 'WEDGWOOD' printed or stencilled in red, black or gold, was by no means consistently used.

When their production of bone china ceased, their London showrooms were closed and their direct trading came to a halt. The production of bone china was reintroduced in 1878 and is discussed later.

FURTHER READING:
Fontaines, J.K. des, (Ed. G. Godden), *Staffordshire Porcelain,* Chapter 14, Granada, 1983.
Reilly, Robin, and Savage, George, *The Dictionary of Wedgwood,* Antique Collectors' Club, 1980.
Reilly, Robin, *Wedgwood,* Macmillan Publishers Ltd., 1989.

NANTGARW & SWANSEA

c.1813-c.1825

William Billingsley had been involved with the decoration and making of porcelain for many years prior to his arrival at Nantgarw, in South Wales. He was first apprenticed at the China Works in Derby in 1774, when he was sixteen years of age.

In 1796 Billingsley had persuaded John Coke to invest in a new porcelain factory at nearby Pinxton. It had always been his ambition to become a producer of porcelain, as well as a fine painter and gilder, but by 1799 the New Pinxton China Factory had not proved to be a financial success, the partnership was dissolved and Billingsley moved on, leaving John Coke to continue. Following some apparently unsuccessful ventures in Mansfield and Torksey he arrived in about 1813 at Nantgarw, where with Samuel Walker as a partner, he established a factory for the production of a soft-paste porcelain, which he hoped would equal that of Sèvres, but his percentage of wasters was so high that within a year he was compelled to abandon his Nantgarw China Works and move to Dillwyn's pottery at Swansea.

Billingsley's Nantgarw wares are comparatively rare and much sought after, especially by the Welsh collectors. When marked they have the name

Swansea porcelain dessert dish, moulded with 'C' scrolls and floral decoration and painted in enamel colours and gilt by William Pollard, made during William Billingsley's period at the factory, c.1814-17. L. 27cm.

By kind permission of A.E. (Jimmy) Jones and Sir Leslie Joseph, authors of *Swansea Porcelain Shapes and Decoration*

Swansea soft-paste porcelain trio, with the painted and gilt decoration most probably added by a London decorator. Unmarked; note the typical form of handle.   Private Collection

Pair of soft-paste porcelain plates, painted in enamel colours and gilt, c.1815-17; the moulded relief pattern was used at Nantgarw and other contemporary porcelain factories. The comparatively sparse decoration and simple gilt rim suggest factory work rather than London. Mark, 'SWANSEA' printed in red. D. 21cm. The plate in centre is marked with 'SWANSEA' impressed together with trident and probably dates a little later. D. 22cm.   Courtesy Phillips, London

Fine Swansea soft-paste porcelain dinner plate, enamelled with flower decoration, the work of William Pollard. D. 26cm.

By kind permission of A.E. (Jimmy) Jones and Sir Leslie Joseph, authors of *Swansea Porcelain Shapes and Decoration*

Soup plate of Swansea soft-paste porcelain, painted in enamel colours and gilt with the 'Gazebo' pattern; note the eight lobed and notched rim. Made during William Billingsley's period at the factory, c.1814-17. D. 24.5cm.

By kind permission of A.E. (Jimmy) Jones and Sir Leslie Jospeh, authors of *Swansea Porcelain Shapes and Decoration*

Pair of finely decorated soft-paste porcelain plates, decorated with enamel flower painting attributed to Henry Morris, within a deep blue rim decorated with gilding. Made by William Billingsley and Samuel Walker at the Swansea factory of L.W. Dillwyn, c.1814-17. D. 24.3cm.

Courtesy Bearnes, Torquay

A soft-paste porcelain sauce tureen, made at Swansea, c.1814-17, during the William Billingsley's period at L.W. Dillwyn's factory, painted with enamel colours and gilt
By kind permission of A.E. (Jimmy) Jones and Sir Leslie Joseph, authors of *Swansea Porcelain Shapes and Decoration*

Swansea porcelain teapot, moulded with basket work and spiral cartouches, with sparse enamel and gilt decoration. L. 17cm.

By kind permission of A.E. (Jimmy) Jones and Sir Leslie Joseph, authors of *Swansea Porcelain Shapes and Decoration*

'NANTGARW' impressed into the clay, over 'C.W' for China Works. The porcelain was well described by the late W.B. Honey as having the translucency of 'sodden snow' and was much favoured by the London 'outside decorators', who purchased the wares in the white glazed condition, after which they were invariably 'overdecorated' with crowded enamel painting and too lavish gilding.

The porcelains made by Billingsley and Walker whilst with Lewis Weston Dillwyn at the Swansea 'Cambrian Pottery', were usually more stable than those produced in Nantgarw and sometimes have a translucency which is likened to the colour of a 'duck-egg', but this is not a sure guide to Swansea wares.

269

Swansea porclain inkstand, with three pen holders and handles in the form of interlocking serpents and eagles, painted with enamel colours and gilt. H. 10cm.
By kind permission of A.E. (Jimmy) Jones and Sir Leslie Joseph, authors of *Swansea Porcelain Shapes and Decoration*

Swansea soft-paste porcelain vase with handles in the form of rams' heads. Painted in enamel colours and gilt by Thomas Baxter, c.1814-17
By kind permission of A.E. (Jimmy) Jones and Sir Leslie Joseph, authors of *Swansea Porcelain Shapes and Decoration*

Swansea soft-paste porcelain vase, moulded with handles in the form of eagles with outstretched wings, painted in enamel colours and gilt in 'Japan' pattern, c.1814-17. H. 13.7cm.
By kind permission of A.E. (Jimmy) Jones and Sir Leslie Joseph, authors of *Swansea Porcelain Shapes and Decoration*

Cream jug of soft-paste porcelain made at Swansea, with moulded floral relief decoration and gilt. Made in the period when William Billingsley was at L.W. Dillwyn's factory, c.1814-17. L. 12.7cm.
By kind permission of A.E. (Jimmy) Jones and Sir Leslie Joseph, authors of *Swansea Porcelain Shapes and Decoration*

Swansea porcelain chamber candlestick of saucer shape, with decorative handle with serpentine head and forked tail, painted in enamel colours and gilt, during William Billingsley's period at Swansea. D. 12.3cm.
By kind permission of A.E. (Jimmy) Jones and Sir Leslie Joseph, authors of *Swansea Porcelain Shapes and Decoration*

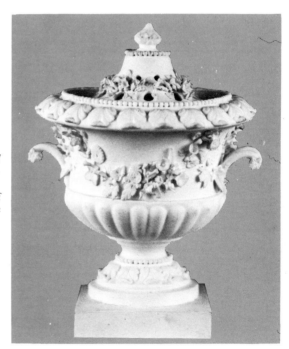

Rare pot-pourri vase of Swansea biscuit soft-paste porcelain, made during the period when William Billingsley and Samuel Walker were at L.W. Dillwyn's factory. H. 13.9cm.
By kind permission of A.E. (Jimmy) Jones and Sir Leslie Joseph, authors of *Swansea Porcelain Shapes and Decoration*

In 1817 Billingsley and Walker returned to Nantgarw and the Swansea works were taken over by T. & J. Bevington & Co. Timothy Bevington and his son John had previously been in partnership with Dillwyn, who now wished to retire. This manufacture was by no means a great success and in 1821 the company, which was comprised of father, son and three other partners, was dissolved. The new partnership of T. & J. Bevington was to continue until 1825, but they may well have restricted their manufactures to earthenware.

A Swansea porcelain dish with gilt twig handles from the Thomas Lloyd service, printed and painted in enamel colours with the 'Mandarin' pattern. The crest of the chained boar is above the motto 'Y DDUW BOR DIOLCH'. From the service made for Thomas Lloyd of Bronwydd, Cardiganshire, probably made to commemorate his marriage to Ann-Davies Thomas of Llwydcoed, Carmarthenshire, in 1819. Mark, 'Swansea' in red. L. 27.8cm.

Courtesy Andrew Hartley Fine Arts, Ilkley

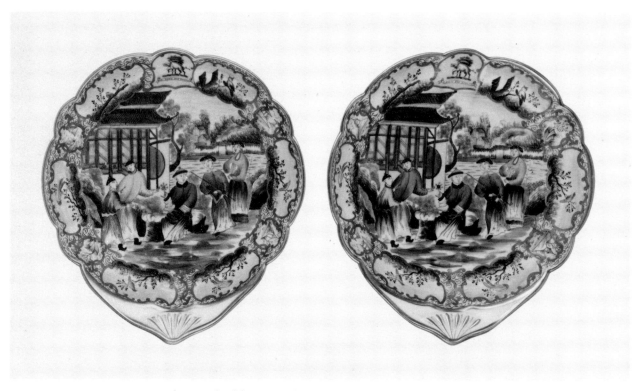

A rare pair of Swansea soft-paste porcelain dessert dishes from the Thomas Lloyd service, printed and painted in enamel colours with the 'Mandarin' pattern. The crest of the boar is above the motto 'Y DDUW BOR DIOLCH'. From the service made for Thomas Lloyd of Bronwydd, Cardiganshire, probably made to commemorate his marriage to Ann-Davies Thomas of Llwydcoed, Carmarthenshire, in 1819. Mark, 'Swansea' in red. L. 27.8cm. Courtesy Phillips, London

Soft-paste porcelain plate made at Nantgarw at William Billingsley's factory, c.1817-20, moulded in relief with a pattern which is seen on wares by other manufacturers during the same period. The gilding on the rim suggests that the painting might well have been added in London. Mark, 'NANTGARW/C.W impressed. (The 'C.W.' stands for 'China Works'.)

Courtesy Phillips, London

Swansea soft-paste porcelain vase, decorated in enamel colours and gilt, c.1820. Decorated by John Powell, who had his own decorating studio in London, c.1810-30. The fine quality Welsh porcelains were in great demand by these ceramic painters who wished to purchase 'blanks'. Marked 'Powell, 91, Wimpole Street'. H. 11cm.

Courtesy Phillips, London

Billingsley and Walker continued to produce their fine porcelain at Nantgarw until 1820, when they moved to join John Rose at Coalport. The premises at Nantgarw were used by the painter, Thomas Pardoe, who continued to decorate the wares left in stock until 1822 when the factory finally closed. In the absence of a genuine mark, the written marks were frequently imitated and it is therefore difficult confidently to attribute the Billingsley and Walker wares, as at times they are so much like those of the Coalport factory, not only in the painting but also in the moulding.

FURTHER READING:

John, W.D., *Nantgarw Porcelain*, Ceramic Book Co., Newport, 1948. Further supplement, 1956; *Swansea Porcelain*, Ceramic Book Co., Newport, 1957.
Nance, E.M., *The Pottery & Porcelain of Swansea & Nantgarw*, Batsford, London, 1942.
Jones, A.E., and Joseph, Sir Leslie, *Swansea Porcelain Shapes and Decoration*, Brown & Sons, Cowbridge, 1988.

HICKS & MEIGH

c.1816-1835

Richard Hicks was born in Shrewsbury, Shropshire, in 1768 and was apprenticed as an engraver to the Caughley Works in Broseley. He moved to Staffordshire some time in the 1790s, and married in 1801, the daughter of the potter, Job Meigh. It is known that his first partnership was with Joseph Boon, an established potter, at Broad Street, Shelton. When Boon left the partnership, Job Meigh junior, Richard Hicks's brother-in-law, took his place, and they appear to have been working together from at least 1803. At first, they are thought only to have produced earthenwares, but certainly by 1816 they were producing some china, as there is a reference to a sale of china to the firm of Minton at this date. Minton had stopped production of their own porcelains between 1816 and 1824 and probably wished to fulfil old orders for their customers.

A government report of 1833 describes a well-run factory employing six hundred people, of which the youngest was a boy of only nine years old. It was quite usual to employ such young persons at this time.

In 1822 the partnership was joined by Johnson, who had been employed as a traveller for the firm, and by 1827 the title of Hicks, Meigh and Johnson was in use. In 1835 it seems that Richard Hicks retired from the business and this partnership came to an end. The factory is then believed to have been purchased by Messrs. Ridgway, Morley, Wear & Co. Richard Hicks died in 1844.

Cup and saucer of bone china, finely decorated with enamel colours and gilt, attributed to Hicks & Meigh of Shelton, Staffordshire, c.1825. D. (saucer) 14.7cm.
Courtesy City Museum & Art Gallery, Stoke-on-Trent

*Teapot attributed to Hicks &
Meigh of Shelton, bearing the
pattern number 1725, typical
of the fine quality wares now
considered to have been made
by these potters, c.1825-30.
Ht. 14cm.*
Courtesy Micawber Publications,
Bridgnorth

So far no marked pieces of porcelain have been reported, which is quite usual,
as at this time, the dealers through which the wares would have been sold would
not have agreed for wares to be marked with the maker's name, as they did not
wish their source of supply to be revealed to their customers. If a firm was large
enough to have its own retail establishment, of course, then their wares would
be proudly marked. Thus, in the absence of marked pieces we have to make do
with the available clues. As the pattern books have unfortunately disappeared,
we have to look to other sources. Descriptions of Hicks's designs occur in
Chamberlain's pattern lists, along with other potters. Manufacturers were keen
to find a popular pattern, and were not adverse to copying those of their rivals.
For instance Pattern No. 2091 in the Chamberlain book refers to 'Coburg,
maroone ground as Hicks, pannels flowers and gold stars as Hicks' and there
are several other references given. Patterns also have been traced through the
shapes and mouldings of marked Hicks & Meigh stone china wares, which
appear to have been repeated in bone china. From these clues a whole range of
wares has been tentatively suggested, which includes dinner, dessert and tea
sets. The pieces are well painted, and the borders are sometimes in rather bold
colours. When gilded, the gilding is generous, but flat, without tooling. The
body and the glaze seem to vary in quality. Cups often have rather large, well
formed handles. Pattern numbers have been noted from 951 to 2349, painted in
red enamel. A few fractional numbers have also been found. There is still much
conjecture in the allocation of wares to this important factory.

FURTHER READING:
Godden, G.A., *Staffordshire Porcelain,* Chapter 17, Granada Publishing, 1983.
Berthoud, M., Article in *Antique Dealer & Collectors Guide,* November, 1988.

Teacup, coffee cup and saucer, of the London shape, moulded in relief and decorated with enamel colours and gilt. Marked CB/341, made by Charles Bourne of Fenton, Staffordshire, c.1825-30. H. (cup) 8.7cm. Courtesy City Museum & Art Gallery, Stoke-on-Trent

Rare figure of a ram in porcelain, painted in enamel colours. Made by Charles Bourne of Fenton, Staffordshire, c.1820-5. L. 8.5cm. Courtesy City Museum & Art Gallery, Stoke-on-Trent

CHARLES BOURNE

c.1817-1830

This fairly modest but interesting pottery was started by two brothers, Ralph and John Bourne, with their brother-in-law William Baker, under the title Bourne, Baker & Bourne. After the death of the two Bourne brothers, John in 1833 and Ralph in 1835, it seems that a third brother, Charles, who may have already been working in the business, took over the concern, and by 1818 he was making both earthenware and china. Notices of the sale of his business between 1829 and 1832, due to his failing health, showed him to be at that time a successful potter, owning the Foley Pottery at Fenton, which consisted of more than six kilns, many buildings and an adjacent house and property.

Wares found are of a bone china. Tea services and dessert services of fashionable shapes of the time were produced, also some magnificent ornamental vases. A few rare animal figures are also in existence.

Marks when found are 'C.B'. sometimes alone, and sometimes shown as a fraction over a pattern number, painted over the glaze. Pattern numbers have been noted from 1 to at least 1017. There is one rare plate in the Victoria & Albert Museum in London, acquired in 1922, which bears the full name and address painted in red, 'Charles Bourne, Foley Potteries, Staffordshire'.

FURTHER READING:
Godden, G.A., *Staffordshire Porcelain,* Chapter 16, Granada Publishing, 1983.

Two bone china tea cups and saucers, unmarked, but the handles suggest they were from the same Staffordshire factory, c.1815-20. The chinoiserie decoration on the left is printed in a crimson enamel, tinted with greens, yellow and blue. The border decoration is of blue enamel loops together with alternating loops in pink lustre, derived from a gold compound. D. (saucer) 14.5cm. That on the right has a similarly decorated bat printed scene, but the border pattern on both saucer and inner cup is of pink lustre. D. (saucer) 14.5cm.

Private Collection

LUSTRE WARES

Early 19th century

Lustre decoration has a long history, for the use of metallic pigments was known to have been used in Egypt on earthenware from the ninth century. This technique which used silver to produce a lustrous yellow or various shades of brown, or copper to give a rich ruby red, was also used on tin glazed wares in Mesopotamia at this same period. It was from the Middle East that the Moorish potters introduced this decoration into Spain at the time of the Moorish occupation, particularly at such centres as Manises and Valencia, and as early as 1154 an Arab traveller wrote of the 'golden pottery of Arragon', referring to the type of wares known today as Hispano Moresque pottery. This type of decorative ware was copied again in the sixteenth century at the maiolica centres of Gubbio and Deruta in Italy.

It was not, however, until the early nineteenth century that lustre decoration became popular in this country, by this time using platinum (which had been discovered in South America in the mid-eighteenth century) to replace silver, and which had the advantage that it did not tarnish. The earlier use of copper gave way to a new technique involving chloride of gold, which was used to produce a pink or purple lustre.

Many British earthenware manufacturers decorated with lustre, among the most prolific being those in the Sunderland area; these are well discussed by Griselda Lewis in her book *A Collector's History of English Pottery*.

Lustre decoration on bone china was also popular, but unfortunately very few of these pieces were marked and it is almost impossible to suggest which factory made them. The simple designs of such firms as Hilditch & Sons were often further embellished with the addition of a little lustre. There were many more sophisticated bone china wares, highlighted with lustre banding and sometimes with fine transfer prints (as illustrated), but all are unmarked. Wedgwood was one of the few companies which did mark their wares and these are discussed in the relevant chapter. Some later factories, such as Shelley Potteries Ltd. and Wiltshaw & Robinson Ltd, which produced 'Carlton Ware', made some interesting lustre wares.

FURTHER READING:
Godden, G.A. and Gibson, M., *Collecting Lustre Ware*, Barrie & Jenkins, 1991.

Porcelain dish from a dessert service, painted in enamel colours, with a predominant orange tone and gilt. Made by Frederick and Ann Peover at Hanley, Staffordshire, c.1818-22. Rare marked examples have the name 'PEOVER' impressed. L. c.30cm.

From the D.R. Pomfret Collection on loan to The City Museum & Art Gallery, Stoke-on-Trent

PEOVER

c.1818-1822

In 1818 Frederick Peover occupied premises in Hanley which he rented from John Glass. He died in 1820 and his wife Ann continued to operate the business until about 1822.

During its short working life, this pottery must have produced quite a considerable range of wares, judging from the few marked pieces which have so far been recognised. The body is of a rather inferior bone china, which tends to show staining, but the decoration on some pieces seems to have a special charm and individuality in its rather unusual painting, whilst other marked pieces, however, could well be mistaken for the wares of the contemporary factories of Derby or Davenport. Dessert and tea wares were produced, and the mark used on these examples is the impressed name of 'PEOVER', sometimes found with a tally mark in the shape of a cross. Although a marked vase is recorded, it would appear to be extremely rare.

FURTHER READING:

Godden, G.A., *Staffordshire Porcelain,* Appendix II, p.459, Granada Publishing Ltd., 1983.

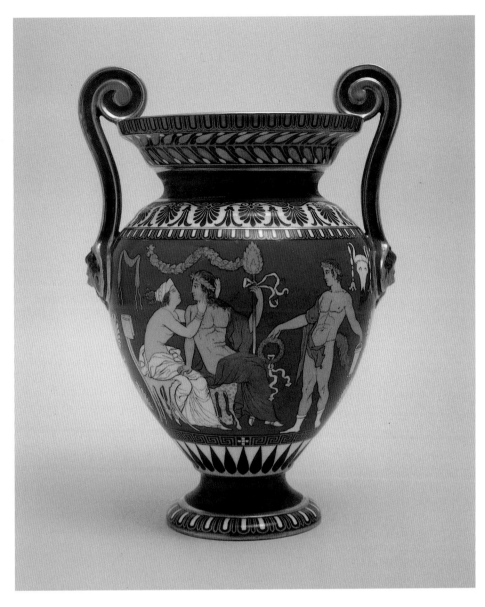

Large porcelain vase, painted in enamel colours to resemble the early Grecian earthenwares depicting classical mythology, of Bacchus and Ariadne on Naxos, a popular legend shown in Titian's painting in the National Gallery. Made by Samuel Alcock & Co. at the Hill Pottery, Burslem, c.1845-50

City Museum & Art Gallery,
Stoke-on-Trent

SAMUEL ALCOCK

c.1822-1859

Despite the fact that the firm of Samuel Alcock was very large by comparison with many contemporary Staffordshire factories, their wide range of porcelains has only in recent years attracted the serious collector, due initially to the research of Mrs. Pat Halfpenny, Keeper of Ceramics at the City Museum & Art Gallery, Stoke-on-Trent, the results of which were published in the *Northern Ceramic Society Journal,* No.2, 1975-6, when among many other details concerning the establishment, she pointed out that four hundred hands were employed in their Burslem factory and their twenty kilns equalled those in use by Minton.

The name of Samuel Alcock is more readily associated with red earthenwares with black decoration in the style of early Grecian wares than with porcelain,

Bone china teapot, decorated in Japanese taste with underglaze blue and enamel colours. Made by Samuel Alcock at the Hill Pottery, Burslem, c.1830. Pattern no. 2000. H. 15.2cm.

Courtesy Mr. & Mrs. P. Miller

Typical early Victorian teapot in bone china, decorated with enamel colours and gilt. Made at Samuel Alcock's Hill Pottery, Burslem, Staffordshire, c.1838-43. Pattern no. 8184. H. 19.6cm.

Courtesy City Museum & Art Gallery, Stoke-on-Trent

and whilst a great deal is known about him as a person, little is known of his porcelain production, which must have been prolific.

In 1839 a group of wares representing their range of production at the time, was buried on the factory site to preserve them for future historians, a novel idea, which unfortunately went wrong, when during demolition work on the site in 1967, they were inadvertently shattered. The fragments, however, were useful as a guide to the wares and proved for example that the popular 'woolly' sheep, a type of figure long considered by some to have been made at the Rockingham factory, were indeed made by Samuel Alcock, some of the

A fine porcelain dessert service painted with polychrome enamel views of Ireland, the locations named on the reverse. The mark, a printed cherub and banner used by Samuel Alcock at the Hill Pottery, Burslem, in the mid-19th century　　　　　　　　　　Courtesy Bearnes, Torquay

fragments were marked with an impressed model number and a workman's number, a useful guide to similar models.

Unfortunately very few of the porcelains made during Alcock's most productive period from about 1830 to 1850 were marked, but in 1843 when writing of the Borough of Stoke on Trent, John Ward highly praised their ornamental china and mentions 'table and tea services, enriched with exquisite landscape paintings and other devices; of vases, fancy bouquettes, articles of toilette and elaborately modelled subjects from history and romance in biscuit china...' Whilst so many of the contemporary firms were producing Parian wares, Alcock made some very well modelled portrait busts in unglazed (biscuit) china, although he did produce many relief moulded jugs in the Parian body.

Samuel Alcock was displaying his wares at the 1851 Exhibition and the similarity to those of Coalport and Rockingham must have accounted for many wrong attributions; probably another instance illustrating that the retailers did not favour selling wares with a mark showing the manufacturer's name, for fear of encouraging the customer to deal direct with the potter for any future orders.

In the absence of a factory mark, Alcock's wares can at times be identified when they bear the 'lozenge' mark, giving the day, month, year and 'parcel' number, indicating the date the form or decoration was registered against 'piracy' with the Patent Office. When the firm of Sir James Duke & Nephews took over Alcock's pottery in 1859, they continued the sequence of pattern numbers in fractional form which had been used by Alcock.

FURTHER READING:
Halfpenny, Pat, *Northern Ceramic Society Journal,* No.2, 1975-6.

Tureen, cover and stand in bone china, decorated in enamel colours and gilt from a very fine service made for the Earl of Shrewsbury in 1827 by H. & R. Daniel of Stoke, Staffordshire. D. 18cm.

City Museum & Art Gallery, Stoke-on-Trent

H. & R. DANIEL
1822-1846

Henry Daniel was originally solely concerned with enamelling at his own small workshop in Hanley until about 1805, when he rented a workshop from Josiah Spode, from whom he purchased undecorated wares, and after adding colours and gilding, he resold the finished articles back to Spode. This was a thriving business, and in 1821 he was known to have a workforce of one hundred and ninety two people, whilst Spode himself was employing only four hundred and

A wide selection of bone china wares made by Henry Daniel at Stoke, c.1822-41, all decorated with enamel painting and gilding. The top row illustrates shapes referred to as Etruscan and First Gadroon; the second row shows the Second Gadroon and Plain Edged teawares; the third row shows the Shrewsbury and C-Scroll teawares and a dessert plate from the Earl of Shrewsbury's service; the fourth row illustrates the Shell and Mayflower tea and dessert wares, whilst in the bottom row are the Ribbed Group teawares and a dessert plate of Pierced Shape.

Courtesy Micawber Publications, Bridgnorth

Teapot of bone china in the C-scroll shape, decorated with pink leaves and gilding. Made by Daniel of Stoke, c.1827. Pattern no. 4413. D. 16.5cm.
Courtesy Micawber Publications, Bridgnorth

Square dish in bone china of ribbed form, decorated in colour with large botanical flower within a green ground. Made by Daniel at Stoke, c.1830. Pattern no. 4988
Courtesy Micawber Publications, Bridgnorth

forty eight. By 1822 he was ready to establish his own factory at London Road, Stoke-on-Trent for the production of bone china. At first the wares of Daniel closely followed those of Spode, he was even using the same pattern numbers, but these are usually painted in gold, unlike those of Spode, which are in enamel colours. There were slight differences in his shapes also, for instance, Daniel's handles tended to be more thickly potted, and his butterfly finials were of a distinctive form and decoration compared to those of Spode and Ridgway. It seems that it was not until 1826, when his son Richard was taken into partnership, that he was able to concentrate on producing his own designs. He was fortunate in having the services of an exceptionally talented flower painter, named William Pollard, whom he employed from 1822 to 1827. The highest point of his career was when he was commissioned in 1827, to produce some particularly lavish services for the Earl of Shrewsbury. These pieces are exceptional for their rich decoration and distinctive moulding. Fortunately many of the surviving pieces were marked, however, this is not the case in most

Coffee cup and saucer in bone china painted with enamel flowers and green panels. Made by Daniel of Stoke, c.1830. Pattern no. 5055. H. (cup) 6.5cm.
Courtesy Micawber Publications, Bridgnorth

Two cream jugs in bone china of Bell shape, c.1836 and 1839, the left painted with a drab ground with plaid pattern, pattern no. 6336, the right having a similar ground with seaweed gilding and printed flowers. Pattern no. 6823. H. 13.5 and 10.5cm.
Courtesy Micawber Publications, Bridgnorth

Plate in bone china of shell shape, painted with a landscape in colour surrounded by a green ground. Inscribed on the reverse 'The Church and Castle of Scurlogstown, Co. of Eastmeath'. Made by Daniel at Stoke, c.1830. Pattern no. 7908. D. 22.5cm.
Courtesy Micawber Publications, Bridgnorth

Dessert plate of bone china of the Shrewsbury shape, made by Daniel of Stoke, c.1830. Decorated with a finely drawn view of Bath, surrounded with a blue ground and a band of unburnished gilding with raised dots. Marked on the reverse 'Bath' and 'Doe and Rogers, Worcester', the decorators. No pattern number. D. 22cm.
Courtesy Micawber Publications, Bridgnorth

Teacup and saucer of the Savoy Shape, of bone china with buff scrolls and enamelled flowers on a green ground. Made by Daniel of Stoke, c.1846. Pattern no. 8812. D. (cup) 10cm.
Courtesy Micawber Publications, Bridgnorth

Large oval dish of bone china, painted with enamel flowers on a white ground. Made by Daniel of Stoke, c.1844. Pattern no. 8115. L. 33.5cm.
Courtesy Micawber Publications, Bridgnorth

of Daniel's wares, therefore it is essential for identification, to study shapes and the decoration and moulding of borders, etc.

When Daniel left Spode in 1822, it is estimated that the pattern numbers had reached between 3400 and 3500, but it is thought that he probably continued the Spode sequence of numbering when manufacturing on his own. Daniel's own patterns appear to start around 3700 and continue into the 8000s usually painted in gold. A pattern number below 3700 should therefore be regarded with care, as it could be the work of either Spode or Daniel. Patterns below approximately 3400 were obviously made prior to 1822.

It is a little confusing to find the name of DANIELL on some wares, including those made by H. & R. Daniel, but this was the name of the London retailer used by H. & R. Daniel, and other potters, and it was often the practice for the retailer to have the wares marked with his name only, to avoid the customer dealing directly with the manufacturer.

FURTHER READING:
Berthoud, Michael, *H. & R. Daniel 1822-1846,* Micawber Publications, Wingham, 1980; *The Daniel Tableware Patterns,* a supplement published in 1982.

JOHN YATES
1822-1843

Today's visitors to antique fairs are often offered porcelain wares attributed to potters whose names a few years back were entirely unknown to the average collector, but now there are many keen researchers who devote all their energies to the study of one particular factory and are generous in passing on their findings.

Among these comparatively new names is that of John Yates of Shelton, who· started potting together with his two sons, John and William, about 1770. It was in about 1822 that the family produced porcelain, a production which continued until 1844. The founder, John Yates, died in 1828, three years after his son William. His son John continued the production and from 1835 until 1843 was together with a partner named May.

The firm obviously produced a wide range of wares, which although not bearing the maker's name, usually had a pattern number ranging from about 1038-1565, although an occasional earlier number has been recorded. Despite the fact that no marked wares have as yet been sighted, the porcelains of Yates are at times attributable through the research of Dr. & Mrs Geoffrey Barnes, who discovered a dessert service given by John Yates to his daughter on the

Trio of bone china, painted in enamel colours, underglaze blue and gilt, with pattern no. 1164. Attributed on the grounds of the moulded rim decoration to John Yates of Shelton, Staffordshire, c.1825-30. D. (saucer) 15.2cm. Courtesy City Museum & Art Gallery, Stoke-on-Trent

occasion of her wedding in 1826. Some of this important key service is still in the possession of a direct descendant of the family

One main distinguishing feature is what appears to be a unique moulded relief seen on the rim, appropriately named by Geoffrey Godden as the 'oak and mistletoe', a decorative form seen on a wide range of dessert wares and tea services with high quality enamel and gilt decoration, all made in a range of porcelain bodies of varying quality. A firm of this duration obviously made many other wares, some of which have been likened in shape to the early productions of H. & R. Daniel (1822-46), yet with considerable differences in their range of pattern numbers, but much still remains to be learned of the wares of Yates.

The reader is cautioned that there were two ceramic retailers trading under the name of Yates, one in Cheltenham and another in Leeds, and marks which include the name of Yates together with that of either of these cities should not be associated with the Shelton factory. As yet no wares have been seen with the sole mark of 'YATES' or 'YATES & MAY'.

FURTHER READING:
Godden, G.A., *Staffordshire Porcelain,* Chapter 20, Granada Publishing, 1983.

French porcelain decorated by T.M. Randall, authenticated by being in possession of one of his direct descendants.
Private Collection

French porcelain decorated by T.M. Randall, authenticated by being in possession of one of his direct descendants.

Private Collection

MADELEY

Shropshire, c.1825-1840

Whether Thomas Martin Randall first learnt his skills as a porcelain decorator by being apprenticed at the Caughley works of Thomas Turner, or at one of the Coalport concerns is not known, but he would have only been about thirteen years of age when the Caughley factory was taken over by John Rose in 1799, so the later Shropshire factory or that of the neighbouring factory of Anstice, Horton & Rose would appear the most likely.

According to Llewellyn Jewitt in *The Ceramic Art of Great Britain,* after working at the Derby factory for a short period in the early nineteenth century, T.M. Randall joined up with Richard Robins to establish a decorating concern near Islington, London, c.1813, where they worked on imported French undecorated porcelain in addition to blanks from various English factories, including Swansea and Nantgarw, which they were able to acquire or had supplied to them by the London retailers, including Mortlock, who commissioned their work. This partnership appears to have successfully continued until c.1825.

Randall then started a decorating establishment at Madeley, Shropshire, where after a short while he also produced a small amount of fine soft-paste porcelain, remaining there until about 1841, when he moved to Shelton, Staffordshire, where it is not known exactly what type of ware he produced or decorated, although he is recorded as making porcelain in 1853, by which time his son had joined the business, which finally closed in 1856, three years prior to his death.

According to various writers over the years, there appears to be little doubt that after leaving Derby, Randall was primarily engaged with applying beautiful enamel painting and gilding to French porcelain blanks in the manner of that seen on the most sought after Sèvres, with turquoise or rose coloured grounds. He employed his nephew John Randall and other skilled painters and gilders, but unfortunately due to the fact that regular factory marks were not used, certain identification of Madeley wares and their limited range of animal figures remains a problem.

ROCKINGHAM

c. 1825-1842

It can confidently be stated that more porcelain made in England during the second quarter of the nineteenth century has been wrongly attributed to the Rockingham factory than to any other. The Rockingham China Works was near Swinton in Yorkshire, on the estate of the Earl Fitzwilliam, who was both the landlord and the patron of the factory. The original factory dated back to about 1745, when an Edward Butler produced a wide range of building and

A dessert plate with the named title 'Northern View of Rotherham', painted on the reverse, c.1830. The outer edge of the border is an interesting feature, showing an acanthus leaf shell moulding. Griffin mark in red. D. 24cm.   Private Collection

A group of tea wares showing five different types of handle known to have been used at the Rockingham factory. The sucrier also shows the crown knob, which is an aid to identification, this is marked with the griffin in puce, used c.1831-42. The other pieces are all marked in red, the colour used c.1826-30.   Private Collection

---

domestic wares from a 'hard brownware', his landlord at the time being the 1st Marquis of Rockingham (*d.*1782). During the second half of the eighteenth century, finer earthenwares were produced under a succession of partners, including John Brameld (*d.*1819).

It was in 1826 that, due to the generosity of the Earl Fitzwilliam, the three sons of John Brameld first began to produce their fine porcelains at Swinton, and in 1830 were commissioned to produce for King William IV, a dessert service of over two hundred pieces at the cost of £5,000, and the term 'Manufacturer to the King' was added to their mark, together with 'Royal

A tray from the Rockingham factory, which produced many fine examples of these wares, c.1826-30. Painted in enamel colours by Thomas Steel, who signed 'T. Steel pinxit'. Marked with the griffin mark in red. W. 40cm.
Courtesy Clifton Park Museum, Rotherham

This vase known as the 'Rhinoceros' vase, is dated 1826 and marked with a red griffin, within the lid. It was made to special order for Wentworth House and, standing 3ft. 9in. (113cm.) high, was reputed to be the largest vase in the country at that date. It is a scent jar decorated with scenes from Don Quixote *painted by John Wager Brameld from designs from Stothard. It may be seen in the Clifton Park Museum, Rotherham. The companion vase is on display at the Victoria & Albert Museum, London*
Courtesy Clifton Park Museum, Rotherham

A group of Rockingham figures, early 19th century, from left to right: 'Paysanne du Canton de Zurich', H.18cm; Griffin impressed 'Simon Pengander', H.16.7cm; Griffin in red, 'Paysan du Canton de Zurich', H.18cm;, Griffin impressed. Simon Pengander was a theatrical character in an early 19th century play, often portrayed by the comedian, John Liston. These figures were probably modelled after contemporary engravings
Courtesy Clifton Park Museum, Rotherham

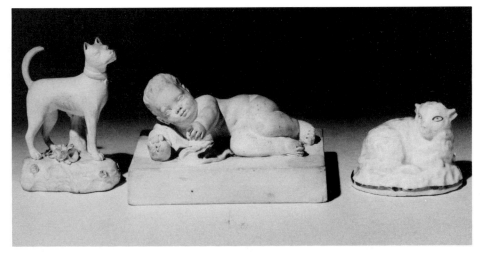

Three Rockingham figures, c.1826-30. The standing pug dog is in the biscuit, and marked with the incised number, 88, and the mark usually seen on figures of the griffin over ROCKINGHAM/ WORKS/BRAMELD. H. c.7.5cm. The biscuit figure of the sleeping child is model no. 65 and has an impressed mark. L. 12cm. The glazed figure of the ewe is model no. 108, and pairs with a ram, with impressed mark. L. 4.5cm.
Courtesy Phillips, London

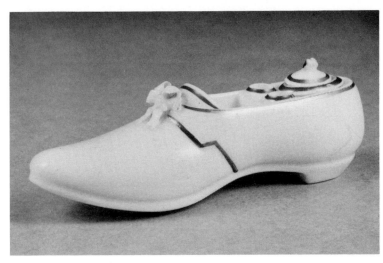

A Rockingham porcelain pen and inkstand, bearing the mark of a red griffin and C 11. The red griffin mark was used from c.1826-30. The significance of the C 1 followed by a number is unknown, but is peculiar to this factory. L. 12.8cm.
Courtesy Lockett Collection

Rockingham Works, Brameld'. The heraldic device of the griffin, also used on earlier pottery, is based on the crest of the Earls Fitzwilliam, heirs to the Marquesses of Rockingham. From about 1826 to 1830 the marks were printed in red, but from 1830 to 1842 the colour was changed to puce. Reproductions of Rockingham porcelains have been made in a hard-paste, with versions of the original marks in a brownish red.

The limited range of Rockingham pattern numbers is certainly a good guide: their tea wares, if numbered, range from about 430 to about 1565, after which a fraction series appears to have been adopted ranging from 2/1 to about 2/100, whilst the dessert services appear to start with pattern numbers from about 415 and continue to about 430. Unfortunately, the original pattern books, which would clarify this approximation, are in private hands and have not been made available to researchers into the history and wares of the factory to permit any serious study. A further reliable guide to genuine Rockingham decorative wares is given when the number is accompanied by the letter and number C1, in either enamel or gilt. The many patterns are not necessarily entirely different and even a variation in the colour of the applied enamels sometimes warranted a different pattern number, as was the case with New Hall. Many of the services and decorative wares are very lavishly shaped and decorated and were obviously

A Rockingham dessert plate, painted with the Royal Arms, as commissioned for the Royal Household of William IV, c.1830. Unmarked. D. 24cm.

Courtesy The Clifton Park Museum, Rotherham

very costly to produce, whereas in contrast many of the tea wares are surprisingly dull.

The question of exactly which figures were made at Rockingham is difficult to establish, although in the recommended book, Terry Lockett lists figures bearing impressed numbers up to 136, which are applied in addition to the griffin mark either impressed or in enamel. Some of the figures are glazed and enamelled in colour, others are left in the white biscuit. All the figures, busts and animal forms are crisply modelled and superior in every way to those of the majority of contemporary Staffordshire figures.

Regrettably, cottages and castles, some in the form of aromatic pastille burners and a variety of animals, such as dogs and sheep, with 'shaggy' fur or fleece, are still wrongly attributed at times to Rockingham, for as yet not a single piece of any of these types has been seen with the Rockingham mark.

One cannot dismiss Rockingham without mention of the two enormous 'Rhinoceros' vases: the first, made in 1826, is forty-four inches high and over one hundred pounds in weight, described by a visitor to the factory at the time as a 'scent jar with hexagonal honeycomb openings for the perfume to escape'. It has a well-moulded figure of a rhinoceros on the lid and is decorated with

A Rockingham dessert plate with moulded scrolled border, gilded with fruiting vines and naturalistic flower sprays, c.1835. Griffin mark in puce and painted number 816. D. 24cm. Private Collection

Figure of a Rockingham sheep lying down, painted in enamel colours and gilt. Mark impressed 'Griffin', made from mould no. 100. L. 7.8cm. It is shown together with unmarked lamb, model no. 109. L. 49cm. Courtesy Terence Lockett

Two finely decorated Rockingham dessert dishes, c.1826-30, painted in enamel colours and gilt; the arrangement of the flowers in a basket suggests the hand of Edwin Steele. The griffin mark is printed in red
Courtesy Phillips, London

This excellent example of a Rockingham tray, c.1830-42, painted with a view of 'Newstead Abbey, Nottinghamshire', has a feature which is quite distinctive, in its double twig handles. Griffin mark in puce. 29.3 x 18.7cm.
Courtesy Sheffield City Museum

scenes from the adventures of Don Quixote, painted by John Wager Brameld. This somewhat damaged vase is now in the Clifton Park Museum in Rotherham. The second similar vase is in the Victoria & Albert Museum and was acquired by the South Kensington Museum in 1859 from the London china dealer Mortlock for 100 guineas; it is painted with flowers by Edwin Steele, according to John Haslem, in consequence the style of painting on this piece helps to identify Steele's work on other Rockingham wares. This vase is well described by the late W.B. Honey, former Keeper of the Ceramics Department of the Victoria & Albert Museum in *English Pottery and Porcelain* (A. & C. Black, London, reprinted 1975), he writes of the vase as having 'Huge paw feet

Rockingham porcelain vase, painted with landscape on a green ground, with finely modelled heads of storks in gilt, c.1830-42. H. 34.2cm.
Courtesy Sheffield City Museum

Rockingham porcelain figure of 'Paysan du Canton de Zurich', painted in enamel colours, c.1826-30. Mark, impressed griffin and incised model number 'No 53'. H. 19.3cm.
Courtesy R.H. Williamson Bequest, Tullie House, Carlisle

A bust of the Earl Fitzwilliam, Patron of the Rockingham Factory, in unglazed porcelain, bisque ware, probably modelled by William Eley, c.1830. Unmarked. H. 30cm.
Courtesy Clifton Park Museum, Rotherham

From a part service of Rockingham porcelain, pattern no. 1461, some saucers with puce griffin mark, c.1838-42. H. (teapot) 19.5cm.
Courtesy City Museum & Art Gallery, Stoke-on-Trent. Gift in memory of Margaret Stewart

A Rockingham cup and saucer, c.1831-42, the saucer only is marked with a puce griffin. The pattern no. is N 1161. D. (saucer) 15cm.
Courtesy Lockett Collection

A Rockingham flower basket, encrusted with applied flowers, painted in enamels and gilt, c.1830-42. Mark, printed griffin in puce. H. 11.2cm. Courtesy Bearnes, Torquay

A porcelain figure of a hound made at the Rockingham factory, c.1830, and bearing the impressed mark of a griffin and Rockingham Works, Brameld. Number 93 incised. H. 5.7cm. Courtesy Lockett Collection

An elaborate flower encrusted vase of rococo shape, made for pot-pourri, painted in enamel colours and gilt, c.1830-42. Mark, griffin in puce. H. 37cm. Courtesy Clifton Park Museum, Rotherham

Part of a Rockingham porcelain tea service, painted in enamel colours and gilt, c.1835. H. (teapot) 19.7cm.
Gift of Mary Pratt and Rachel Lorking in memory of their mother to the City Museum & Art Gallery, Stoke-on-Trent

Miniature porcelain teapot, with relief floral decoration and painted in enamel colours. Made at the Rockingham factory in Yorkshire, c.1835-40. H. 7.5cm.
Courtesy City Museum & Art Gallery, Stoke-on-Trent

beneath a monstrous body smothered in oak leaves and twigs...The painting on this vase (that decorated by Steele) is also typical: hot in colour and laboured in handling, but not without a vulgar abundance and excess that reveal an unmistakable vitality if little taste'. In fairness this opinion should not be used as a pointer to other Rockingham wares, as neither of these vases bear the Rockingham mark, but this is not unusual for the London retailers preferred to have either their own name added or for the pieces to be left unmarked.

It was probably due to undertaking the manufacture of the many extravagant services for royalty and nobility that they ran into financial difficulties which forced the closure of the works in 1842, when the brothers Brameld were in debt to the Earl Fitzwilliam for the sum of £4,500.

Isaac Baguley, who had formerly managed the Brameld's gilding shop, retained a small part of the factory in which to carry on working as a decorator

An underglaze blue printed teapot, c.1835, unmarked, but identified as Rockingham, by the shape of the handle and the unusual crown finial on the lid. The pattern is known as the Two Temples pattern
Courtesy Lockett Collection

of other people's wares, and possibly some old Rockingham stock, especially that decorated with a fine brown glaze, which was an ideal ground for gilt decoration. Isaac Baguley died in 1855, but his son continued the business until 1865, when he moved to Mexborough, where he continued to use the name 'ROCKINGHAM WORKS, MEXBRO' in his printed mark which included the name BAGULEY until his death in 1891.

FURTHER READING:
Rice, D.G., *The Illustrated Guide to Rockingham Pottery & Porcelain*, Barrie & Jenkins, 1971.
Eaglestone, A.A., and Lockett, T.A., *The Rockingham Pottery*, David & Charles, 1973.
Cox, Alwyn and Angela, *Rockingham Pottery & Porcelain 1745-1842*, Faber & Faber, 1983.

JOHN BREEZE

Tunstall, Staffordshire, c.1828-1830

Among the many unfamiliar names of potters to sometimes be attributed to well decorated bone china wares on offer at today's antique fairs, is that of Breeze, of which there are at least four entries as potters in the Staffordshire rate records. This raises the problem as to which of these concerns are the table wares with the painted mark of 'BREEZE' together with a pattern number, to be attributed. Judging from the form and style of decoration seen on these named examples, John Breeze & Co, working at Cobridge and/or Tunstall, c.1828-30, would seem the most likely potter to have made the example illustrated.

A well decorated porcelain dish painted in enamel colours and gilt. Attributed to John Breeze, who was working c.1828-30 in Cobridge or Tunstall, or both. Painted with the name Breeze and the pattern no. 10. L. 28cm.   Courtesy City Museum & Art Gallery, Stoke-on-Trent

Chapter 3
Victorian Porcelain Factories
c.1837 - c.1900

COPELAND & GARRETT   COPELAND
1833-1847   *1847-present*

Following the death of Josiah Spode III in 1827, the company continued to be administered by two relatives, Hugh Henshall Williamson and Thomas Fenton, but they were not well acquainted with the production of ceramic wares and the running of the company was left in the capable hands of William Taylor Copeland, a partner in their London business.

The Copelands were a Staffordshire family; the grandfather had a farm near the Longton Hall porcelain factory and might well have had his own small pottery to produce the red earthenware vessels used on the farm and in the kitchen, as so many farmers did in the area.

William Taylor Copeland's father became involved with the industry when he became a partner to Josiah Spode II and William Spode in their London business in 1805. By the time he died in 1826 he had accumulated a large sum of money, which enabled his son, William Taylor Copeland, to purchase the Spode company in 1833, although he spent the remainder of his life in London,

Three superb examples of Copeland's jewelled porcelain. All pieces are the work of William Ball, c.1870. The cup and saucer are of eggshell thickness. Marked 'COPELAND' under interlaced Cs. H. (vase) 16.5cm.
Private Collection

303

Tea cup, coffee cup and saucer of bone china, painted in enamel colours and gilt on a fawn ground, c.1833. The initials 'C & G' for Copeland and Garrett (1833-47) are an early form of mark used at the start of the partnership, together with pattern number 4723

Courtesy Spode Museum
Collection

A Copeland & Garrett dessert plate painted with enamel coloured scene, titled 'Loch Voil' within a cream coloured border, the moulded rim decorated in gilt, c.1835-40. Red painted pattern number 5603 and COPELAND AND GARRETT within a crowned wreath printed in green. D. 24cm. Courtesy Andrew Hartley Fine Arts, Ilkley

where in 1835 he became Lord Mayor. From 1837 to 1852 and 1857 to 1865 he was the Conservative member of Parliament for Stoke. Although not too active in Parliamentary debates, etc., he was very concerned with the well-being of his constituents and was a keen supporter of the establishment of art schools for the promotion of better design in the industry and when the Potteries School of Design was opened in 1847, for the tutoring of boys and girls over the age of twelve years, he and the firm of Copeland and Garrett were subscribers.

It was in 1833 that William Taylor Copeland purchased not only the London business but also the Stoke factory and at this time took into partnership Thomas Garrett who was obviously involved with the London business of Spode from at least 1826, little is known of the part he had played in the company, but it is suggested that he might well have been their principal

Three examples of 'jewelled' porcelain, made by Copeland, c.1880-90. The jewelled effect of inlaid precious and semiprecious stones, such as first used at Sèvres, is achieved by using heavily applied 'drops' of translucent or opaque enamels. The vase is signed by W. Ball and the 'Primula' shaped plate by H. Milward. H. (vase) 13cm.
Courtesy Spode Museum

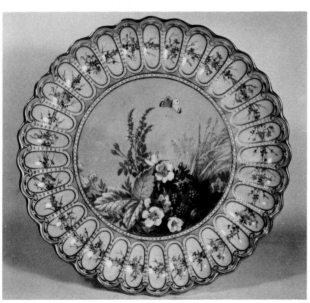

Copeland bone china plate of the 'Chelsea' shape, the centre floral decoration is the signed work of C.F. Hürten. Marked, 'COPELAND'S CHINA' with impressed potting mark for January, 1890. Dia. 23.5cm.
Courtesy Spode Museum Collection

traveller. After becoming a partner he seemed to have been responsible for the actual production in Stoke, in co-operation with Thomas Battam, the Art Director of the firm. The partnership was dissolved in 1847, and Garrett died in London in 1865.

During the Copeland and Garrett period the factory made great strides, more adjacent land was purchased and within three years they were using twenty-five ovens, only three less than Davenport. By 1842, when there was a commission into the employment of children in factories, Copeland and Garrett were employing a total of seven hundred and eighty hands, seventy-seven of whom were children under the age of fifteen years. An article in the *Penny Magazine* of 1843 describing the factory said 'The works...appear more like a small town than a manufactory'. By 1867, one year before the death of William Taylor

Dessert plate, Belinda shape, painted in enamel colours with a scene of Ponti Rotti, Rome. Possibly painted by William Birbeck, c.1885. Marked with 'COPELAND' under two interlaced Cs and F/82. D. 21cm.
Private Collection

Copeland, his four sons, William, Alfred, Edward and Richard Pirie were taken into partnership and the new title of W.T. Copeland & Sons was adopted. By 1896, Richard Pirie was the only son still remaining with the firm, continuing until his death in 1913. His sons, Ronald and Gresham, continued the business until they retired in 1956. Production continued under their sons until 1966, when the company was purchased by the Carborundum Co. Ltd. After a few years the company again changed hands when it was purchased by Royal Worcester Ltd., who in 1976 merged the two companies to form Royal Worcester Spode Ltd. There were further changes of ownership and since 1988 Spode Ltd. and Royal Worcester Ltd. operate as separate concerns under The Porcelain and Fine China Companies Ltd.

It was during the Copeland & Garrett period (1833-47) that highly decorated wares, influenced by the fashion for revived rococo, were produced in quantity, in addition to all the usual table services. Many other decorative and useful wares were introduced to enhance the Victorian homes, including door furniture and toilet services, the latter being in great demand, when the only running water was that carried by the maid.

Copeland bone china plate, painted in enamels and gilt, attributed to W. Yale, who was a scenic painter working at the factory towards the end of the 19th century. Marked on reverse, 'Greenwich/ from the Thames' in purple script and the SPODE/fretted square with 'C'/Copeland in underglaze green, with U/84 impressed. D. 23.7cm.   Private Collection

In this same period Parian ware was enjoying great popularity. These wares are discussed in a separate chapter, although it should be mentioned here that Copeland and Garrett appear to have been the first manufacturers to make and market small scale porcelain statuary that resembled the texture and appearance of marble.

The series of pattern numbers started by Spode in about 1800 was continued until 1852 and it is estimated that at the time Copeland and Garrett took over the number reached was in the region of 5300, continuing to about 7600 by the end of the partnership. Further rather involved series of numbers were introduced for specific wares, which will be covered in great detail by Robert Copeland, who is still actively concerned with the company, in a book he is in the course of preparing.

From 1847 the production under W.T. Copeland was to flourish, involving a great number of new patterns and shapes, although many of the table wares were made for a more practical purpose rather than to delight the eye and the decoration was often confined to the borders. There was great rivalry between the major British porcelain makers at the series of International Exhibitions,

Copeland bone china pot-pourri jar and cover in the form of an incense burner, a form that was in use in 1913. Painted in enamel colours and gilt, signed by T. Worrell. Mark, SPODE/COPELAND'S CHINA/ENGLAND. H. 32cm.
Courtesy Bearnes, Torquay

where, as seen from contemporary illustrations, the very volume of the wares exhibited on their stands tended to distract from the highly skilled painting and gilding on the individual pieces.

It was not until during the 1860s that the management permitted some of their outstanding painters and gilders to sign their work and today these wares are amongst the most sought after collectors' items, especially when made to the order of a notability. Among the many fine painters engaged at Copelands those especially worthy of note during the Victorian period include David Evans, C.F. Hürton, Lucien Besche, all specialising in floral work, Daniel Lucas and W. Yale in landscapes, whilst Samuel Alcock was a superb figure painter. At this time highly skilled painters were in great demand and consequently rather a nomadic group, whose work can often be identified on the wares of other factories, including Minton, Derby, Coalport, Doulton and Worcester.

Although today the majority of bone china wares are decorated by the application of multicoloured transfers which have been produced by lithography or silk screen printing, which after soaking in water can be carefully slid on to the warm, glazed ceramic ware, however highly talented painters are still available in the major factories when hand painting is required.

FURTHER READING:
Whiter, L., *Spode. A History of the Family, Factory and Wares from 1783 to 1833,* Barrie & Jenkins, 1970.
Copeland, Robert (Ed. G. Godden), 'Spode Porcelain 1797-1833 and the succeeding firm', Chapter 8, *Staffordshire Porcelain,* Granada, 1983.
Exhibition catalogue, *Spode-Copeland 1733-1983,* City Museum and Art Gallery, Stoke-on-Trent, 1983.

Porcelain figure made by John and Rebecca Lloyd of Shelton, Staffordshire, c.1840-50. Marked 'LLOYD/SHELTON' impressed, painted in enamel colours. H. 33cm.

Courtesy City Museum & Art Gallery, Stoke-on-Trent

J. & R. LLOYD
c.1834-1852

There are few Staffordshire figures of porcelain which can be attributed to a definite manufacturer, consequently those which can be named become extremely important collectors' items; this is certainly the case with those recorded which have the impressed mark of 'LLOYD/SHELTON' on the reverse.

The earliest recorded portrait figures are those of 'Albert' and 'Victoria & Princess Royal', produced by John & Rebecca Lloyd in their factory at Shelton, which was in operation from around 1834 until 1852. The figures, which match, probably date to 1841, one year after the birth of the Princess Royal.

The Lloyds made many of their early figures in both earthenware and porcelain, some of the latter with open bases, which is a feature only rarely seen on earthenware models. It is interesting to note that among their range of figures these potters also made porcelain chimney-piece ornaments of various sized spaniel dogs, of the type still being made to this day, and also models of French poodles, with rough curly hair (made by applying finely shredded clay), the type which for many years were wrongly attributed to the Rockingham factory. Following the death of John Lloyd, his wife Rebecca continued the production until 1852.

COALPORT

c.1837-1926-present

As Coalport moved into the Victorian years their wares began to show a closer resemblance to those of Rockingham, and it is only during recent years that the variation in the range of pattern numbers has been used as a guide, and many Coalport pieces, which in the past have been wrongly attributed, can now be correctly identified.

Part of a dinner service, produced by Coalport in the early 19th century, in their lavish 'Japan' style, c.1805. Fragments of this pattern were found during excavations on the Coalport site

Courtesy Bearnes, Torquay

This is a particularly impressive example of a pastille burner, the original 'air freshener', possibly made by Coalport in the early 19th century. The pastille would have been placed inside the house, and when lit would have exuded a pleasant odour. W. 23cm.

Courtesy Bearnes, Torquay

310

Miniature chamber candlestick made by John Rose & Co., of Coalport, decorated in coloured enamels and gilt, c.1825. Printed with the mark introduced after 1820, when John Rose was awarded the Gold Medal by The Society of Arts, for his introduction of a glaze which did not contain lead, and which had such a beneficial effect on the health of the potters concerned, who had invariably suffered from lead poisoning prior to this date. D. 9.5cm.
Courtesy Bearnes, Torquay

Coalport watch stand and plinth, decorated in enamel colours and gilt, with a light green ground, c.1825-45. Mark, 'Coalport' written in script in underglaze blue. A drawing of what would appear to be this model, without plinth, appears in the design book of William Hedley (who was the chief travelling saleman for John Rose & Co., Coalport), described as 'New watch stand' 8½in. 18s. H. 43cm.
Courtesy Bearnes, Torquay

John Rose died in 1841, four years after Queen Victoria ascended the throne; he was succeeded by his nephew, W.F. Rose, and William Pugh, who together were shortly to steer the factory in a new direction, when they looked towards eighteenth century Sèvres for their inspiration, even to the extent of sometimes copying the famous crossed 'L's' cypher of the Royal monogram. These fine reproductions were so good, that when displayed behind the barriers in stately homes, often with poor lighting, it is difficult to separate the genuine French wares from the reproductions, and during the nineteenth century many Coalport decorative pieces were mistakenly purchased as soft-paste Sèvres. The only real guide, except for a close examination of the body, is the quality of the gilding, as that used at Vincennes and Sèvres cannot be matched. Many of the popular ground colours were successfully reproduced including the underglaze blue (*bleu lapis*), the rich blue enamel (*bleu nouveau*), the turquoise (*bleu céleste*) and the pink (*rose*), popularly called *rose Pompadour,* a term not mentioned in the records of the factory.

The Victoria & Albert Museum is especially rich in these Coalport pieces, due to the early association of the South Kensington Museum with the Great Exhibition of 1851. The outstanding painter of these wares was John Randall (*b.*1810), whose father, T.M. Randall, was responsible for redecorating some of

A pair of Coalport vases for pot-pourri, c.1840. The perfume would have escaped from the perforated lids; an inner cover is sometimes found, which would have preserved the contents, when not in use. Though unmarked, this pattern is recorded in a Travellers' Design Book used from about 1820 to 1840. H. 24cm.
Courtesy Bearnes, Torquay

Though lacking a factory mark, the design for the form of this Coalport part dessert service, was registered at the Patent Office in November 1849
Courtesy Bearnes, Torquay

the genuine eighteenth century Sèvres porcelain which was sold from the factory from the time of the Revolution. John Randall worked at Coalport from about 1835 until he retired in 1881, by which time his painting of figures, flowers and birds had become famous in the field of British porcelain painting.

There were of course many other accomplished painters at Coalport, including William Cook, specialising in fruit and flowers, James Rouse, favouring figures and pastoral subjects, during his long stay (1830-65), and Percy Simpson, who painted birds and landscapes well into this century, his father Thomas having been the foreman painter. From 1890 to 1932 Thomas

An extravagantly decorated plate in colour by Josiah Rushton, a fine figure painter, who prior to moving to Coalport in about 1871 had been painting at Royal Worcester. He painted a series of similar plates featuring well-known court characters of the previous century; this example is of Lady Sarah Bunbury, after a Reynolds' original. The series was exhibited by Coalport at the 1893 Chicago Exhibition. D. 23.5cm.
Courtesy Phillips, London

Coalport vase in bone china, painted with enamel colours and gilt, c.1891-1920, a few years before the Coalport company moved in 1926 from Shropshire to Shelton, Stoke-on-Trent. They now operate at the Coalport China Ltd. at Fenton, but since 1967 have been part of the Wedgwood Group. Ht. 17.8cm.
Courtesy City Museum & Art Gallery, Stoke-on-Trent

John Bott was the Art Director at Coalport, he was the son of the more famous Thomas Bott who excelled in his reproductions of Limoges enamels during his years as a painter at the Worcester factory.

The production continued under the name of John Rose & Co. until 1889, when under the new owner, Peter Bruff, it was renamed Coalport China Company, continuing to operate in Shropshire until 1926. In about 1920 Coalport had been purchased by Cauldon Potteries Ltd. and in 1926 was moved to the Cauldon Works at Shelton, Staffordshire. In 1936 a new takeover brought in George Jones, from which date Coalport, Cauldon and George Jones were trading as one, under the name of the Crescent Pottery until 1950, when the trade name of Coalport was revived. In 1958 the pottery was closed

Miniature Coalport cabaret with 'jewelled' decoration consisting of enamel to simulate pearls on a turquoise ground. Exhibited at the 1893 Chicago World Fair, where Coalport wares were awarded a gold medal. Mark, Crown/Coalport/A.D. 1750 printed in green. Courtesy Phillips, London

and a new owner, E. Brain, purchased Coalport and George Jones, and moved the production to Fenton, whilst Cauldon Potteries Ltd were purchased by Pountney of Bristol, and from 1963 all the products were called Coalport.

In 1967 the Wedgwood Group became the new owners and since 1988 some of the former Coalport tablewares are made under the trade mark of Wedgwood, whilst Coalport wares are restricted to figures and giftwares.

FURTHER READING:

Godden, G.A., *Coalport & Coalbrookdale Porcelains,* (new edition) Antique Collectors' Club, 1981; *Victorian Porcelain,* Herbert Jenkins, 1961.
Niblett, Kathy, *Dynamic Designs, The British Pottery Industry 1940-1990,* Exhibition at City Museum & Art Gallery, Stoke-on-Trent, 1990.

G.F. BOWERS

c.1841-1871

Among the many Staffordshire ceramic manufacturers whose fine quality wares won recognition at the Great Exhibition of 1851 was that of George Frederick Bowers, who was producing both earthenware and bone china at his own pottery of Brownhills Works, Tunstall and also at another pottery in the area, where he was in partnership with Challinor and Wooliscroft, a partnership which ceased in 1849.

The designs deposited with the Patent Office at the time of the registration have enabled some of their otherwise unmarked porcelain to be recognised. Bowers produced a wide range of wares, including dessert services and tea wares, many of which were decorated with transfer prints further decorated with hand tinting in enamel colours, a style of decoration requiring only the skills of the engraver of the copperplates used to produce the paper prints, enabling unskilled painters or learners to fill in the design as required.

G.F. Bowers was yet another firm that adopted the fractional form of numbering their patterns, which approximated to about 100 a year during their earlier period. The son Frederick Thomas Bowers was less successful than his father and within three years of his taking over the business it failed in 1871.

Bone china teapot, painted in enamel colours and gilt on a buff ground. Made by George F. Bowers at Tunstall, c.1845. The shape was registered at the Patent Office 14 December, 1843. Mark, '239. Worcester'. H. 19.7cm.
Courtesy Mr. and Mrs. P. Miller

Cup and saucer in bone china, painted in enamel colours and gilt with pattern number 2/742. The design for this form was registered at the Patent Office by G.F. Bowers & Co. of Tunstall, Staffordshire, on 20 June 1848. (Parcel No. 4). D. (saucer) 15cm.
Courtesy City Museum & Art Gallery, Stoke-on-Trent

J. & M.P. BELL (Glasgow Pottery)
1841-1910

There must be little doubt that the Scottish ceramic factory best known for its production of fine bone china was that established in 1841 by two brothers, John and Matthew Person Bell, although by 1880 both brothers had died, the production was continued until 1910, after which the concern traded solely as merchants until finally closing in 1941.

From the start they made a wide variety of ceramic bodies and at the 1851 Great Exhibition in Hyde Park, they showed earthenware, stoneware, porcelain and a selection of Parian ware figures and other ornamental wares, for which they received an honourable mention. In *The Ceramic Art of Great Britain* by Llewellynn Jewitt, published in 1878, he wrote of their wares as being of a 'superior class — equal to most English makes; while some of the tea-services are of tall classic form and of excellent taste in colour and decoration'.

The wares of this factory are well represented in the catalogue of the exhibition held in Glasgow during August, 1990, entitled 'Glimpses of Glasgow's Pottery Tradition 1800-1900', where apart from a wide range of earthenwares with printed designs, some of which were registered at the Patent Office, were shown several moulded Parian ware jugs, all bearing a form of the J. & M.P. Bell & Co. mark, to which was added 'Ltd' in 1881.

Tea wares of bone china, painted in enamel colours and gilt, made by the Glasgow firm of J. & M.P. Bell, c.1870, at the Glasgow Pottery, the cups of classical shape with high handles.
Private Collection

Two porcelain comports, painted in enamel colours, with green borders, c.1870. The view on the right is of Garelochhead, that on the left is an unidentified river scene. Mark, on named piece. J.B. in bell impressed, for J. & M.P. Bell of the Glasgow Potteries. D. 23.5cm.

Private Collection

Their bone china plates were usually decorated with a well painted, named view of a Scottish beauty spot, such as Loch Katrine, Loch Lomond or the Trossachs, although flowers were occasionally painted.

Other Scottish factories which attempted to produce and market bone china, included Verreville and the Saracen Pottery, where Nautilus Porcelain ware was made, but these factories tended to concentrate on pottery, which seemingly enjoyed more success than their porcelains, which were only produced for very short periods.

FURTHER READING:
Jewitt, Llewellynn, *Ceramic Art of Great Britain,* Virtue & Co., London, 1878.
Fleming, Arnold, *Scottish Pottery,* Maclehose, Jackson & Co., Glasgow, 1923.
McVeigh, Patrick, *Scottish East Coast Potteries 1750-1840,* John Donald, Edinburgh, 1979.

PARIAN CHINA

c.1842-early 20th century

Parian ware is a porcellaneous material, which shows some translucency; it has a matt and yet silky surface, which does not require a glaze. The material should not be confused with bisque ware, which is simply an unglazed porcelain with a body which is at times porous in comparison, and a little chalky in texture.

The credit for the early development of Parian ware seems to belong to Thomas Battam, the Art Director of Messrs. Copeland and Garrett, shared with John Mountford, who had previously been employed as a figure maker at the Derby factory. It was suggested by John Haslem in his book *The Old Derby China Factory* published in 1876 that Mountford accidentally invented the Parian body whilst trying to rediscover the lost recipe of the old Derby biscuit ware.

One of the first and most successful Copeland & Garrett productions in Parian ware, was this figure of 'Narcissus', date 1846. Copied from a statue by John Gibson, commissioned by the Art Union of London and bearing a special mark including the name and date. H. 31cm.

Private Collection

Called 'The Bitten Tongue', this Parian mustard pot was designed by John Bell for Summerly's Art Manufactures, c.1847 Courtesy Minton Museum, Royal Doulton Ltd

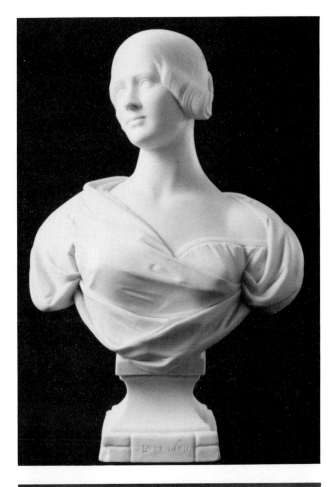

Parian portrait bust of the actress and singer Jenny Lind, modelled by Samuel Joseph in 1847. Theatrical figures were a favourite subject with Minton and included such famous people as Henry Irving, Sarah Bernhardt and Mrs Siddons
Courtesy Minton Museum, Royal Doulton Ltd

This Parian ware figure 'The Distressed Mother' after the original by Sir Richard Westmacott, was especially made for the Summerly's Art Manufactures, c.1847. This sculptor was one of many from whom Henry Cole commissioned designs, c.1847-50   Courtesy Minton Museum, Royal Doulton Ltd

This Parian figure was introduced by Wedgwood in 1849. It represents Ariadne, who gave her lover Theseus a sword to kill the Minotaur and then find his way out of the labyrinth with a thread. H. 23cm.
Courtesy Wedgwood Museum Trustees, Barlaston, Stoke-on-Trent

319

Parian ware was used at Minton for a variety of wares other than figures. This font is based on that at St. Mary Magdalene, Oxford, and it is suggested that these miniature fonts were made for the baptism of infants who were too ill to be taken to the church. This version was made c.1850, and was also produced in bone china or stoneware. H. 14.3cm.

Courtesy Minton Museum, Royal Doulton Ltd

Minton made a variety of sixty-eight busts and fifty portrait figures, apart from their huge production of other figures, all in Parian ware from the late 1840s. This figure of Princess Beatrice appears in their figure shape book as number 366   Courtesy Minton Museum, Royal Doulton Ltd

There were other claimants to the discovery, including the firm of Minton, but certainly by 1846 it was the firm of Copeland & Garrett which was successful in marketing this new ware. The material itself was likened to marble, and one of their first productions was a copy of John Gibson's statue of 'Narcissus', reproduced by E.R. Stephens, and commissioned by the Art Union of London. This figure, as with other Art Union pieces, bore a special mark, including the name and date, in this case 1846.

The Art Union of London was formed in 1836 to promote sales of works of art, and to encourage membership; lotteries were organised yearly, for which prizes were given. These prizes were mainly in the form of contemporary paintings from the Royal Academy, but lesser awards were also made, and what could be more appropriate than to provide these miniature statues, for the Victorian parlour. There is no doubt that the interest and encouragement shown by the Art Union of London, followed by others in many other parts of

This Parian figure of Miranda was produced by Minton, and modelled by John Bell for the Felix Summerly's Art Manufactures. The model, introduced in January 1850, became very popular and was even selected as a prize for the Art Union. It is interesting to note that the garland of sea shells was moulded separately, and hangs as a loose adornment. Year Mark Imp. 1876. H. 38cm.

Private Collection

This Parian figure was produced by Minton in the 19th century and was so popular that it was still in production at the beginning of the 20th century. It is a copy of a marble statue by the American sculptor Hiram Powers, and was considered to be one of the gems of the Great Exhibition held in Hyde Park in 1851, warranting its own specially erected canopy.

Minton Museum, Royal Doulton Ltd.

Britain, was a tremendous help in promoting the popularity of Parian wares.

Under the pseudonym of 'Felix Summerly', Henry Cole, the Director of the South Kensington Museum (which from 1899 became known as the Victoria & Albert Museum), also helped to popularise these new wares, for in 1847, he established the Summerly's Art Manufactures, a business aimed at improving public taste, by producing wares designed by well-known artists of the day. Queen Victoria was interested in the scheme, and purchased some of the most important pieces. Unfortunately difficulties arose with the manufacturers, and the wares did not sell easily. Henry Cole also became deeply involved in the organisation and planning of the Great Exhibition, and in 1850, after only three years in business, the company came to an end. It was, however, responsible for the production of some fine wares, including the figure of 'Dorothea', from Cervantes' *Don Quixote,* modelled by John Bell, and manufactured by Minton.

PARIAN CHINA

Two Parian busts marked C. Delpech and made by W. & T. Copeland for the Art Union of London. The bust of Apollo on the left was produced in 1861 and is a copy of a statue 'Apollo Belvedere' which is in the Vatican, Rome. The bust of Clytie on the right, published in 1855, is after a Greco-Roman marble in the British Museum, London. It is fitting that these busts should be shown together, as according to mythology Clytie was beloved by Apollo, turned into a sunflower, and forever followed his path in the sky, with her beautiful head. H. (Apollo) 38cm. (Clytie) 35cm.

Courtesy Bearnes, Torquay

Pair of Parian figures, made by Bates, Brown-Westhead Moore & Co., c.1859-61, representing Euterpe, the muse of music, and Thalia, the muse of comedy. Bates was in partnership with Brown-Westhead & Co. from c.1858-61, after which date it became Brown-Westhead, Moore & Co. H. 37.5cm.

Courtesy Bearnes, Torquay

Large Copeland Parian ware group, entitled 'Go to SLEEP'. Marked, J. DURHAM Sc. Copyright Reserved 1862. Joseph Durham R.A. (1814-1877) allowed much of his original work to be reproduced by Copeland, including busts of Queen Victoria and the Prince Consort in 1855. H. 48cm. Private Collection

An interesting though unmarked Parian group, factory unknown, c.1860. H. 35cm. Courtesy Bearnes, Torquay

This Parian bust was made by Messrs. W.T. Copeland for the Ceramic & Crystal Palace Art Union in 1861. Known as the 'Veiled Bride', it is copied from an original sculpture by Rafaelle Monti (1818-1881). This bust was one of their most popular productions. H. 37cm. Courtesy City Museum & Art Gallery, Stoke-on-Trent

A Parian group from Kerr & Binns Worcester period, of Faust and Margaret from a set of three groups of lovers; the others in the series are of Romeo and Juliet and Henda and Hafed. These figures were produced from 1862. Printed mark in light blue. H. 33cm.   Courtesy Bearnes, Torquay

Parian figure of Psyche, modelled by Albert Ernest Carrier, and produced by Minton in 1864. Painted in pale matt colours and gold. Impressed marks and date code. H. 42cm.

Courtesy Bearnes, Torquay

This figure was a great success, and was reproduced for many years, adding greatly to the popularity of the new material. A special mark was used on these wares of 'F.S.' in a monogram raised on a pad.

The Victorian era was the age of the great exhibitions, which were held in many prestigious cities throughout the world, including New York in 1853, Paris in 1855, Vienna in 1873 and Melbourne in 1879. These, among other major cities, became shop windows for British products throughout the world. The most spectacular, however, must have been the Great Exhibition of 1851, which was held in Hyde Park in London. It was on this occasion that the most magnificent display of Parian ware was exhibited by all the leading manufacturers. Queen Victoria was particularly impressed by a fine dessert service, produced by Messrs. Minton. The service was of two materials, incorporating in the centrepieces, figures of Parian, supporting dishes of bone china, lavishly decorated in turquoise and gold, reminiscent of the best work of the Sèvres factory. The Queen purchased the service, and later gave it to the Emperor of Austria; it is now on display in the Schönbrunn Palace in Vienna.

A duplicate piece from the service may be seen in the Victoria & Albert Museum in London.

Parian ware was expensive to produce, involving great skills. The figures were moulded, and in some intricate groups as many as fifty separate pieces were used. As the figures were prone to excessive shrinkage during firing, from as much as 25% to 33%, they had to be supported by props made of the same material, the end of the props which touched the figure were coated with flint dust, to prevent them adhering. Great care had to be taken during the week allowed for drying out, in order to be certain that there were no signs of slipping or warping. Firing the wares was also a hazardous procedure. The temperature was taken to 1100 degrees centigrade, which was maintained for at least sixty hours. After being allowed to cool, the props were removed, the figures were 'tidied up', and then placed within a saggar filled with sand, and again placed into the kiln for a second higher firing, which turned the material into a vitrified mass.

Of great help to the manufacturers of figures at this time was a machine invented by Benjamin Cheverton, for which he was granted a patent in 1844. This machine allowed sculpture of any size to be accurately reduced to the scale required by the potter. Cheverton usually worked from his own studio, and produced the master models, usually in alabaster, from which the manufacturers could make their models. This amazing machine can be seen in the Science Museum, South Kensington, London.

Not all Parian ware was left in the white; at times gilding was used to highlight certain parts of the figure, and Messrs. Minton were particularly successful in adding delicate colours to their pieces. Coloured wares, however, did not really appear generally, until after the Great Exhibition. In some cases the mixture itself was tinted, especially in the case of hollow wares such as jugs and vases, which were also made. The interiors of the useful wares were glazed in most cases.

The standard of the principal manufacturers was exceedingly high, not only in workmanship, but also in their aesthetic approach. Much care was taken to produce accurate figures in classical style, and well-known artists and modellers were employed, such as John Bell and Léon Arnoux, who modelled for Minton. John Henry Foley, A.R.A., who modelled for Messrs. Copeland, and John Gibson, R.A., known for his famous work 'Narcissus' as mentioned previously. Popular figures of the day were also produced, including musicians, politicians, religious groups and figures of Royalty, all reflecting the life of the times.

The leading manufacturers used special trade names for their Parian wares. Messrs. Copeland & Garrett and W.T. Copeland named their wares 'Statuary Porcelain', whilst Wedgwood took the name 'Carrara' from the marble quarries in Northern Italy. Kerr & Binns named their wares 'Irish Statuary Porcelain', obviously because they obtained their felspar used in the production from Ireland. It was the firm of Minton, however, who were responsible for the name 'Parian', named after the marble quarried on the Greek island of 'Paros',

This portrait bust of Queen Victoria, in Parian, was made by Robinson & Leadbeater to commemorate her jubilee in 1897. H. 41cm. Courtesy City Museum & Art Gallery, Stoke-on-Trent

This Parian figure is a good example of an added tint used to highlight the body; in this case, the figure is draped in a pale green robe. Made at the Royal Worcester Factory, the 'Bather Surprised' is taken from an original model by Sir Thomas Brock. The figure was first produced in 1902. Impressed marks. H. 66.5cm.
Courtesy Bearnes, Torquay

Two early Goss Parian ware busts; the unglazed bust of Gladstone on the left was made in the 'First Period' of W.H. Goss and is dated 1876. H. 16.7cm. The bust on the right is of the Earl of Granville, and bears the same date. These busts were considered to be above average, and excellent likenesses.
Courtesy Nicholas J. Pine of Goss & Crested China Ltd

This figure of Lady Godiva, made in the late 19th century by W.H. Goss, is of exceptional quality.
H. 16.5cm. Courtesy City Museum & Art Gallery, Stoke-on-Trent

which became the popular name for the whole range of wares.

Among the other manufacturers engaged in the production of Parian ware, were the Belleek Pottery Ltd., who mainly glazed their wares, and Robinson & Leadbeater, who confined their production almost solely to this type of porcelain.

There were many other firms who were engaged to a lesser degree in the manufacture of Parian; almost one hundred are listed, but by the turn of the century its popularity had waned, although some Parian is known to have been produced in smaller quantities at Minton's up to 1939.

FURTHER READING:

Godden, G.A., *Victorian Porcelain,* Herbert Jenkins Ltd., 1961.
Shinn, Charles and Dorrie, *The Illustrated Guide to Victorian Parian Ware,* Barrie & Jenkins, 1971.
Atterbury, P., *The Parian Phenomenon,* Richard Dennis, 1988.

A range of bone china miniatures, made at Minton from the 1830s until c.1920. The pieces illustrated show a jug of c.1840 and a teapot and loving cup of c.1890. The sizes of these miniatures, made for display rather than playthings, range from 7 to 12cm.
Courtesy Minton Museum, Royal Doulton Ltd

'Easy Johnny', a porcelain figure, is unmarked but attributed to Minton, c.1830-40. It has a 'nodding' head and is fashioned after the Meissen figure modelled by J.J. Kaendler in 1737 of Joseph Fröhlich, the court jester at the court of Augustus in Dresden, Saxony (lacking the hat on the original). H. 17.9cm.
R.H. Williamson Bequest, Tullie House, Carlisle

MINTON

1845-present

Following the death of Herbert Minton in 1858, the two remaining partners, Michael Daintry Hollins and Colin Campbell, took Robert Minton Campbell, a nephew of the founder, into partnership. There were ten prosperous years until 1868, when following a dispute the partnership was dissolved, with Hollins leaving with a 'golden handshake' of £30,000. Hollins established his own tile production, for which Minton had already built up a high reputation, having during the 1840s supplied tiles for the Chapter House at Westminster, Osborne House, the home of Queen Victoria on the Isle of Wight, and the Houses of Parliament.

From the early Victorian period Minton produced not only a wide range of Parian ware, but also made many unglazed bisque flowers, on which the Continental technique of using real lace was often used in their decoration. In this very simple operation the lace was saturated in slip (watered down clay) and attached where required; during the firing the fabric burnt away leaving a perfect reproduction in porcelain.

By the 1860s the firm of Minton had built up a reputation unmatched in Britain and their products were highly acclaimed at all the International Exhibitions where their wares were exhibited. Léon Arnoux (b.1816) was the first of a long line of Continental ceramic designers and artists to be employed by the firm, when in about 1848 he was appointed chemist, and later Art Director, but his greatest influence is seen on the coloured glazed earthenwares, 'Majolica', which received such high praise at the 1851 Exhibition in Hyde

Two bone china plates from a service made for Lord Milton. The scenes from life in North West Canada are painted from the drawings made by his companion, Dr. Cheadle, on their expedition in 1862-3 to find the North West Passage by land. Each piece is decorated with Lord Milton's monogram. A second service without the monogram was made for Dr. Cheadle and is still with his descendants. The service shows a very early use of acid etched gilding
Courtesy Minton Museum, Royal Doulton Ltd

Pot-pourri vase in Minton bone china, fashioned after an 18th century Sèvres original, painted in enamel colours with a rose ground and gilding, c.1870. H. 25.8cm.　Courtesy Bearnes, Torquay

A design for a spill vase by Christopher Dresser for Minton, c.1867. Dresser (1834-1904) supplied Minton with designs for a wide range of wares, only some of which were put into production
Courtesy Minton Museum, Royal Doulton Ltd

Park. Although he retired in 1892 he was associated with the factory until his death in 1902. His value to the factory is reflected in his high salary of £1,500, which was about four times that of their finest painters.

Thomas Allen (1831-1915) was apprenticed to Minton at a very early age. He specialised in painting figures on Sèvres style vases, c.1854-75, when he became Chief Designer to Josiah Wedgwood & Sons. This vase illustrates the Four Seasons and was exhibited at the 1851 Exhibition. H. 50.8cm.

Courtesy Minton Museum, Royal Doulton Ltd

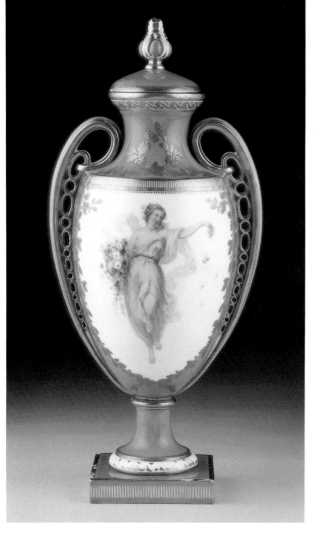

Thomas Allen (1831-1915) was apprenticed to Minton at a very early age. He specialised in painting figures on Sèvres style vases, c.1854-75, when he became Chief Designer to Josiah Wedgwood & Sons. This vase, symbolic of Spring, is from a pair of vases illustrating the Four Seasons, which were exhibited at the 1851 Exhibition Courtesy Minton Museum, Royal Doulton Ltd

A covered bowl of glazed and enamelled bone china, with Parian ware figures and finial. This piece matches a service that was made for the 1851 Exhibition and was then presented by Queen Victoria to the Emperor of Austria. H. 25.5cm. Courtesy The Victorian & Albert Museum

Among the other Continental painters employed, was Christian Henk, who was painting landscapes and figure subjects in the style of Sèvres, from about 1854 into the early 1880s, but being unsigned, his work is sometimes difficult to attribute with certainty. Another German painter and designer was Ludwig

Comport and plate of bone china from a dessert service painted by Antonin Boullemier, after Angelica Kaufmann, in 1878. Comports, or raised dishes, were popular with hostesses to give a variation in the height of table settings, during the 19th century. Minton produced over fifty comports in a variety of shapes
Courtesy Minton Museum, Royal Doulton Ltd

Jahn, who became Henk's son-in-law, and specialised in figure subjects after such painters as Watteau and Raphael; he was active from about 1862 to the early 1870s and was later to return as Art Director from 1893 to 1903, having been Art Director for Brownfields in the meantime. It is interesting to note that from 1903 to 1911 he was Curator at the Hanley Museum, now the City Museum & Art Gallery, the foremost ceramic museum in Britain. Another outstanding painter, whose work is much in demand today, was Antonin Boullemier, whose father had been a decorator at Sèvres, where he himself served his apprenticeship as a figure painter, before migrating to England in about 1871 and being engaged at Minton's from c.1872-1900, where his paintings of portraits, cupids and mythological subjects reflected his earlier association with Sèvres, although some of his later work of contemporary scenes make a pleasing change. His two sons, Henri and Lucien, were both active at Minton's from the late nineteenth century to the early twentieth century, painting very much in the same manner as their father. In the early 1870s another Paris trained figure painter, Desiré Leroy, was employed for about sixteen years before moving to Royal Crown Derby; Leroy and his work are discussed in more detail under Royal Crown Derby.

William Mussill, an Austrian, was also an active painter at Minton from about 1872, his most admired work resulting from his original sketches made from nature and local landscapes, flowers and birds.

Today 'china painting' is a popular occupation with large numbers of people, both with independent professionals and amateurs, who purchase the glazed readily available blanks in either a hard-paste or bone china, but this employment or hobby is by no means new. It was in 1871 that Colin Campbell established the London Art Pottery Studio in South Kensington, under the direction of the talented ceramic painter, W.S. Coleman, who had already built

One of a pair of Minton dessert plates, with pierced gilt border and painted in white enamel on a turquoise ground, signed by the painter Leroy. Marks, 'MINTONS' impressed together with the impressed year cypher for 1877, printed with the name and address of 'A.B. DANIELL & SON, 46 Wigmore Street, LONDON', the retailer, who continued in business until 1917. D. 24cm. Courtesy Andrew Hartley Fine Arts, Ilkley

Minton bone china vase, decorated and signed by L.A. Birks, with pâte-sur-pâte panel on a dark blue ground, depicting a cherub on a globe in white on a green ground, heavily decorated in gilt, c.1875. H. 26cm. Courtesy Bearnes, Torquay

Pair of Minton bone-china 'moon flasks', decorated in the pâte-sur-pâte technique by Louis Marc Solon. The putto on the left with buckets being symbolic of Water and that on the right with burning torches, Fire. Made in about 1890. H. 26.5cm.

Bearnes of Torquay

up a high reputation as a designer and watercolour artist before being employed by Minton in 1869.

The *Art Journal* of 1870 states that Mr. Coleman 'will select a few skilled painters from Stoke and students from the National Art Training Schools at Kensington and conduct a class for practical china painting. . .it is hoped that with its facilities, eminent artists (ladies especially) may be induced to paint porcelain and majolica'. Despite a very encouraging start the venture was soon to prove a very expensive experiment and few tears were shed by the Stoke management when the studio was burnt down in 1875. Many of the amateurs attending these classes made a practice of signing and dating their work, but collectors are warned that these signatures are most unlikely to appear in any ceramic mark book and are mostly on earthenware.

It was from about 1872 that the name of MINTON, which was included in the majority of their marks, was changed to MINTONS, although on their present day Fine Bone China, the word MINTON is again used, together with the pattern name in many instances.

Without doubt the name most associated with the later nineteenth century Minton's porcelain is that of Louis Marc Solon (*b*.1835), yet another French

Without the opportunity of handling it would be hard to identify these Oriental style vases as Minton, c.1870. It was their Art Director Joseph François Léon Arnoux (1816-1912) who was responsible for introducing these fine monochrome glazes. Courtesy Minton Museum, Royal Doulton Ltd

A pair of Minton bone china teacups and saucers, decorated with figures in enamel colours amidst profusely applied gilding in Japanese taste. Mark on saucers 'MINTONS' and year mark for 1876 impressed, with purple printed mark on all four pieces of 'A.B. DANIELL & SON. Wigmore Street, London', the retailer. D. (saucer) 13.5cm. Private Collection

Rare Minton coffee can and saucer, decorated in pâte-sur-pâte technique and signed with the initials L.B. for Lawrence Birks, one of the few artists trained by Louis Marc Solon whom he allowed to sign their work. Mark (on saucer), 'MINTONS' and year symbol for 1876 impressed and printed mark of 'MINTONS' on globe under a crown in gold on cup and saucer. D. (saucer) 11.5cm. Private Collection

trained designer and artist. The event that persuaded so many of these people to migrate at that time was doubtless the Franco-German War (1870-1) when the French were heavily defeated and Paris sustained a four months siege. Solon

Two bone china plates from a Minton dessert service painted in colour with cherubs playing on a variety of sea shells, c.1880, by Antonin Boullemier (1840-1900), who was active as a Minton painter, c.1872-1900
Courtesy Minton Museum, Royal Doulton Ltd

During the 1880s, in common with many contemporary factories, Minton produced many wares in Japanese taste. Europeans became aware of these Far Eastern pieces following the opening up of Japan to trade by Commander Perry, the American naval officer, in 1854 and their displays at the International Exhibition in 1862. The pierced decoration filled with glaze was at one time mistakenly thought to be achieved by inserting rice grains into the body before firing, which then burnt away leaving the resulting aperture to be filled with glaze, hence the term 'rice-grain' decoration
Courtesy Minton Museum, Royal Doulton Ltd

A Minton bone china vase of about 1890, made in the form of a well-known Sèvres model designed by J.-C. Duplessis, who was employed at the factory from 1754 to 1774. An original in the Wallace Collection painted by C.-N. Dodin is 37.7cm high and may have belonged to Madame de Pompadour
Courtesy Minton Museum, Royal Doulton Ltd

From the 1830s Minton made some outstanding reproductions of Sèvres in their fine bone china; this centrepiece, termed a vaisseau à mât, *dates to c.1900, and was made originally as a pot-pourri. Such wares were produced at Mintons in the 1920s. The masted vessel is thought to be derived from the arms of the city of Paris. The original is 44cm. high*

Courtesy Minton Museum, Royal Doulton Ltd

A popular shape, first produced at Sèvres and known as the vase hollandois, *enabled one to change the water in the separate base without disturbing the flower arrangement. Made at Mintons in bone china, c.1900 and painted by L. Boullemier in the manner of Morin, the famous French decorator. H. 19.5cm.*

Courtesy Minton Museum Royal Doulton Ltd

claimed to have perfected his technique of decorating in *pâte-sur-pâte* at Sèvres in 1862 before joining Minton's in 1870, although it is known that some Minton wares were produced by this technique as early as the late 1850s. This laborious and highly skilled method of decoration involved the use of Parian clay slips, which were applied in layers on to the unfired tinted body of the ware until sufficient depth of clay was built up to enable the modeller to carve the work as a bas-relief. This technique was different from the method employed by Wedgwood and some of his contemporaries, where the contrasting colour decorations were merely casts taken from the moulds and sprigged on to the surface of the ware, possibly with a certain amount of hand finishing. Recent research described in *The Dictionary of Minton* by Paul Atterbury and Maureen Batkin, suggests however that a certain amount of casting did take place. Such was the demand for these wares, despite their high price, that Solon alone was not capable of supplying the market and he was compelled to accept a group of assistants who often did work bearing the master's name, although eventually some, such as Lawrence Birks, Frederick Rhead and Charles Toft, were permitted to apply their own signatures to their modelling. Although Solon continued to work for Minton up to his retirement at the age of sixty-nine, he continued to work independently until his death in 1913.

There were dark years at Mintons and from 1886 to 1900 the company made large annual losses and would have failed but for the timely help of the former Art Director, Léon Arnoux, who was called back from retirement at the age of eighty-four and with the skills of newly appointed Art Director, Léon Solon, and his very able assistant John Wadsworth, the company survived. The main influence of this management is seen on the earthenware of the Secessionist movement, which introduced a style inspired by the Continental *art nouveau*.

Following the difficult post-war years, it was the greatly loved Reginald Haggar (*d.* 1988) who was faced with a very demanding task when he arrived at the factory in 1929. Shortly afterwards he became the Art Director and introduced many modern style patterns and shapes before leaving in 1935, after a further series of annual losses. Under the directorship of John Wadsworth there was a slight improvement in 1936, but it was not until 1941, after the output of Mintons was confined solely to fine china, that sufficient confidence was gained in the factory to bring about a merger in 1968 with Doulton's, known from 1973 as Royal Doulton Tableware Ltd, and from 1984 as Royal Doulton Ltd.

FURTHER READING:

Atterbury, Paul and Batkin, Maureen, *The Dictionary of Minton,* Antique Collectors' Club, 1990.

Godden, G.A., *Victorian Porcelain,* Barrie & Jenkins, 1961.

From 1842 the firm of Minton adopted the practice of applying an impressed mark to show the year of manufacture, usually in addition to the full factory mark in use at the time. When filled in with glaze these marks are at times difficult to read correctly, but if held before a transmitted light it becomes easier.

This dating method was stopped in 1942, when the 'V' for Victory was used, during World War II.

From 1943 the more conventional system was used consisting of sets of three cyphers indicating the month, the potter's mark and the year, for example '52' indicates the year 1952, etc.

YEARLY MARKS OF MINTONS LTD.
1842–1942

1842	1843	1844	1845	1846	1892	1893	1894	1895	1896
1847	1848	1849	1850	1851	1897	1898	1899	1900	1901
1852	1853	1854	1855	1856	1902	1903	1904	1905	1906
1857	1858	1859	1860	1861	1907	1908	1909	1910	1911
1862	1863	1864	1865	1866	1912	1913	1914	1915	1916
1867	1868	1869	1870	1871	1917	1918	1919	1920	1921
1872	1873	1874	1875	1876	1922	1923	1924	1925	1926
1877	1878	1879	1880	1881	1927	1928	1929	1930	1931
1882	1883	1884	1885	1886	1932	1933	1934	1935	1936
1887	1888	1889	1890	1891	1937	1938	1939	1940	1941
							1942		

THE KING STREET FACTORY, DERBY
c.1848-1935

The original Nottingham Road works of the Derby factory was occupied by the son-in-law of Robert Bloor (the former owner who was forced to retire through mental illness in 1828), until 1848, when it was closed.

Much of the equipment was purchased by Samuel Boyle, who was already operating a china and earthenware pottery at Fenton, Staffordshire, having just moved from Stoke. At this same time Sampson Hancock, who had previously worked at the failed factory, got together with five of the former Derby workers

A pair of Derby pedestal vases, painted in enamel colours and gilt with bouquets of flowers, both back and front, in a dark blue ground, early 19th century. The swan handles appear to be very rare and are not pictured in the major books on Derby wares. Marked with the crown, crossed batons and D, in red. H. 24.8cm.

Courtesy Bearnes, Torquay

Three campana shaped vases, painted in enamel and gilt and made at Derby, early 19th century. The large vase is inscribed 'Near Windley, Derbyshire'. H. 20.5cm. The two smaller vases are inscribed 'In Cumberland' and 'In Wales'. Mark, crown, crossed batons and D in red

Courtesy Bearnes, Torquay

339

Rare shaped coffee pot, made at Derby and dated 1809. The landscapes in the reserves are attributed to John and Robert Brewer and named on base 'Castle at Spoleto' and 'The approach to the Cascade at Ferni'. Mark, crown, crossed batons and 'D' in red   Courtesy Royal Crown Derby Museum

Derby porcelain dessert dish and vase, painted in enamel colours and gilt, attributed to Richard Dobson, who specialised in 'carelessly drawn' brightly coloured birds, working at Derby, c.1813-20, during the Robert Bloor period. Mark, circular Bloor/Derby in red enamel. W. (dessert dish) 24cm.   Courtesy Phillips, London

Two dessert dishes and inkstand, made at Derby, c.1815-20. The dish on the left has an unusual moulded border, with gilt decoration on a dark blue ground, possibly painted by Robert Brewer with a 'View of Germany'. L. 29.2cm. The dish on the right, also possibly by Brewer, is entitled 'In Devonshire'. L. 22.4cm. The inkstand is decorated with gilt on a dark blue ground and an unidentified landscape. L. 29.5cm.

Courtesy Bearnes, Torquay

and together they established their own factory with some of the material still available. In fact he claimed at the time to be 'transplanting the Nottingham Road works to my present factory — King Street'. This new factory first operated under the name of Locker & Co., Late Bloor. William Locker had formerly been the Chief Clerk of the Bloor Works, but when he died in 1859, George Stevenson, a draper, was taken into partnership and the company continued under various partnership titles until 1863, when for a three year period it became Stevenson & Hancock. The old mark of the Derby factory was adopted, comprising a crown over crossed batons over a letter 'D', with three dots at either end of the batons, but replacing the dots with the initials 'S' and

A rare elongated campana shaped vase, the blue ground is heavily decorated with gilt and has a scene in enamel colours of Linmore in Ireland, which is attributed to the painter John Brewer, c.1812-15. Made by Robert Bloor & Co. of Derby. Marked with crown, crossed batons and 'D' in red enamel
Courtesy Royal Crown Derby Museum

This model of a peacock was first modelled by John Whitaker, jun., at the Nottingham Road factory, c.1829. Whitaker was apprenticed to learn modelling and figure making in 1818, and became superintendent of the figure makers on the retirement of Samuel Keys in 1830. He remained at the factory until the closure in 1848, and for the last six years was foreman of the entire potting department. This same model of Peacock among Flowers, is still produced at the Royal Crown Derby factory. H. c.13cm.
Courtesy Royal Crown Derby Porcelain Company

The series of figures symbolic of the 'Four Elements' first appear to have been made at the Derby Porcelain factory, c.1773, when they were modelled by Pierre Stephan. After this factory came to an end in 1848 some of the workers went to a new, smaller factory in nearby King Street, where they continued to produce wares in the Derby tradition. Among these various partnerships were Stevenson & Hancock, who were operating from c.1862-6. These four figures were made at that time and are marked with the crown, crossed batons and D mark in red, with S and H on either side of mark. H. 17cm.

Courtesy Bearnes, Torquay

341

Derby plate made for Mr. John Trotter of Dyrham Park, near Barnet, Hertfordshire. The floral decoration is attributed to Moses Webster, c.1820-5; this is a fairly common pattern and only the pieces marked with the crown, crossed batons and 'D' in gold rather than red are considered to have come from Mr. Trotter's service. D. 24.5cm. Courtesy of Royal Crown Derby Museum

A pair of ornate Derby vases decorated with applied fruit and flowers and landscape paintings attributed to Daniel Lucas, sen., who came to Derby from Davenport, c.1820. Made during the Robert Bloor period, c.1840. Mark, crown over Gothic 'D' in red enamel. H. 25.5cm. Courtesy Royal Crown Derby Museum

A pair of rare Derby porcelain musicians, painted in enamel colours and gilt, made during the Robert Bloor period, c.1825. They are modelled after those made at the Chelsea factory, c.1755, who in turn were probably copying Meissen figures. Mark, a crown over DERBY and number 32 in red enamel. H. 16.5cm. Courtesy Royal Crown Derby Museum

Pair of porcelain figures, known as 'The French Shepherd and Shepherdess' painted in the strong enamel colours of the 1825-35 period, later described in the King Street factory list of 1934 as 'English Shepherd and Shepherdess', the latter has the printed circular mark of Bloor and both have number 57 incised. H. 14cm. Courtesy Royal Crown Derby Museum

Derby porcelain basket, with landscape in enamel colours attributed to Edward Prince, a landscape painter at the Derby works until its closure in 1848. The ground colour is pale blue. Mark, a crown over Gothic 'D'. Made during the Robert Bloor period, c.1835-40. L. 13cm.

Courtesy Royal Crown Derby Museum

A rare Derby covered urn, thought to be an unrecorded shape. The floral panels are attributed to the hand of John Brewer, whilst the high quality gilt decoration is by Samuel Keys, sen., whose number '1' is painted on the foot rim. Made during the Duesbury and Kean period, c.1810. Mark, crown, crossed batons and 'D' in red. H. 33cm.

Courtesy David Holborough Collection, Royal Crown Derby Museum

'H' (Stevenson & Hancock). When Stevenson died the same mark was continued in use, for the same initials were those of Sampson Hancock, under whose name the company continued, although under various relatives and partners, until being purchased by the Royal Crown Derby concern in 1935.

From the time of the establishment of the new factory their wares followed very much the same patterns as those the original partners had been familiar with at the early factory, on dinner, dessert and tea services. Ornamental wares were all in the popular Japan styles, which is a pattern most commonly associated with Derby even today. The fact that both Sampson Hancock and James Hall had formerly been engaged as flower painters also accounts for the high quality of their wares decorated with floral subjects.

This small factory found it difficult to produce enough wares to satisfy their retailers and purchased white wares from other manufacturers including Aynsley, Minton, Worcester Royal Porcelain Company, Josiah Wedgwood (where by 1878 the production of bone china had again started), Coalport and several lesser known manufacturers. These undecorated white wares were sold so very cheaply that one is surprised that the profit would have been sufficient to warrant assisting rival productions in this way.

Among the accomplished painters working at the King Street factory were several who had formerly served their apprenticeship at the Nottingham Road works; these included Edward Prince, a fine landscape painter working from 1863, and James Rouse, sen., a very versatile painter, whose speciality was fruit and flowers, and who after seven years with Hancock left to work at the new Crown Derby Porcelain Company in Osmaston Road in 1882 at the age of eighty-one. Joseph Broughton, apprenticed at the early age of eleven, specialised in Japan patterns, whilst many others too numerous to mention produced flower encrusted wares and figures, including the popular Derby Dwarfs, peacocks, tithe groups, shepherds, gardeners, etc.

In his excellent book *Royal Crown Derby,* John Twitchett points out the fact that this factory did not add the word 'England' to their mark from 1891, which so many other factories did, in order to comply with the requirements of the American McKinley Tariff & Trades Act and consequently the same 'S & H mark mentioned could indicate any date from 1862 up to the time of their merger with the new factory in 1935. The establishment of this small, but most successful factory enables the city of Derby to claim an unbroken history of porcelain manufacture over the past two hundred and forty years.

FURTHER READING:
Twitchett, John, *Royal Crown Derby,* Barrie & Jenkins, 1976; 2nd Edn., 1980; 3rd Edn. published by Antique Collectors' Club, 1988.

KERR & BINNS

1851-1862

It was the ambition of R.W. Binns to produce the same high quality wares that had once been associated with the earlier Worcester factory, and in his book *Worcester China. . . 1852-1897,* he wrote that his aim 'was to exalt the name and enhance the reputation of Worcester porcelain that the new proprietors applied themselves. They felt at the same time that if this work were to be accomplished it must be upon new lines; to revive old styles by old hands would neither show progress or meet the requirements of a newly educated and critical public, a change was imperative'.

A selection of pieces from the famous Shakespeare service made by Kerr & Binns, Worcester, in 1853, when it was exhibited at the Dublin Exhibition. The service was designed by W.B. Kirk and decorated by Thomas Bott. The figure subjects are in Parian ware featuring various characters from A Midsummer Night's Dream, *such as Titania and Oberon. H. (candelabra) 68cm.*

Courtesy Phillips, London

To accomplish this the factory was practically rebuilt and some fine designers and decorators employed, producing such wares as the famous 'Shakespeare' dessert service, which included Parian ware groups depicting characters from *A Midsummer Night's Dream,* designed and modelled by W.B. Kirk, and shown at the Dublin Exhibition in 1853.

Perhaps the most original work in the Kerr & Binns period was that reproducing Limoges enamels of the late fifteenth and sixteenth centuries, when such outstanding painters as Léonard Limosin (or Limousin) were engaged in painting secular work on metal forms in the Mannerist style. These were very fine and much admired wares at the time and not as Llewellynn Jewitt describes them in *The Ceramic Art of Great Britain* in 1878, as 'a coating of porcelain over sheets of metal', a rather derogatory opinion of a fine art even admired by François I and Henri II, who made Limosin, enamel painter to the King. The Kerr & Binns painter, Thomas Bott, who made such a fine job of decorating the bone china reproductions of these early French wares, had previously been employed as a glass painter prior to joining the Worcester concern in 1853, unfortunately too late for the 1851 Exhibition, but his work was later seen and highly praised by Queen Victoria and the Prince Consort.

It was in the Paris International Exhibition of 1855 that the new wares and ceramic bodies made by Kerr & Binns were so highly appreciated 'from those of the highest and most costly character down to articles for ordinary and daily use' (*Art Journal,* 1856).

It was in this same period that the ivory tinted wares were introduced and used for the production of busts, figures, and ornamental pieces. Jewitt is again scathing about the French wares when he compares the early 'Jewelled Porcelain' of Sèvres, introduced about 1773, which he described as 'tinselly', yet highly praises those somewhat similarly decorated wares of Kerr & Binns, such as the déjeuner set made for the Countess of Dudley as a wedding gift.

It was in 1852 that the now familiar mark of Worcester was introduced, consisting of four cursive 'W's within a circle, around '51', for 1751, the date of the establishment of the Worcester factory; this mark was retained in 1862 by the Royal Worcester Company, who merely added a crown above the circle.

FURTHER READING:
Binns, R.W., *Worcester China, A Record of the Work of Forty-five Years 1852-1897,* B. Quaritch, London, 1897.

ADDERLEYS

1852-present

It is again to the invaluable volumes of Jewitt that we turn to learn of the firm of Adderley, first established at the Daisy Bank Pottery in 1852.

A whole succession of potters, including Charles Mason & Co., produced earthenwares and stonewares in this late eighteenth century pottery before 1852, when it was purchased by the partnership of Hulse, Nixon & Adderley. By 1874 both Hulse & Nixon had died, leaving William Alsager Adderley as the

---

Bone china figure of an English robin, painted in natural colours. Mark of Royal Adderley Floral factory, a title used from 1973. The factory started c.1945 and since 1973 has become part of Royal Doulton Ltd. H. 12cm.

Linnet in bone china, made at the Royal Worcester factory in 1942, modelled by Eva L. Soper, and made in unlimited numbers. H. 12.2cm.   Private Collection

sole proprietor, who according to Jewitt was producing china and earthenware for the home, Canadian and New Zealand, as well as for Continental markets. The operation was conducted on a grand scale, their wares consisting of 'breakfast, tea and dessert services, Déjeuner and trinket sets, etc, both plain and ornamental of superior quality'. Jewitt also tells us that no distinctive marks were used on the early wares, a fact that may well account for these exports not being mentioned by Mrs Elizabeth Collard in her excellent book *Nineteenth Century Pottery & Porcelain in Canada,* published in Montreal by the McGill University Press in 1967.

It was probably nearer the 1880s before the printed or impressed initials 'W A A' were used, becoming 'W A A & Co.' in 1886, at the same time as the trade mark of a sailing ship was adopted, probably suggested by their large export trade.

From 1906 the firm was known as Adderleys Ltd. and a variety of marks were used all including the name of the firm until 1947, when Adderleys were purchased by the Lawley Group Ltd. The more recent concern of Adderley Floral China was established in 1945 at Sutherland Road, Longton, producing wares under the trade names of Adderley Floral or Royal Adderley. Today both Adderleys Ltd. and Adderley Floral China are part of a large conglomerate of companies under Royal Doulton, made up from nineteen potteries from Allied English Potteries, with a further four from Doulton and Company.

FURTHER READING:
Jewitt, Llewellynn, *The Ceramic Art of Great Britain,* Virtue & Co., 1878.
Niblett, Kathy, *Dynamic Design,* Exhibition at City Museum & Art Gallery, Stoke-on-Trent, 1990.

Coffee cup and saucer, decorated with lavish gilding over a dark blue ground, made by Aynsley China Ltd., whose work since their beginnings, c.1856, has always been considered to be of the finest quality. Made in 1979. D. (saucer) 12.7cm.
Courtesy City Museum & Art Gallery, Stoke-on-Trent

AYNSLEY

c.1856-present

There was a John Aynsley recorded as a potter at Lane End, Staffordshire, from *c.*1797-1809, but there is no evidence of his having produced porcelain during the early 'bone-china' years and it is another John Aynsley, with whom we are concerned, who was the founder of the firm in Longton from about 1856, of whom Jewitt writes in *The Ceramic Art of Great Britain* in 1878 as making 'China of a superior character' in his Portland Works, at Sutherland Road, Longton.

Today Aynsley wares are proudly exhibited and named at many of the more modest antique fairs, but it must be remembered that the majority of these pieces were made in this century and most bear the word 'England' in the mark, denoting they were made after 1891 in order to comply with the American McKinley Tariff Act, which required the country of origin to be applied to imported wares.

The firm has a very long and confusing history and from 1864 were trading from the Portland Works under the trade name of Aynsley; they became a limited company in 1933 and were quoted on the Stock Exchange in 1948. It was in 1970, after being taken over by Waterford Glass Company, Eire, that the company was renamed Aynsley China Limited, after which they purchased two Longton potteries, Sydney Works in 1973 and Alsager Works in 1980. They were associated for a short while with Josiah Wedgwood & Sons, when that firm was taken over by Waterford Glass, but the following year purchased their independence under the name of Aynsley Group Plc.

Today, following the purchase of the trade names and patterns from Hammersley China Ltd. and Palissy Pottery Ltd. from the owners, The Porcelain and Fine China Companies Ltd., who today are also the owners of Spode and Royal Worcester, they trade under the names of both Aynsley and Hammersley.

FURTHER READING:

Jewitt, Llewellynn, *The Ceramic Art of Great Britain,* Virtue & Co., 1878.
Niblett, Kathy, *Dynamic Design,* Exhibition at City Museum & Art Gallery, Stoke-on-Trent, 1990.

Figure of Fagin, the character from Oliver Twist *by Charles Dickens. Bone china made by Aynsley China Ltd, Lane End, Longton, 1979. H. 23.5cm.*

City Museum & Art Gallery, Stoke-on-Trent

SHELLEY POTTERIES

1857-present

Over recent years the fine bone china produced by the Shelley factory has become highly collectable and is to be seen on offer at most antique fairs. The firm dates back to about 1857, when Henry Wileman first built the Foley China Works at Fenton, where he produced largely unidentified wares until his death in 1864, when he was succeeded by his two sons, James Francis and Charles. Charles retired in 1870 and James continued alone until taking J.B. Shelley into partnership in about 1872, producing both earthenware and porcelain, under the name of Wileman & Co, with the trade name of 'Foley China'.

In 1884 James Wileman retired and J.B. Shelley continued making very average wares until the late 1890s, by which time his son Percy Shelley was taking a very active part in the production and saw how necessary it was to improve the quality and design of their wares if they were to remain competitive. Percy began by engaging talented painters and designers under the directorship of Frederick Rhead, who remained with the firm for nine years. It was after the arrival of his successor in 1905 that more attention was paid to fine china. The new Director was Walter Slater, who had previously worked at both Doulton's and Minton's. In about 1919 Slater was joined by his son Eric, who during his art school training was greatly influenced by the famous and talented Gordon Forsyth, Superintendent of Art Instruction, at the Stoke-on-Trent School of Art. In 1926 the now sought after Queen Anne shape tea wares were introduced, decorated with the Sunrise and Tall Trees pattern, a style of painting that remained in production for many years; in all over 170 various patterns were applied to Queen Anne shaped wares.

It was in about 1930 that two new shapes were introduced, entitled the Vogue and Mode, which appear to be very impracticable for holding hot liquids, being an inverted cone balanced on a very narrow foot, with a solid triangular handle, which could easily slip, but were nevertheless forms quickly imitated by several other major factories. These top-heavy items were subject to much criticism and by 1933 had given way to the new Regent pattern, with comfortable supported ring shaped handles on well-balanced geometric shapes, decorated in the currently popular soft pastel colours. The present day collector favours the less common and short-lived Art Deco styles of the Vogue and Mode.

In 1925 the firm was renamed 'Shelleys', changing to Shelleys Potteries Ltd. in 1929 and to Shelley China Ltd. in 1965, a year before the company was taken over by the Allied English Potteries, who merged with Doulton & Co. Ltd. in 1972, and operate today as Royal Doulton. There is a collectors' club, the Shelley Group, formed in 1986, particulars of which can be obtained from the Curator, Sir Henry Doulton Museum, Royal Doulton, Nile Street, Burslem, Staffs.

FURTHER READING:
Watkins, Harvey and Senft, *Shelley Potteries,* Barrie & Jenkins, 1980.

WILLIAM HENRY GOSS

c.1858-1931

Porcelain souvenirs, that not too long ago were brought home as presents for the parents of children who had been on a Sunday School treat, are now serious collectors' items. We are of course talking of the so-called 'crested' china, first made by William Henry Goss of Stoke-on-Trent. Prior to starting his own factory in 1858, he was the chief designer and modeller for the firm of W.T. Copeland, where he would have become familiar with their production of Parian ware, which was the porcelain body he himself chose to use for his early ornamental wares. These finely produced pieces soon became so popular that it was necessary for him in 1872 to move into larger premises, where in 1883 he was joined by his son Adolphus. It was Adolphus who saw the potential trade in the manufacture of cheap miniature souvenir wares for the 'tripper' and holiday maker. These pieces were often modelled after genuine historical wares,

Typical range of larger Goss models, up to 10cm high, top left to right: Steyning Sea Urchin, with arms of Manor of Bramber; Burton Beer Barrel, with arms of Burton upon Trent; Dark Sack Bottle, with arms of Dartmouth, and Bournemouth Pilgrim Bottle, with arms of Bournemouth. Bottom row, left to right: Winchester Pot, arms of City of Winchester, Bournemouth Ancient Egyptian Lamp, Bournemouth; the Nose of Brasenose, Brasenose College, Oxford
Courtesy Nicholas J. Pine of Goss & Crested China Ltd

Termed an 'OLD FLEMISH MELK POT', this example of W.H. Goss, was made in the 'Second Period', 1900-20. The arms are those of the Borough of Keighley
Courtesy Nicholas J. Pine of Goss & Crested China Ltd

A finely potted example of the 'Second Period' wares of W.H. Goss, 1900-20. Depicting the Bartlow Ewer of Saffron Walden, the seemingly unrelated crest is that of Bournemouth and St. George
Courtesy Nicholas J. Pine of Goss & Crested China Ltd

buildings or monuments associated with the town or city, whose coat of arms, in bright enamel colours, was skilfully applied to the piece.

Prior to the death of William Goss in 1906 at the age of seventy-three, his other two sons had joined the business, which was now world-wide and employed over 1,000 agencies in Britain alone. Following the decline in trade during the First World War, the firm was taken over by the Stoke firm of Arkinstall & Sons, who used the trade name of 'Arcadian China'. They continued the production of Goss-type crested wares, which were marked 'Goss England' until about 1940 at the Goss factory, although Arkinstall & Sons became a branch of Cauldon Ltd in 1925.

Among the most collectable of Goss pieces are those which were modelled after the earlier historical antiques to be seen in or associated in some way with the place named, of which there are over 600 recorded; all bear a necessarily brief description regarding the original, which is at times to be seen in the local museum. Of equal interest are the pieces depicting cottages or buildings which have since disappeared.

Some especially interesting models are those of aircraft, ships, guns, tanks and personalities associated with the Great War, many of which were also made

The Chicken Rock Lighthouse, Isle of Man, made by W.H. Goss during the 'Second Period', 1900-20. The coat of arms, though, is that of Cowes, the yachting resort on the Isle of Wight
Courtesy Nicholas J. Pine of Goss & Crested China Ltd

Four commemorative pieces of Goss type porcelain, some made by firms that were taken over by H.T Robinson by 1931. Top left: Biplane, a design registered at the Patent Office by Wiltshaw & Robinson of Stoke in 1916, painted in colour with the arms of Swansea. Top right: a monoplane, by Willow Art China, Longton, painted with the arms of Ludlow. Bottom left: a dirigible, inscribed 'Zeppelin H.M.S. DESTROYED BY LIEUTENANT ROBINSON V.C. AT CUFFLEY, ESSEX, SEPT 3rd 1916, painted with the arms of Brighton, mark illegible. L. 17.3cm. Bottom right: Monoplane, Arcadian China, trade name of Arkinstall & Sons of Stoke-on-Trent, c.1904-25, painted with the arms of Dovercourt   Simon Warren Collection

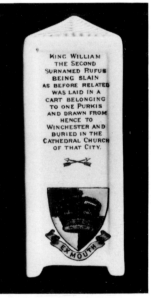

Porcelain figure of 'Barbara' fully painted in enamel colours. The mark printed in black is the usual Goss mark of a Goshawk over GOSS/ENGLAND. This mark was continued by Harold Taylor Robinson after he took over the original firm of W.H. Goss Ltd in 1931 and assumed the name of Goss China Co. Ltd. This figure was made just prior to the factory closing in 1939-40. H. 12cm.   Private Collection

Holiday mementoes were popular from the late 18th century, when the Lowestoft porcelain factory was producing 'Trifles' from Lowestoft, which today are very costly collectors' items. The Victorian or Edwardian holiday maker was able to purchase a wide range of souvenir wares usually modelled after an historical artefact or historical event associated with the city or area of which the enamelled coat of arms was painted. This replica of the famous Rufus Stone recording the death of King William II, was made by W.H. Goss, c.1900-20
Courtesy Nicholas J. Pine of Goss & Crested China Ltd

by such other Staffordshire pottery firms as Wiltshaw & Robinson, using the trade name of Carlton Ware, A.B. Jones (Grafton China), Shelley (late Foley), Charles Ford (Swan China) and H.T. Robinson (Willow Art China).

The Shire Publication by Nicholas Pine, *Goss and other crested china*, gives a most useful list of places where collections of crested wares can be seen, and particulars of major dealers and collectors' clubs catering for those seeking these often still modestly priced items.

FURTHER READING:

Andrews, Sandy, *Crested China,* Milestone Publications, 1980.
Andrews, Sandy and Pine, Nicholas, *The Price Guide to Crested China,* Milestone Publications, 1984.
Jarvis, J.J., *Goss Record War Edition,* Milestone Publications, 1979 (reprinted).
Ward, Roland, *The Price Guide to the Models of W.H. Goss,* Antique Collectors' Club, 1981.

SIR JAMES DUKE & NEPHEWS

c.1860-1864

When the Hill Top Pottery, Burslem, was vacated by the company of Samuel Alcock & Co. in 1859, the factory and the production was taken over and continued by Sir James Duke (a former Lord Mayor of London and an M.P. for the City of London until 1865), but the porcelain production was run by his two nephews, C. & J. Hill. The 'take-over' from Alcock was seemingly on a very friendly basis and the Alcock series of pattern numbers was continued, sometimes as fractions under the number '6'.

Llewellynn Jewitt in *The Ceramic Art of Great Britain,* published in 1878, was full of praise for their wares, both in bone china and earthenware, for which they received awards in the 1862 London exhibition. The production came to a halt in 1864, when they were succeeded by The Hill Pottery Co., a short-lived concern, which according to their letterheading made porcelain and Parian wares, in addition to a variety of other bodies, but their exact detailed history is very confusing and of comparatively little importance.

FURTHER READING:
Jewitt, Llewellynn, *The Ceramic Art of Great Britain,* Virtue & Co., London, 1878.

Plate in bone china, painted in enamel colours and gilt. Made by the Burslem firm at the Hill Pottery of Sir James Duke & Nephews, c.1860-4. Pattern number 4/2699. The high number is due to this firm continuing the sequence of those used by Samuel Alcock & Co., the previous proprietors. D. 22.8cm.

City Museum & Art Gallery, Stoke-on-Trent

BROWN-WESTHEAD, MOORE & CO.
c.1861-1904

This company, formed in 1861, took over the premises formerly occupied by John Ridgway & Co., at Cauldon Place, Hanley, Staffordshire. They also owned the Royal Victoria Works, in Hanley.

By the year 1881 the company were employing some 1,800 people, they had showrooms in Hamburg, Paris and New York, and in 1889 they exhibited at the Paris Exhibition. Leading artists were employed such as Thomas John Bott, who painted in the manner of his father's reproductions in porcelain of Limoges enamels, and Antonin Boullemier who had been trained at the Sèvres factory and had also been employed by the Minton company. Indeed the wares of this concern have much in common with many of the contemporary productions of Minton.

In *The Ceramic Art of Great Britain,* Llewellynn Jewitt well describes the costly china wares made for members of the Royal family, including the Prince of

Bone china plate with moulded beaded rim. The design of this plate was one of four registered with the Patent Office by Brown-Westhead, Moore & Co. on 1st February, 1870. This firm was operating in Hanley, Staffordshire, c.1861-1904. Pattern number B/3385. D. 23.5cm.

Private Collection

An uncommon form of dessert dish, design registered with the Patent Office on February 1st, 1870. Parcel No. 6. Painted in enamel colours by G. Pederson. Made by Brown, Westhead, Moore & Co., of Hanley. D. 23cm.

Courtesy City Museum & Art Gallery, Stoke-on-Trent

Wales and the Duchess of Edinburgh, in addition to services made for the Imperial family of Russia. They were known to have used the title 'Potters to Her Majesty Queen Victoria by Special Appointment'.

The highly decorated wares were produced in bone china, and Parian wares of a fine quality were also manufactured.

Very few pieces are marked, but when found, are printed with the full title, or with initials only, within a shield. Some pieces bear the Patent Office registration mark, and pattern numbers under a letter 'A' 'B' or 'C', and some have been noted up to the letter 'L'.

The firm of Cauldon Ltd. took over the works at Cauldon Place in 1905, after the closure of Brown-Westhead, Moore & Co. in 1904.

FURTHER READING:

Godden, G.A., *Staffordshire Porcelain*, Granada Publishing, 1983; *Encyclopaedia of British Porcelain Manufacturers*, Barrie & Jenkins, 1988.
Jewitt, Llewellynn, *The Ceramic Art of Great Britain*, Virtue & Co., 1878.

WORCESTER ROYAL PORCELAIN CO. LTD.

1862-present

The porcelains made at the original Worcester porcelain factory, which was started by Dr. Wall and his partners in 1751, are almost certainly the most popular of British porcelains today, with many fine collections, both public and private, in Britain, Canada, Australia and the U.S.A., to name just the major countries. Following the death of Dr. Wall in 1776, the factory continued under

Two Worcester porcelain vases as shown at the South Kensington International Exhibition in 1871 and at the Vienna Universal Exhibition in 1873, illustrating the making of porcelain in Japan, 'The Potter at His Wheel' and 'The Painting of the Ware'. The series of six vessels was designed by R.W. Binns, modelled by James Hadley and decorated by James Callowhill. Date mark for 1872. H. 26cm.

Courtesy Phillips, London

A Royal Worcester dessert service, painted with butterflies by Charles Fergus Binns. Impressed marks, one inscribed C.F. Binns, May 31st 1873, the others with initials and dates. D. 22.7cm.

Courtesy Bearnes, Torquay

357

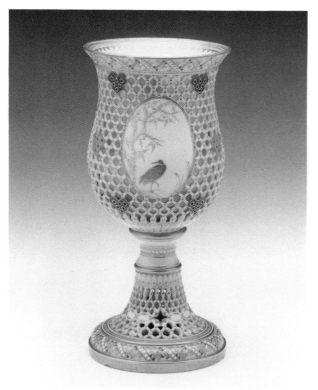

This Royal Worcester goblet is probably the work of George Owen, who was renowned for his reticulated work. The ogee bowl is painted in gold and enamels on a pierced eggshell blue ground, the rim and foot painted over a pink ground. Printed mark, c.1875. H. 19.4cm.   Courtesy Bearnes, Torquay

Figure of a boy cricketer, painted in enamel colours. Modelled by James Hadley, who from 1875 worked as a freelance modeller, but mostly for the Royal Worcester Porcelain Company, where he had been previously employed. Marks, both impressed and printed. H. 20cm.   Courtesy Phillips, London

The well-known Aesthetic Teapot in bone china made by the Royal Worcester Porcelain Co. in 1882, painted in greens and yellows. Marked on base, 'Fearful consequences through the laws of Natural Selection and Evolution of living up to one's teapot'. Male on one side, female on the other. H. 15.2cm.
Courtesy Phillips, London

the direction of William Davis, until he too died in 1783. The factory was then purchased by Thomas Flight, who together with his sons ran the factory until 1793, when Martin Barr became a partner and we begin the confusing change of partnerships: Flight & Barr, 1793-1807, Barr, Flight & Barr, 1807-13, and Flight, Barr & Barr, 1813-40, when they were merged with the nearby factory of Chamberlain, and their vacated factory at Warmstry House was devoted to the manufacture of tiles. After twelve years, during which time both the quality and sales of their productions declined, the factory passed into the hands of W.H. Kerr and R.W. Binns (1851-62) and for a further ten years the factory

A Royal Worcester plate from the 'Queen Victoria Service', c.1904. Produced in glazed Parian, known at the time as 'Ivory Porcelain', possibly the work of William Hale. It is known that wares showing the same intricate border were specially commissioned for Queen Victoria. Mark, in red W. 7029. D. 24cm.   Private Collection

produced some very commendable wares, including a service made for Queen Victoria. In 1862 a new company was formed by Mr. Binns, giving birth to the now famous Worcester Royal Porcelain Company Limited, which continues to flourish today, despite suffering some very difficult periods financially in their earlier years.

The new factory was to reap the benefit of being able to continue to employ many of the fine potters, painters and gilders who had been on the staff of the Kerr & Binns factory and even the latter's mark of the four interlaced 'W's' in a circle surrounding a small crescent and '51' was continued as a mark, with just the addition of a crown above. Although too late for the great 1851 Exhibition in Hyde Park, the new company was able to launch a fine range of wares at the 1862 International Exhibition held in London, including their new Ivory Porcelain, which was a glazed Parian ware, from which they made a series of groups, busts and ornamental wares. This material also became very popular for tableware services, some of which were made for presentation to royalty. Mr. Binns himself was a great admirer of the newly available Japanese porcelains and amassed a large collection of these and other Oriental wares, which he used to acquaint his designers with the popular taste of the day.

A pair of Royal Worcester wall pockets, depicting boys netting fruit trees. These are predominantly painted in blue and gold. Printed and impressed marks with the date code for 1882. H. 21.5cm.
Courtesy Bearnes, Torquay

A pair of Royal Worcester figures, each holding a bird, representing 'Joy' and 'Sorrow', in polychrome, on a glazed Parian body. These figures were particularly popular at this period. Impressed marks, c.1885. H. 25.5cm.
Courtesy Bearnes, Torquay

A pair of Royal Worcester vases, each one finely painted, one with a jay, and the other with an owl. Printed mark and date code for 1885. H. 49.5cm.
Courtesy Bearnes, Torquay

It was at the Vienna Exhibition in 1873 that the highly original porcelain creations of Thomas Bott were so well received, and which if not handled, could well be mistaken for the original sixteenth century Limoges enamels. The Worcester wares were also greatly admired at the Paris Exhibition of 1878,

This Royal Worcester vase was painted by Harry Stinton, and shows a scene of long horned cattle grazing in a mountainous landscape. Printed mark and date code for 1888. H. 18cm.
Courtesy Bearnes, Torquay

Worcester porcelain ewer, moulded with scale pattern and painted in enamel colours and gilt. The gilding bears the mark of Frederick Henry Davis and the Worcester factory mark and date code for 1883. H. 28.5cm.
Courtesy Bearnes, Torquay

A pair of Royal Worcester vases, finely decorated with ferns in gold relief, on an ivory ground. Printed mark and date code for 1890. H. 32cm.
Courtesy Bearnes, Torquay

when large decorative vases inspired by the Italian Renaissance earned a gold medal and a cross of The Legion of Honour for Mr. Binns himself. It was at this time that the names of so many Worcester designers and painters, whose work is so sought after today, were first brought to the attention of the public.

During the last decade of the nineteenth century the factory continued to maintain a high reputation and their wares were exhibited all over the world, as far afield as Chicago and Melbourne. It was during this period that the early forms of lithographic transfers were introduced, but due to the low wages paid to the painters, many of whom were female, the new techniques were not generally adopted and hand painting of a very high quality was continued, as well illustrated here, with the flying swans, birds and landscapes of Charles Baldwyn and others of his period.

The number of employees had risen from about seventy-five in 1862 to about 700 in 1887, although at times there was insufficient work to keep all their best painters busy and it was necessary for some of them to seek renumerative spare-time activities to make a modest wage.

Many articles have been written on the delicate and highly skilled work of George Owen, who specialised in reticulated, or pierced, decoration, which was a very long and tedious operation often requiring several months' work on a single piece, during which time the clay had to be kept in a sufficiently moist condition to enable the fine bladed knife to be used without risk to the piece. George Owen, who was working during the later years of the nineteenth century, is said to have incised his name under the base, or on the side of his work.

One cannot leave the nineteenth century without drawing attention to the remarkable Stinton family, eight of whom were engaged in the decoration of porcelain, either at Grainger's factory or the Royal Worcester. The most famous and accomplished must be John Stinton, who was born in 1854, and his son Harry (*b.* 1882) who worked at the factory from 1896 until 1963, dying five years later at the age of eighty-six years. Harry Stinton's landscapes, which invariably include Highland cattle, are among the most sought after twentieth century porcelains of their type and make very high prices, as do those of his father, John, who first painted for Grainger and lived to the age of 102. The talented painters employed at Worcester during this period are too numerous to mention and one cannot do better than refer to Henry Sandon's *Royal Worcester Porcelains from 1862 to the Present Day,* in which he writes as though he knew them all personally.

R.W. Binns retired in 1897 and died three years later, as the production entered the twentieth century. His position as Art Director was filled by his younger son William Moore Binns.

Another famous name associated with the Worcester Royal Porcelain Company is of course Harry Davis, who was employed from 1898 until 1969, only one year before his death in 1970 at the age of eighty-five. Regrettably not all their accomplished painters enjoyed such a long life as those mentioned. Both

Reticulated, or pierced ware, was made by George Owen, working for the Royal Worcester Company. This is not signed by him, but is most likely to be by his hand. The ground colour is white, the handle, spout and cover, have applied blue beads. Months of work was involved in this process, which required great skill. Impressed mark, c.1890. H. 12cm.

Courtesy Bearnes, Torquay

A pair of Royal Worcester figures, from a series of Eastern Water Carriers, produced in glazed Parian. Printed mark, c.1891. H. 25.5cm.

Courtesy Bearnes, Torquay

the father and grandfather of Harry Davis were employed at the factory, his grandfather, Joseph, being a very fine gilder. Harry painted a wide variety of landscapes, including some delightful views of London, which he copied from picture postcards which he purchased on a trip to the city, but his preference would appear to be for landscapes which included sheep.

It was during the depressions of the late 1920s and the early 1930s that the company ran into some very difficult financial periods, but it was in 1934 that a series of limited editions in the form of Service Plates painted with copies of Audubon's *Birds of America* were produced. Service Plates had been in use over a long period and consisted of beautifully decorated plates which were placed before the guests at table, to be discussed and admired whilst waiting for the first course of a meal to be served. Shortly afterwards a limited series of figures of King George V and Queen Mary were published in readiness for the celebration of their Silver Jubilee in 1935, but these proved to be less popular than the more animated groups of equestrian figures modelled by Doris

A group of various wares of the Royal Worcester Company, all with the so-called 'Blush ivory' ground colour, painted with enamel colours and gilt, c.1893-1908, and very popular with today's collectors. All are marked with the usual crowned Worcester device with yearly date code. H. (pot-pourri) 27.5cm.
Courtesy Phillips, London

A Royal Worcester vase painted in enamel colours and gold, on a cream ground, with finely moulded handles in the form of heads. Printed mark and date code for 1899. H. 56cm.

Courtesy Bearnes, Torquay

Lindner, and the first of the series of American birds modelled by Dorothy Doughty, which immediately became collectors' items, as the limited editions were comparatively small. Her first model in the series of Redstarts on Hemlock were published in 1935 in an edition of only sixty-six, whilst some of the later models were produced in editions of up to 500.

The Worcester factory remained busy during the difficult war years, during which time they operated with a very reduced staff and although decorative wares for home consumption were not available, export wares, such as Dorothy Doughty's birds which were made for the American market, were in great demand and remained so, well into the post-war years, when Miss Doughty spent some time in the U.S.A. studying the American birds from life in their natural habitat. These models remained in great demand until the time of her death in 1962, after which a similar series of game birds and fish were issued, modelled by Ronald Van Ruyckevelt, who had previously worked with Miss Doughty.

It was during the early post-war years that figures modelled by Doris Lindner again went into production, continuing into the 1960s when some of her best work of equestrian figures, cattle and horses, including the beautiful Palomino horse (1971) were produced. The outstanding feature of all these models discussed is that they were painted in a true likeness with matt enamel colours, which especially in the case of the birds captured a very near to nature appearance.

In 1974 the Worcester Royal Porcelain Co. Ltd., acquired the Spode company and in 1976 the two companies merged to form Royal Worcester Spode Ltd., but since December 1988 the two companies have operated separately.

FURTHER READING:

Sandon, Henry, *Royal Worcester Porcelain from 1862 to the Present Day,* Barrie & Jenkins, 1975.

E.J.D. BODLEY

c.1875-1892

Edwin James Drew Bodley first became known as a potter during his short lived partnership with T.R. Diggory, at the Hill Pottery, Burslem, where Diggory had been producing bone china together with George Alcock, c.1867-70. From 1871, when Diggory retired, E.J.D. Bodley first produced both earthenware and china under the name of Bodley & Son, but from 1875 he was trading solely under his own name.

The fine quality bone china produced by Bodley maintained the high standard of the former occupiers of the factory and in view of the high fractional pattern numbers seen on the wares bearing the impressed or printed name or initials of Bodley, it would appear that he continued the sequence of numbers initially started by Samuel Alcock, who had occupied the factory from 1840.

Many of these wares are datable due to the designs having been registered under his name at the Patent Office from 1876, shortly after he commenced to produce wares independently.

Typical late Victorian porcelain jug, with relief moulded decoration, made by the Burslem firm of Edwin J.D. Bodley in the late 19th century. Edwin Bodley occupied part of the Old Hill Pottery, which had been vacated by Samuel Alcock, first with a partner and alone from about 1875 until 1892. High pattern numbers suggest a continuation of those used by Alcock, rather than a very large production of his own wares. H. 14cm.

City Museum & Art Gallery, Stoke-on-Trent

BELLEEK POTTERY

c.1863-present day

This, our only Irish pottery to be discussed, is situated in County Fermanagh, Northern Ireland, and it lies on the River Erne, close to the sea. This situation was a great asset to the factory, for not only did it provide water power for their great water-wheel, but also it was invaluable for the transportation of finished wares, and the raw materials such as the china clay from Cornwall also needed in the manufacture of porcelain. Their other natural advantage was the felspar available on the land. It was from here that Kerr & Binns of Worcester obtained supplies of felspar for use in their Parian ware, which they even named 'Irish Statuary Porcelain'. It was following the sale of felspar, and realising the potential of this material that Robert Armstrong, an architect from Dublin, with the financial help of his friend David McBirney, founded the pottery, which at first traded under the name of McBirney & Armstrong, and later that of David McBirney & Co. This name ceased in 1884 when it became the Belleek Pottery Works Co. Ltd., until 1919, from which date it was known as the Belleek Pottery Ltd., the name it retains today.

Many fine wares were produced under R.W. Armstrong, who acted as Art Director, especially those depicting marine forms. Elaborate services were

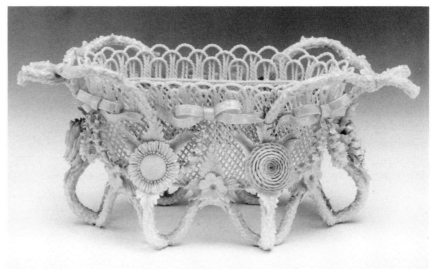

A nautilus shell supported on coral from the Belleek Pottery in Co. Fermanagh, Northern Ireland. These pieces were copied from marine life, and were particularly suited to the delicate porcelain, combined with the sparkling glaze. R.W. Armstrong, the Art Director, is said to have introduced these shell patterns. Printed mark in brick red. H. 20.5cm.　　Courtesy Bearnes, Torquay

This type of ware could only be the product of the Belleek Pottery, Co. Fermanagh, Northern Ireland. The intricate treatment of woven basketware, with added flowers and ribbons, looking so vulnerable, are a tribute to the craftsmen involved. Mark, Belleek, Co. Fermanagh. W. 31cm.

Courtesy Bearnes, Torquay

This tea service is typical of the porcelain produced by the Belleek Pottery, Co. Fermanagh, Northern Ireland, but it is difficult to do justice in a photograph, to the fine delicate porcelain, and the iridescent glaze, which are the hallmarks of these wares. Late 19th century. Printed mark in black
Courtesy Bearnes, Torquay

This basket from the Belleek Pottery, Co. Fermanagh, Northern Ireland, is the type of popular ware, which is still in production today. Early 20th century. W. 13.4cm.
Courtesy City Museum & Art Gallery, Stoke-on-Trent

made for Queen Victoria and the Prince of Wales; included in these services were magnificent centrepieces, incorporating both glazed and unglazed Parian, modelled with mermaids and seahorses. Many shell forms were accurately copied and produced as cups and vases, and tea sets in the shape of sea urchins were made. The glaze was particularly suited to this theme, as it has a lovely iridescent sparkle, reminiscent of sea spray. Basket forms were also a speciality of this pottery, which were finely woven and often profusely decorated with delicately fashioned flowers.

Other more humble wares were produced, however, for the home, and even for use in the electrical industry, as the fine hard paste was particularly suitable for this purpose. Apart from the production of Parian ware, a small amount of bone china was also made.

A variety of printed marks were used, of various colours, although black is the most common. The mark comprises a tower, harp and an Irish wolfhound over the word 'BELLEEK', in a ribbon, and indicates the earliest period, before the words 'Co. Fermanagh, Ireland' were added *c.*1890. In about 1927 'Deanta in Erinn', the Irish for 'Made in Ireland' was further added, but today only 'Ireland' is included with the standard wolfhound mark described.

A version of the mark from the Belleek Pottery, Co. Fermanagh, Northern Ireland. The words 'Fermanagh, Ireland', were added in 1891 to comply with the American McKinley Tariff Act, which required the name of the country of manufacture to be applied to all imports. Mark printed in black, but other colours are found

Several American firms produced a type of Belleek from the late nineteenth century, and confusingly both the Willits Manufacturing Co. and the Colombian Art Pottery Co., incorporated the word 'BELLEEK' in their marks.

FURTHER READING:
Shinn, Charles and Dorrie, *The Illustrated Guide to Parian China,* Barrie & Jenkins Ltd, 1971.
Smith, G.M., *Belleek Porcelain & Pottery, A Handbook for the Collector,* Toucan Press, Guernsey, C.I., 1979.
Godden, G.A., *Encyclopaedia of British Porcelain Manufacturers,* Barrie & Jenkins Ltd, 1988.

POWELL & BISHOP & Various Partnerships
c.1866-1939

Prior to 1865 Powell and Bishop were in a fourteen year partnership with William Livesley at Miles Bank, Hanley, where they produced a wide range of wares in various ceramic bodies. On the retirement of Livesley, the firm continued under the name of Powell & Bishop, by which time the partnership was producing wares from three factories.

Powell and Bishop had the Waterloo Works, close to their mill on the canal side, erected solely for their china production, although the decoration was all applied at their major factory, the Stafford Street Works.

Their china merited very high praise from Llewellynn Jewitt, who was writing *The Ceramic Art of Great Britain* at the time; he praised the quality of the body and glaze, and the beauty of their designs of dessert and tea services, which he thought at times appeared to be inlaid with ormolu (gilt-bronze).

The high quality gilding of their wares was doubtless due to their being the

Plate of bone china, decorated with enamel colours and gilt on a crimson ground. Made by Bishop & Stonier, c.1890. This firm is better known for the production of earthenware. Mark, an impressed caduceus. D. 23.8cm. R.H. Williamson Bequest, Tullie House, Carlisle

'Sole workers of, and possess the exclusive right to and in, a patented process of printing in gold and colours, originally purchased by their firm from some Austrians, by whom it was invented'. Jewitt then likens the quality of this unique gilding to that seen on mediaeval illuminated manuscripts. He similarly lauds their toilet services decorated with transfer printing, lustre, enamelling and gilding, with special comment on the shapes of their ewers, jugs and table flower pots. Their wares earned many medals at major exhibitions in London, Amsterdam and Paris, but with such a script writer as Jewitt for their advertising this is not surprising.

In 1878 a third partner, John Stonier, entered the firm, and their new title Powell, Bishop & Stonier was used until 1891, after which it was Bishop & Stonier until the death of the latter in 1900, when James Bishop continued alone until 1939. The new collector may well be bewildered to see their china marked with the name of a well-known gravy powder, but 'BISTO' is merely the trade name and abbreviation for Bishop and Stonier; other marks used by this firm include the name or initials of the current partners, often together with the caduceus mark, the mark of Hermes, messenger of the gods, which was registered in 1876 and used until their closure.

FURTHER READING:
Jewitt, Llewellynn, *The Ceramic Art of Great Britain,* Virtue & Co., 1878.

C.J.C. BAILEY, FULHAM

c.1873-1891

From 1864 Charles Bailey was concerned mostly with the manufacture of stonewares and terracotta, but is known to have made some experimental porcelain wares with the name 'FULHAM' impressed and sometimes the initials C.J.C.B. in monogram form from c.1873.

The origin of Fulham porcelain has at times, without any evidence, been associated with John Dwight, who was making salt glazed stoneware at Fulham from 1672, but may well have been endeavouring to produce porcelain as well.

A rare porcelain salt made by C.J.C. Bailey in Fulham, London, c.1873-91. It is made from a material much akin to bone china. Impressed 'FULHAM'. H. 8cm. Private Collection

THE DERBY CROWN PORCELAIN CO.

c.1875-present

The early Nottingham Road Derby Porcelain company, established by William Duesbury in 1756, was to continue under various proprietors, including Robert Bloor, until finally closing down in 1848. The gap was almost immediately closed with the opening of a new factory in nearby King Street by a group of six workers who had previously worked at the early factory; this very successful venture, initially Locker & Co., late Bloor, continued until 1935. A further new factory was established in 1875 by a Staffordshire potter, Edward Phillips, and William Litherland, a Liverpool glass and china retailer, with a capital of £67,850, a considerable sum at that period. According to Llewellynn Jewitt, writing in his second edition of *The Ceramic Art of Great Britain,* published in 1883, the factory in 1877 under Edward Phillips was employing 400 hands, had

Royal Crown Derby porcelain plate decorated and signed by Désiré Leroy and dated to 1906. Leroy started his career at the famous Sèvres factory in France where he served his apprenticeship from 1851, by the age of twenty-two (1862) he was considered the finest ceramic artist in the world. He came to England in 1878 and worked for Minton until moving to Derby in 1890

Courtesy Royal Crown Derby Museum

erected three biscuit ovens and three glost ovens and was producing a very wide range of wares in china, Parian and vitrified stoneware. 'Dinner, Tea, Breakfast, Toilet, Trinket and Dejeuner and a variety of other useful wares are made...In Parian: Busts, Statuettes and groups are produced in considerable variety. Specialities are vases, principally of Persian and Indianesque character...with a profusion of raised gilt ornament...The eggshell china cups and saucers thus decorated being far beyond those of other houses'.

Despite all these new, lavish wares Cassell's *Magazine of Art* reported in 1884 that 'the promoters of the revival of the manufacture of Derby China have respected with becoming reverence the artistic tradition of the ''old Derby'' school, and reproduced its more famous patterns, they have not been content to remain mere plagiarists in porcelain...'

Raised gold work, such as praised by Jewitt, remains a favourite feature of their present day dinner services, tea wares and dessert services and the work of many of the decorators of their early years is eagerly sought today, although sometimes difficult to attribute with any degree of certainty. Among the highly accomplished flower painters were Joseph Peach, C. Newbold Wright, Radford

Coffee cup and saucer of extremely thin 'egg-shell' bone china, decorated with raised gilding and cupids in enamel colour by James Platts, a painter at Derby Crown Porcelain, c.1880, who specialised in figure painting   Courtesy Royal Crown Derby Museum

A duplicate of one of the original plates made by Derby Crown Porcelain in a twenty-six piece service presented to the Rt. Hon. W.E. Gladstone, M.P., by the Liberal Working Men of Derby in 1883. The landscape is of Pickering Tor; the landscapes of the service were painted by Count Holtzendorf and most of the flowers by James Rouse, sen   Courtesy Royal Crown Derby Museum

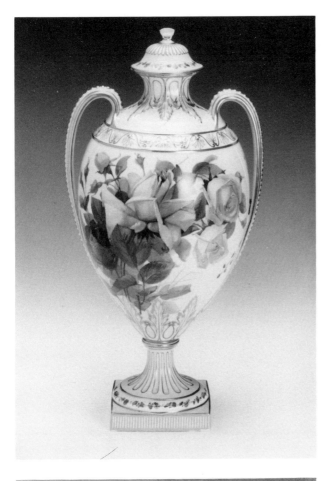

This fine classical shaped vase is referred to as the Kedleston and numbered 394. It featured in the 1909 sale catalogue of the collection of William Bemrose, the founder director of the factory, where it was stated to be 'The first piece bearing the Royal Arms' and to have been painted by Richard Pilsbury, who was at the factory, c.1882-92. H. 43cm. Made at Royal Crown Derby

Courtesy Bearnes, Torquay

A vase with shell form neck with entwined ropes, painted in enamel colours with a shipping scene by W.E.J. Dean, c.1897. These later painters had the advantage of studying photographic records, and Dean took trips on trawlers to gather material which made his paintings so genuine. He was employed at Derby from the late 1890s until his death in 1956. Shape 877. H. 22.4cm.

Courtesy Royal Crown Derby Museum

A rare Royal Crown Derby reticulated vase of ivory coloured bone china, c.1878. Reticulated is an alternative word for pierced: the process calls for very experienced and skilled workers who cut through the outer wall of double-walled vessels whilst the clay is still in a 'leather' hard condition, any slip of the thin bladed knife would be very difficult to make good

Courtesy Royal Crown Derby Museum

Royal Crown Derby porcelain plate of the Ely shape. Painted in enamel colours by Albert Gregory, by whom it is signed and dated 1911. Gregory, who was a bachelor, was probably the finest natural flower painter to be employed at the Royal Crown Derby factory, where he arrived from Minton, c.1890 and apart from a short break in the U.S.A. in 1908, was a very prolific painter into the early decades of the 20th century   Courtesy Royal Crown Derby Museum

and H. Stoner. Many of the figures previously made during the early nineteenth century were continued, especially the most popular, including the Mansion House Dwarfs, and those depicting the antics of Dr. Syntax, modelled by Edward and Samuel Keys after the illustrations by Rowlandson in the book published by William Combe.

It was in 1890 that 'Her Majesty had been graciously inclined, at the solicitation of the venerable Duke of Devonshire K.G. Lord Lieutenant of the County and Lord High Steward of Derby, to confer upon these works the title of ''Royal'' (and the use of the Royal Arms)' published in *The Gentlewoman* in 1891. Queen Victoria was obviously impressed by a pair of large vases given to her by the Ladies of Derby to commemorate her Jubilee, together with a plaque painted with her portrait.

From that time the title of the factory became The Royal Crown Derby Porcelain Company, and was considered to be probably the most modern in Europe, but their wares were never cheap. As far back as 1777, when Dr. Johnson and James Boswell paid a visit to the old Derby China Works, they commented that beautiful as the wares were, they cost as much as silver. The two were probably disgruntled at not receiving a gift, as was customary with so many other visiting V.I.Ps.

Possibly the best known of all the Royal Crown Derby Porcelain Company painters was Désiré Leroy, who after serving his apprenticeship at Sèvres from

the age of eleven, came to England in 1878, when he was thirty-eight years old, to accept an engagement with the firm of Minton. His work, which was shown in the Paris Exhibition in the same year, was highly praised in the Report of the Society of Arts as 'deserving of great praise, as instanced in a couple of card-trays with groups of flowers in the centre'. In 1890 Leroy began working for the Royal Crown Derby Porcelain Company, where he remained until his death in 1908. The beauty of his work reflects very clearly his association with the French factory and an article on his work in the *Pall Mall Magazine* in December 1906, made a very true forecast when discussing his painting that 'There can be little doubt that when his work is "antique" it will be worth its weight in gold, for everything that comes from his cunning hand is a unique gem of art in itself'. He was obviously highly paid and arrived in a cab to work at the factory, wearing a silk hat and carrying a cane.

In addition to their large range of lavish wares, the production of Toys, or miniatures was introduced in 1904, usually decorated with the so-called 'Imari' Japanese styles. These delightful pieces of useless nonsense remained in production until about 1940 and are eagerly sought today despite the very high prices, the range includes teapots, sugar boxes, creamers, cups and saucers, flat

Part of a Royal Crown Derby tea service, painted in underglaze blue, red and gilt with the so-called 'Witches' pattern. The mark includes the date code for 1899, with the exception of the two tea plates, which date to 1913. Made at Royal Crown Derby

Courtesy Bearnes, Torquay

There appears to have been slight variations in the suggested year cyphers which were used at the Osmaston Road factory of the Derby Crown Porcelain Company in their earlier years, but those published here by John Twitchett, Curator of the Royal Crown Derby Museum, are believed to be correct to within one year.

From 1887 to 1890 the mark used was two 'D's in monogram form under a crown, with the simple line, year cypher from 1880; from 1890 to 1940, the same mark was used under 'ROYAL CROWN DERBY' with the appropriate year mark. From 1940 to 1945 'ROYAL CROWN DERBY', 'MADE IN ENGLAND' and Patent Office Registration number, was below the mark. From 1964 to 1975, the mark read 'DERBY CHINA' over the usual mark, under which was written 'ROYAL CROWN DERBY/ENGLISH BONE CHINA' plus year mark.

The year 1976 saw another change with crown and double 'D' monogram within a circle, reading ROYAL CROWN DERBY ENGLISH BONE CHINA with year mark in Roman numbers. To comply with the American McKinley Tariff Act, the word 'ENGLAND' was added to their mark from 1891 until about 1921 when the full term 'MADE IN ENGLAND' was used.

irons, saucepans, coal buckets, watering cans, vases and a host of other novel shapes.

The Derby Crown Porcelain Co. and the Royal Crown Derby Porcelain Co. were fairly consistent in marking their wares and from 1882 a year cypher of a device or Roman numerals together with their interlaced 'D' under a crown was applied, usually in red enamel, a mark first introduced in 1877. 'England' was added to this mark from about 1890 and the full term 'Made in England' in about 1921. From 1964 'English Bone China' was also added.

In 1964 The Royal Crown Derby Porcelain Company was merged with the Lawley group, which became the Allied English Potteries, owned by S. Pearson and Sons Ltd. In 1971 Pearson acquired Doulton & Co. Ltd. and in 1973 the companies were again merged to form Royal Doulton Tableware Limited.

FURTHER READING:

Twitchett, John and Bailey, Betty, *Royal Crown Derby,* Barrie & Jenkins, London, 1976; 3rd Edn. Antique Collectors' Club, Woodbridge, 1988.

TABLE OF DERBY YEAR-MARKS

1880	1881	1882	1883	1884	1885	1886
1887	1888	1889	1890	1891	1892	1893
1894	1895	1896	1897	1898	1899	1900
1901	1902	1903	1904	1905	1906	1907
1908	1909	1910	1911	1912	1913	1914

1915	1916	1917	1918	1919	1920	1921
1922	1923	1924	1925	1926	1927	1928
1929	1930	1931	1932	1933	1934	1935
1936	1937	1938	1939	1940	1941	1942
1943	1944	1945	1946	1947	1948	1949
VI	VII	VIII	IX	X	XI	etc.

376

HADLEY

c.1875-1905

Perhaps the most successful of the 'breakaway' porcelain producers in Worcester was James Hadley, who was first employed as a modeller by Kerr & Binns, although his finest work must be that which he produced during his thirteen years with the Royal Worcester concern until 1875, when he decided to work independently as a modeller and designer, although most of his work was still for the Royal Worcester Company.

The models produced by Hadley during his independent period were clearly incised with his full signature, 'J. Hadley', with the 'J' and 'H' sometimes being written in the form of a monogram, all of which can be clearly read on the multitude of wares produced by Royal Worcester from his original models. He produced a great variety of figures and decorative useful wares, but perhaps his best known and sought after pieces are those fashioned in the then popular Japanese taste, among which are some exceptional relief moulded vases showing the various stages in the production of the original Oriental porcelains.

It was 1896 before James Hadley, together with his three sons, decided to establish their own small factory and produce multiple wares from their own models, employing some of the Royal Worcester workers; but this period of complete independence lasted only until 1905, when two years before the death of the founder, James Hadley, they were amalgamated with the major Worcester company under the direction of two of his sons.

FURTHER READING:
Sandon, H., *Royal Worcester Porcelain,* Barrie & Jenkins, 1973.

JOSIAH WEDGWOOD
1878-present

It was probably due to the competition of the fine hard-paste porcelain being made in France that Josiah Wedgwood II decided to halt his production of bone china in about 1830 and concentrate on the manufacture of Queen's Ware (creamware) and Jasper. It was not until 1878, when the factory was under the management of Francis Wedgwood, the third son of Josiah II, that the manufacture of bone china was revived at Etruria, where the production was to remain, until the 1930s, when the directors decided that the time had come to abandon the now very outdated building, which over the years had sunk eight feet, due to subsidence caused by the underlying coal mining. They therefore decided to move to a country estate near the village of Barlaston, which was six miles away and build a new modern factory in clean and dust free surroundings, so essential for the production of fine wares.

The foundation stone of the new factory was laid in 1938, with production starting in 1940, but the outbreak of the Second World War in the previous year was to prevent the completion of the works, although the manufacture continued of valuable export orders, mostly for the U.S.A., which accounted for about 80% of the output. Barlaston was the first ceramic factory in this

A group of Wedgwood wares in bone china after its reintroduction in 1878
Courtesy the Wedgwood Museum Trustees, Barlaston, Stoke-on-Trent

378

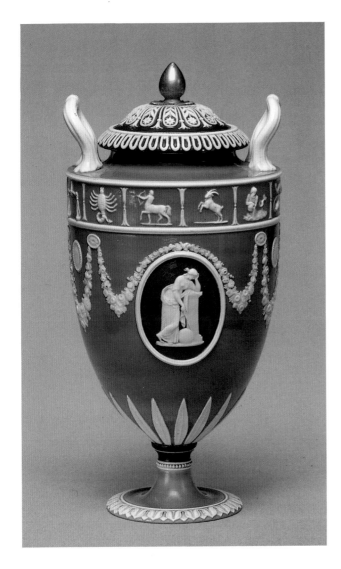

A Wedgwood vase and cover in Classical style, with a border showing signs of the Zodiac. In glazed Parian with enamelled ground. 'Victoria Ware', 1875
Courtesy The Wedgwood Museum Trustees, Barlaston, Stoke-on-Trent

country to be equipped with electric tunnel ovens, which meant the smoky coal fired bottle kilns and the clumsy saggars, in which the wares were stacked for firing, were outdated. Now the wares for either biscuiting or glazing, are skilfully stacked on wheel trolleys and are slowly moved on rails through an electrically heated tunnel for about one hundred yards. Within the tunnel the maximum temperature required was reached, after which the contents slowly cooled until emerging comparatively cold at the exit of the tunnel, ready to be removed for glazing or decorating.

Following the appointment of John E. Goodwin in 1902 as Art Director, many of the old designs which would have been fully approved by the first Josiah, were modified and reissued in the current taste of the twentieth century. This trend was ably continued by Goodwin's successor, Victor Skellern, who held the post from 1934 to 1966 and summed up his aims so well, when he wrote 'that the designer's task is often less to ''create'' the absolutely new, than to adapt and develop, always with regard to the contemporaneous world in which he operates as technician and artist'.

One of the most talented artists during this period was Millicent Taplin, who, after training at the Burslem School of Art, joined Wedgwood in 1927,

A bone china table centre of marine form from the Wedgwood factory, c.1894
Courtesy the Wedgwood Museum Trustees, Barlaston,
Stoke-on-Trent

becoming head of the hand painting department in 1958, having excelled in designing for lithographic reproduction. The year 1966 saw the appointment of Peter Wall (who had trained at the Royal College of Art) as the new Art Director; he left in 1968 to take up the post of Head of the School of Ceramics at Birmingham Polytechnic. Peter Wall was replaced by Robert Minken, who had also trained at the Royal College of Art, and at the present time holds the post of Design Director. Both these Directors have produced wares during their term of office which will certainly number among the 'antiques of the future'.

It was during Goodwin's time as Art Director that some new exciting experiments were to take place at Wedgwoods, which were far removed from their traditional wares. James Hodgkiss was experimenting in the production of an Oriental inspired blue glaze as a basis for colourful printing, gilding and lustre decoration: this was the glaze upon which Daisy Makeig-Jones was to apply her now sought after 'Fairyland lustres'. 'Daisy' began her apprenticeship with Wedgwood in 1909 and within a few years had evolved a then unique style of painting flowers, birds and animals, which were soon to develop into the animated Fairyland scenes (popularised in print by such artists as Arthur Rackham and Dulac), a style in which she continued to excel in up to her retirement in 1931. It is surprising that such wares, embracing so much detailed and painstaking work could be produced commercially at a profit.

It was in 1948 that the firm of Wedgwood, then under the Chairmanship of Josiah V, opened a showroom in the West End of London, soon to be followed by what was at that time a novel form of marketing, having an independent retail shop within the premises of a large well-established store, a venture that proved so successful that by 1980, 112 such centres were marketing Wedgwood wares throughout the world, as far afield as Australia and Japan. The London showroom in Wigmore Street was closed in 1990.

Josiah V, who died in 1968, was the last company Chairman who was a direct descendant from Josiah I (*d.*1795), the founder of the original pottery in 1759 at Ivy House Works, Burslem. Just prior to the death of Josiah V, a new Chairman had been appointed, Arthur Bryan, who had joined the firm in 1947 as a management trainee, and under whose guidance the company has flourished, and by 1990 had absorbed no less than eighteen other companies, including The Goldsmiths & Silversmiths Association of London.

It was Arthur Bryan who said 'A successful manufacturing potter must be prepared to put on the market designs that are ahead of the time and not seek an immediate return' and it was Susie Cooper, probably the best known ceramic designer of this century, who was very aware of this recipe for success. After studying at the Burslem School of Art under Gordon Forsyth, Susie Cooper was employed as a decorator for A.E. Gray & Co. from 1922 until 1929, when she set up her own business, where she planned to have the opportunity to take part in the designing of the wares upon which to paint her simple, yet popular designs, which often show her familiarity with textile designs. Initially she was still buying wares 'in the white' for herself and her staff to decorate as well as commissioning some useful and decorative shapes from other manufacturers. This venture was to prove unsatisfactory and she moved to Crown Works, Burslem, a new factory of Wood & Sons; there she was given the opportunity to both design and decorate wares under her own name, which almost immediately achieved wide popularity and even Queen Mary numbered among her customers.

In 1966 The Susie Cooper Pottery, now in partnership with R.H. & S.L. Plant, was taken over by Wedgwood. Susie Cooper is still engaged as a freelance designer for the group, and the mark of their bone china includes the note that the piece is a 'Susie Cooper Design'.

The twentieth century firm of Wedgwood has continued the tradition, started by Josiah I, of employing freelance designers and the list includes such well-known names as Dame Laura Knight, Eric Ravilious, Arnold Machin (later a full-time modeller for the company), Laurence Whistler and Eduardo Paolozzi. This practice continues today with promising designers being invited to work at their Design Studio.

Today, in the face of keen home and overseas competition, Wedgwood have gone into the market of producing 'Series' and 'Limited Editions'. Their first Christmas Plate was issued in 1969, soon followed by a wide range of annual best sellers for such events as 'Mother's Day' or 'Father's Day'; other 'Limited Editions' sometimes number up to 5,000.

The latter part of the twentieth century has certainly seen a great revival in the world-wide prosperity of Josiah Wedgwood & Sons Ltd., but whether Josiah I would have given his approval to all their current productions and presented his wife, Sarah, with a Mother's Day Plate, we'll fortunately never know, although we must remember that when writing of her accomplishments he said 'I speak from experience in Female taste, without which I should have made but a poor figure among my Potts, not one of which, of any consequence, is finished without the approbation of my Sally'.

FURTHER READING:

des Fontaines, Una, *Wedgwood Fairyland Lustre,* Sotheby Parke Bernet, London, 1975.
City Museum & Art Gallery, Stoke-on-Trent, *Wedgwood of Etruria & Barlaston,* 250th Anniversary Exhibition, 1980.

DOULTON

1884-present

The firm of Doulton was first established in 1815, when John Doulton as a young man of twenty-two years risked his life savings of £100 to buy a partnership in a small pottery at Lambeth, owned by Martha Jones, the widow of the former proprietor, who also took a John Watts into partnership at the same time, the firm becoming Jones, Watts and Doulton. The bulk of their wares consisted of salt glazed stoneware jugs and mugs, sometimes modelled in the form of such famous and well-known characters as Nelson, Wellington and Napoleon and a large variety of purely domestic or commercial vessels including humble bottles for boot blacking. After the retirement of Mrs Jones in 1820, the two remaining partners continued as Doulton and Watts and

An elaborate bone china table centrepiece by Doulton & Co., modelled by Charles J. Noke, with raised gilding by William Hodkinson, exhibited at the 1893 Chicago Exhibition

Courtesy Royal Doulton Ltd

Shell shaped dish painted in enamel colours by David Dewsbury at the Royal Doulton factory, Burslem, c.1910. This accomplished painter joined Doulton in 1889 at the age of thirty-seven; the most admired examples of his work are those painted with orchids, usually on Doulton's Luscian Wares, a fine bone china with a new matching glaze introduced by John Slater, c.1900, which produced 'a rich soft effect by the skilful blending of various colours painted on the glaze — orchids and other flowers by Dewsbury . . .' (Pottery Gazette, May 1898) Courtesy Royal Doulton Ltd

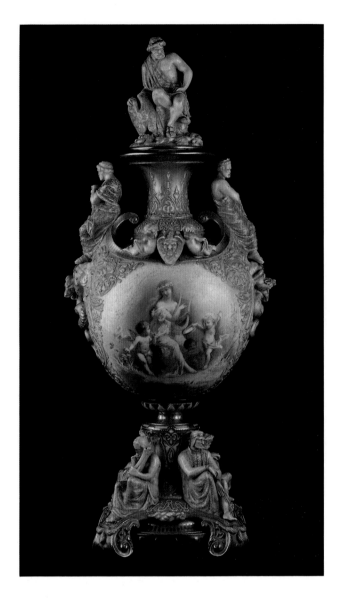

'The Dante Vase' was modelled by Charles J. Noke, for the 1893 Chicago Exhibition, four years after he had joined Doulton's at Burslem, at the age of thirty-one, having received his training at Worcester where he was apprenticed c.1874. He became the Art Director in 1914. The painted scenes from Dante's Inferno *are by C. Labarre and G. White*

Courtesy Royal Doulton Ltd

prospered so well due to the demand for their acid resisting stoneware for industrial use, that it became necessary to move into larger premises, which became known as the Lambeth Pottery, near Lambeth Palace.

It was in 1835 that John Doulton's second son, Henry, became an apprentice and was soon to be involved with their production of sanitary wares of all types, which included the now famous drainage pipes for which there was a great demand by health authorities throughout the country. The story of the Lambeth decorative stonewares and earthenwares is fully discussed in *A Collector's History of English Pottery* by Griselda Lewis.

In 1878, five years after the death of the founder, John Doulton, his son Henry and his brother James decided to take a major interest in the Burslem pottery of Pinder, Bourne and Co., but following disagreement between the partners in 1882 the partnership was dissolved and the firm became Doulton & Co., Burslem.

Although they experienced some difficulties in the beginning, the wares on exhibition today in the Sir Henry Doulton Gallery, attached to the Burslem factory, are a fitting reminder of their artistic achievements under the direction

DOULTON

of John Slater, who had been trained at Minton by the famous Léon Arnoux, and a young but highly talented general manager, John Cuthbert Bailey.

It was in 1884 that a new wing was attached to the Burslem factory for the production of a fine quality bone china, perfected by Slater and necessitating the recruitment of new staff skilled in all the various branches involved in the production of beautifully decorated bone china table and ornamental wares, which were soon to enjoy a world-wide demand. These late nineteenth century wares, when signed by such painters as Joseph Birbeck, Percy Curnock, Edward Raby and a host of others are in great demand by today's collectors. These artistic achievements under Henry Doulton were recognised in 1887 when he was knighted by Queen Victoria, the first potter to receive such an honour. Following the death of Henry Doulton in 1897, at the age of seventy-seven years, the business was formed into a limited company under the direction of his son, Henry Lewis Doulton.

It was in 1901 that King Edward VII presented the chairman of the company with the Royal Warrant and the company continued to stride ahead under the artistic direction of Charles J. Noke, who had been trained at Worcester under James Hadley.

Perhaps among the most popular of all Doulton wares today are their bone china figures, which they started to produce under Charles J. Noke in 1913. To date they have marketed several thousand different models, some of which are at times withdrawn, whilst new figures are constantly being issued. The 1990 directory of new models includes a limited edition of 2,500 models of Her Majesty Queen Elizabeth the Queen Mother, in commemoration of her 90th birthday, modelled by Eric Griffiths, Doulton's Art Director of Sculpture, priced at £250.

In this same year a new series of 'Pretty Ladies' was issued at a more modest price of about £90; this same series is also produced in miniature, modelled by Douglas V. Tootle, Peter Gee, John Bromley, Leslie Harradine and Peggy Davies (d. 1989). The larger figures average about 20cm. high, whilst the miniatures are about 10cm. The range of their newly issued figures is wide, but of outstanding attraction is a collection of sculptures decorated in *rouge flambé*, a colour so much admired on early Chinese wares of the Kangxi period (1662-1722); the choice of subjects is so fitting for the colour and includes Confucius, modelled by Peter Gee and The Genie by Robert L. Tabbenor.

Character jugs, influenced by 'Good Sir Toby' continue to appeal to the collector and seven new faces have appeared as jugs, including Guy Fawkes by William K. Harper and the Lord Mayor of London by Stanley James Spencer. A further series which will almost certainly be in demand for gifts are The Angler, The Gardener and The Golfer.

FURTHER READING:
Eyles, Desmond, *The Doulton Burslem Wares,* Barrie & Jenkins, 1980.
Eyles, Desmond and Dennis, Richard, *Royal Doulton Figures,* Royal Doulton Ltd., 1978.

PLANT BROS.

c.1889-present

This long established firm started operations at Stanley Works, Bagnell Street, Longton, where they remained until c.1898, when they were combined with R.H. & S.L. Plant at the Tuscan Works, Forester Street, Longton, trading under the name of Tuscan China until 1966 when they were taken over by the Wedgwood Group.

The later history of the firm, founded in 1759 by Josiah Wedgwood, becomes extremely complicated and since being taken over in 1986 by the Waterford Glass plc. of Eire was renamed Waterford Wedgwood. By 1990 R.H. & S.L. Plant was just one of eighteen formerly independent ceramic companies now within the group. They had adopted the trade name of TUSCAN CHINA soon after the turn of the century and the majority of their wares, both useful and decorative, were stamped with marks which included this name, continuing until 1971 when the term ROYAL TUSCAN was used and in 1989 the factory was also renamed Royal Tuscan.

Their decorative and useful wares made up to the outbreak of the Second World War in 1939, were of a good quality, but hardly ranked as 'collectable', yet today under the guidance of Wedgwood, their designs are of a very fine quality and well rival those of some contemporary factories such as Rosenthal. In 1990 an exciting exhibition was held in the City Museum & Art Gallery, Stoke-on-Trent, entitled 'Dynamic Designs, The British Pottery Industry 1940-1990' which included examples of their recent wares.

LOCKE & CO

1896-1915

A further late and short-lived Worcester factory was that started in about 1896 by Edward Walter Locke, who had formerly worked as a manager for the Royal China Works of Grainger.

Locke, with the financial support of two local men, appears to have catered for the lower price range wares, although very much under the influence of the finer and earlier wares of both Grainger and the Royal Worcester Company. Their productions were described in the *Pottery Gazette* of 1899 as a 'very large assortment of fancy goods at very moderate prices'.

The wares of Locke & Co. usually bore the hand written or impressed name of the firm together with 'WORCESTER' or the printed globe of the world with 'LOCKE & CO./WORCESTER/ENGLAND'. The later version of 'LOCKE & Co./ SHRUB HILL WORKS/WORCESTER' over England was a form of mark introduced to comply with the result of a legal battle brought about in 1902 by the Royal Worcester Company, who objected to Locke marketing his wares as 'Worcester Porcelain'.

Production was obviously halted by the outbreak of the Great War in 1914; the factory was sold and the pottery production ceased in 1915.

Coffee service, porcelain with white pâte-sur-pâte *decoration on a salmon pink ground, thought to be the work of Kate Locke. Made by Locke & Co. of Worcester, c.1900-4. This Worcester company closed in 1915*
Courtesy Phillips, London

PARAGON CHINA COMPANY

1919-present

Paragon China Ltd. was not established until about 1920, and if we are to accept that the term 'antique' should not be applied to wares less than 100 years old, then despite receiving Royal Warrants from three generations of the Royal family, Paragon porcelain should not be offered for sale at Antique Fairs. Their marks all include the word 'Paragon' together with a reference to the Royal patron at the time of their production.

The Star China Company was established in 1899 at St. Gregory pottery works, Longton, moving to Atlas, Longton, a pottery previously known as Sutherland Works, in 1903, where the trade name Paragon China was adopted. In 1919 the Star China Company was renamed the Paragon China Company, using the trade name of Paragon Fine Bone China, and became a limited company in 1930, known for a short period as Royal Paragon China Limited.

In 1960 Paragon was taken over by Thomas C. Wild & Son Ltd., who in 1964 became part of the Allied English Potteries and today operate as part of the Royal Albert China Division under Royal Doulton. Their production consisted mainly of tea and breakfast wares for the Australian, New Zealand and South African markets, but was later expanded to include dinner services for export to North and South America.

Paragon China Co. of Longton, have a long history of making fine porcelain. The Atlas China Company, founded in 1899, adopted the trade name of The Paragon China in 1903. The high standard of their productions has justified Royal Warrants from the last three Queens and the company has built up a tradition of producing wares to commemorate Royal occasions. This bone china loving cup was made in 1986 to celebrate the Royal Wedding of Prince Andrew and Sarah Ferguson

Courtesy Royal Doulton Ltd

Chapter 4
20th Century Industrial Wares

Designs in industrially produced porcelains changed little in the early years of the 1900s. Art Nouveau, with its writhing style, looking rather like 'stretched chewing-gum', was adopted by such firms as Doulton and Minton, but owed little to the British designers in Staffordshire. The firm of Doulton also produced a new range of wares which they named 'Flambé', in which they used glazes in exciting new combinations of red, green and blue, which by the second decade, showed increasing influence of the monochromes produced in the Far East from the Song dynasty (960-1279). These wares were exceptional, however, and most firms produced traditional patterns to cater for popular taste.

Whilst production of table wares and other fine porcelains had been brought to a halt on the Continent during the First World War years, British industry had continued to produce wares primarily for export to the colonies and the U.S.A. Following the war there were many changes in Britain, especially in the social structure: stronger trade unions were demanding better conditions and wages for all workers, including those in the pottery industry, particularly for the female decorators, whose poor wages had encouraged management to use hand decoration in preference to using lithographic transfer prints, although

Left, teapot of bone china made by W. T. Copeland of Stoke-on-Trent. The 'Apollo' design is on a 'Royal College' shape, the work of Neal French and David White in 1958. From 1958 to 1972 Neal French was a modeller and designer at Royal Worcester Ltd   Private Collection

Right, can-shaped coffee pot of bone china, by Susie Cooper in 1957. Despite having her own ceramic company from 1929 to 1980, this foremost designer found time to produce designs for Josiah Wedgwood & Sons, Ltd., who made this coffee pot. H. 23cm.
Courtesy City Museum & Art Gallery, Stoke-on-Trent

388

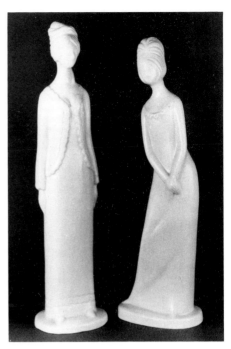

The St. Edward plate of bone china, decorated by coloured transfer prints designed by Harold Holdway in 1965, in a limited edition of 900, a number chosen in celebration of the 900th anniversary of the foundation of Westminster Abbey. Published with the approval of Her Majesty The Queen and the authority of the Dean and Chapter of Westminster. Made by W. T. Copeland, Stoke-on-Trent. D. 26.9cm. Private Collection

Pair of white glazed porcelain figures of Diana and Priscilla, from the 'Young Elizabethans' series, modelled in 1965 by Pauline Shone. Marked, 'Spode/BONE CHINA/ENGLAND'. H. 25.5 and 27cm. Private Collection

Royal Crown Derby coffee cup and saucer of bone china decorated with lavish raised and chaised gilding. Part of a service commissioned by Tiffany's for James Deering, which took eighteen months to complete by a team of gilders under George Hemstock in the early years of this century. H. 6.4cm.
Courtesy Royal Crown Derby Museum

Porcelain plate painted with enamel colours by Arnold Machin, who for a short while was at the King Street factory of Sampson Hancock. This plate is from a service presented to Henry Blogg, Coxswain of the Cromer Lifeboat, by Mr. and Mrs. Paget in 1934. Mark of Sampson Hancock in puce and dated 1934
Courtesy Royal Crown Derby Museum

Royal Crown Derby bone china plate painted with enamel colours by C.M. Pell whose signature it bears, c.1968. Mary Pell is known for her hunting scenes and botanical painting, such as this clematis. She was employed at the Osmaston Road factory from 1965 to 1970 and later became well known for her watercolours John Twitchett Collection

Royal Crown Derby have chosen their 'Duesbury' shape for the attractive 'Quail' pattern, the feathers of which are in shades of blue, red and gold, in a highly original treatment of bone china Courtesy Royal Crown Derby Porcelain Co. Ltd

A popular design in current production at Royal Crown Derby is 'Cloisonné', suggested by the Oriental technique where wires are fused to a metal form providing the separated compartments into which coloured enamels are contained to form the design. Here the colours of rich iron-red, chrome green, ivory, blue-black and gold, are applied to the surface of the glaze with transfers Courtesy Royal Crown Derby Porcelain Co. Ltd

This bone china table ware design by Royal Crown Derby is 'Ambassador', the rim decoration of which is in cobalt blue and gold interspersed with red stylised flowers, with gold lining on the edges Courtesy Royal Crown Derby Porcelain Co. Ltd

Among the many wares being produced by the Royal Crown Derby factory today are these of the Pearly King and Queen, from their 'Royal Cats' collection

Courtesy Royal Crown Derby Porcelain Co. Ltd

Royal Crown Derby bone china group of a boy and girl playing leap frog, modelled by Arnold Mikelson, who was working at the Derby factory from about 1950 and during the course of his stay produced a variety of about sixty models, mostly of birds (model no. F.548). Royal Crown Derby mark in red enamel

Courtesy Royal Crown Derby Museum

these had been available from the late 1890s. In general, caution was followed in decoration, with the exception of one or two smaller firms such as that of Shelley, who ventured into the fashionable 'jazzy', angular style of Art Deco. Another exception is found in the work of Daisy Makeig-Jones, who was a designer for the Wedgwood company from 1917 until the early 1930s, where she produced distinctive designs of fairyland scenes following book illustrations from such artists as Arthur Rackham and Edmund Dulac. Experiments to improve design were also carried out by such small firms as Gray & Brain (Foley China), who commissioned leading artists such as Laura Knight, Graham Sutherland and others, to produce new patterns. Fine as these new wares were, the names of outstanding artists of the day meant little to the general public upon whom the companies relied to achieve their principal sales, and the mainstream of the pottery industry followed a conservative and safe route, which was probably sensible for those difficult times, but offered little competition to their Continental competitors.

Table wares were the main product of the industry, but 'fancy' wares were also produced, some of which have now already become collectors' items. Doulton's introduced their range of popular figures as early as 1913, some

Another popular Royal Crown Derby figure was that of the robin, the work of Arnold Mikelson,
of recent manufacture (model no. F.558) Courtesy Royal Crown Derby Porcelain Co. Ltd

With the popularity of bird-watching today such figures should well be in great demand, although
these models of budgerigars by Arnold Mikelson would suggest that they have escaped from captivity
(model no. F.555) Courtesy Royal Crown Derby Porcelain Co. Ltd

The famous birds modelled by Dorothy Doughty for the Worcester factory set a new fashion and
it was not long before many other factories were employing fine modellers to make similar series of
animals and birds. The work of Arnold Mikelson is outstanding and here is his 'Brown Owl' of
comparatively recent manufacture (model no. F.525)

Courtesy Royal Crown Derby Porcelain Co. Ltd

Royal Crown Derby bone china model by Arnold Mikelson of 'Blue Tit and Chicks', painted in
enamel colours (model no. F.529). The list in Royal Crown Derby *by John Twitchett and Betty*
Bailey, of the figures made at the factory, include sixty which are the work of this same modeller

Courtesy Royal Crown Derby Porcelain Co. Ltd

Royal Crown Derby model by Arnold Mikelson of 'Thrush Chicks' (nicely balanced by a performing caterpillar), in bone china painted in natural enamel colours of recent manufacture (model no. F542)
Courtesy Royal Crown Derby Porcelain Co. Ltd

Royal Crown Derby 'Chelsea Birds' in bone china painted in colour, c.1976. Modelled by Arnold Mikelson, a Latvian, who was employed at the Derby factory from about 1947, where he produced a wide range of bird models, prior to emigrating to Canada where he continued to sculpt in wood
Courtesy Royal Crown Derby Porcelain Company

Pair of Mansion House dwarfs in bone china painted in enamel colours, a popular model first produced at the original Derby factory at Nottingham Road and still in production today at Osmaston Road. The Mansion House Dwarfs should carry advertising material on their large hats, and are not to be confused with the original Meissen figures of dwarfs, which were in turn copied at Chelsea, c.1755
Courtesy Royal Crown Derby Museum

Octagonal plates are in demand both for table settings and for use as decorative wall plaques, these as illustrated are today in current production at Derby. D. 23cm.
Courtesy Royal Crown Derby Porcelain Co. Ltd

Japan patterns have of course been used by many different porcelain factories, but it is still a pattern most commonly associated with Derby. This current condiment set in their famous 'Old Imari' is decorated in cobalt, red and gold
Courtesy Royal Crown Derby Porcelain Co. Ltd

The shape of the early so-called 'Ginger Jars' as exported from China from the 18th century onwards has remained popular. Today the jars are made by the Royal Crown Derby Porcelain Co. Ltd. in three patterns and three sizes; shown here (left to right) are 'Aves', 'Posy' and 'Old Imari'
Courtesy Royal Crown Derby Porcelain Co. Ltd

John Hugh Plant was a painter of Coalport and Wedgwood before joining the firm of Doulton in 1902; his signature is to be found on many fine pieces painted in a wide variety of subjects. He specialised in views of Venice, but was also an accomplished painter of fish, as seen on this example of his work, c.1905
Courtesy Royal Doulton Ltd

Porcelain dish made by Royal Doulton and painted in enamel colours by J.H. Plant, who was engaged c.1902-20. He specialised in painting castles, but on work which required less hand painting he sometimes used the name J. Hughes   Courtesy Royal Doulton Ltd

Portrait bust of Edward VII, painted in enamel colours by George White in 1902 at Royal Doulton, where he was employd from 1885 until 1912. White was their chief figure painter whose work appeared on vases shown at the 1893 Chicago Exhibition   Courtesy Royal Doulton Ltd

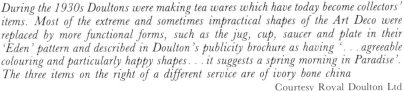

During the 1930s Doultons were making tea wares which have today become collectors' items. Most of the extreme and sometimes impractical shapes of the Art Deco were replaced by more functional forms, such as the jug, cup, saucer and plate in their 'Eden' pattern and described in Doulton's publicity brochure as having '...agreeable colouring and particularly happy shapes...it suggests a spring morning in Paradise'. The three items on the right of a different service are of ivory bone china   Courtesy Royal Doulton Ltd

In the early 1930s a most successful line of animal models was introduced under the title 'Championship Dogs', all modelled by Frederick T. Daws, from 1931 to 1985. Daws was a former student of the Lambeth School of Art who visited kennels to model from life. Almost all his models were produced in three different sizes: illustrated here are the 'Bulldog', 1074, L. 7.9cm., 'Springer Spaniel', 2517, L. 9.5cm., and 'Collie', 1058, L. 12.7cm.   Courtesy Royal Doulton Ltd

This porcelain coffee pot, cup, saucer and plate are made in Royal Doulton English Translucent China, now known as English Fine China, a form of English hard-paste, which is much whiter than that made by foreign manufacturers. 'Morning Star' dates to 1966 and is decorated with overglaze printing, designed by Joseph W. Ledger, ARCA, who was appointed Art Director for Doulton in 1955. H. 18.7cm.   Courtesy Royal Doulton Ltd

The series of table wares in Doulton's bone china, entitled 'Reynard the Fox', proved very popular with the hunting fraternity, and were in production from 1953 to 1975
Courtesy Bearnes, Torquay

This early and sought after Doulton figure of 'Darling' which was in production for fifteen years, was named after being seen by the late Queen Mary, who exclaimed 'Isn't he a darling'. The modeller was Charles Vyse, who was appointed to Doultons as early as 1896, leaving to establish his own studio in Chelsea in 1919. This figure was introduced in 1913 and withdrawn in 1928, and is still one of the most sought after collectors' items. H. 19cm.
Courtesy Royal Doulton Ltd

These two table lamps decorated with Royal Doulton figures feature Genevieve (H.N. 1962) which was withdrawn from production in 1962, and Katrina (H.N. 2327) which was withdrawn in 1969. H. 44.5 and 49.5cm.
Courtesy Bearnes, Torquay

designed by outside artists, and many by talented full-time modellers, as discussed under Doulton.

During the Second World War the home customer had to be content with plain wares, as decoration was restricted to wares for export only. It was not until the early 1950s that restrictions were lifted by the Board of Trade, and the industry was once more allowed to produce new shapes and also decorate their wares. Unfortunately our potteries had become run down during this period, and had to face both Japanese and European competition, by this time working from their newly organised factories. The solution appeared to be for British manufacturers to pool money and resources by merging or forming combines, which many of them did, providing a new pattern of group industries, such as the Wedgwood, Spode and Doulton groups, which later again altered. Spode are now owned by Royal Worcester Ltd., although since 1988 have operated independently, whilst the great firm of Wedgwood was taken over by the Waterford Glass Group Plc in 1986, and in 1989 were renamed Waterford

There can be little doubt that among the most universally collected wares today are Royal Doulton figures, a vast range to which new models are constantly being added, whilst the production of others is frequently being halted, thus immediately creating sought after collectors' items. One of the pioneer modellers in this field was Leslie Harradine (1887-1965) who, inspired by the famous George Tinworth, first created a series of Dickens characters in salt glazed stoneware, later produced in porcelain. Illustrated here are six of his popular figures. Top row, left to right: Hunts Lady, 1926-38, HN1201, H. 21cm.; Swimmer, 1928-38, HN1270, H. 19cm.; Gloria, 1932-8, HN1700, H. 17cm. Bottom row, left to right: Sunshine Girl, 1929-38, HN1344, H. 12.7cm.; Siesta, 1928-38, HN1305, H. 12cm.; Scotties, 1928-38, HN1281, H. 13.3cm.

Courtesy Royal Doulton Ltd

Over the last two years Doultons have reissued some of the figures modelled originally by Peggy Davies from as early as 1947 as miniatures, which are about half the size of the early models. From left to right top and bottom row: Christmas Morn, HN3212, H. 10cm.; Elaine, HN3214, H. 9.5cm.; Southern Belle, HN3174, H. 10cm.; Sunday Best, HN3218, H. 9.5cm.; Fragrance, HN3220, H. 9cm.; Kirsty, HN3213, H. 9.5cm.; Fair Lady, HN3216, H. 9.5cm.; Sara, HN3219, H. 9.5cm.; Ninette, HN3215, H. 9cm. The larger versions are still available

Courtesy Royal Doulton Ltd

Newly issued in 1990 are these three figures in Doulton's 'Pretty Ladies' series, the top figure, modelled by Douglas V. Tootle, is Fiona, H. 18cm.; bottom left, Cheryl, by the same modeller, H. 19cm.; bottom right, Annabel, modelled by Robert Tabbenor, H. 14cm.

Courtesy Royal Doulton Ltd

Commemorative plate, beaker and loving cup made to celebrate the marriage of Charles, Prince of Wales, to Lady Diana Spencer on 29th July 1981. Printed with enamel colours and gilt
Courtesy Royal Doulton Ltd

Commemorative plate made by Royal Doulton Ltd. to celebrate the Royal Wedding of Prince Andrew and Miss Sarah Ferguson on 23rd July, 1986, at Westminster Abbey, printed and painted in enamel colours and gilt
Courtesy Royal Doulton Ltd

Catering for all ages, Royal Doulton Ltd. market figures and table wares modelled or painted in their 'Bunnykins' series, which have been available for over fifty years, to which they are constantly adding. The two pieces illustrated, with specially created scenes by Walter Hayward, were presented to HRH the Princess of Wales when she visited the pottery as a gift for HRH Prince William
Courtesy Royal Doulton Ltd

Royal Doulton Ltd. have added to their range of wares in the 'Bunnykins' series with mugs and plates as gifts at a christening, showing members of the popular rabbit family gathered around the church font
Courtesy Royal Doulton Ltd

This fine figure of 'Leopard on Rock' painted in enamel colours (No.2638) was first issued in 1952, it is still in production in 1990, but the modeller does not appear to have been recorded. L. 29.2cm.

Courtesy Royal Doulton Ltd

Helen of Troy, immortalised by Homer and Christopher Marlowe, modelled by Peggy Davies, was the second figure in her series 'Femmes Fatales'. Helen was the beautiful wife of the Spartan King Menelaus, but her lover, Paris, carried her off to Troy with much treasure, thus precipitating the Trojan War. Other figures in the series include Cleopatra and the Queen of Sheba. Modelled in 1981 in a limited edition of 750. H. 23.4cm.

Courtesy Royal Doulton Ltd

Tz'u-hsi, the Empress Dowager of the Celestial Empire of China, who ruled from behind the throne from 1861 to 1908, born the daughter of a minor mandarin in 1835, was ruthless and malicious and responsible for the fall of the Ch'ing Dynasty. She well deserves her place in the series of 'Femmes Fatales' modelled for Royal Doulton by Peggy Davies in 1983. H. 20.3cm.

Courtesy Royal Doulton Ltd

Doulton's prolific modeller, Peggy Davies, has been producing a very attractive series called initially 'Dancers of the World' since the late 1970s, including such colourful and animated figures as the 'Scottish Highland Dancer', 'Philippine Dancer', 'Indian Temple Dancer' and 'Spanish Flamenco Dancer', the series are in limited editions of 750 world-wide. 'The Breton Dancer' as illustrated was first issued in 1981. H. 21.5cm.

Courtesy Royal Doulton Ltd

A group of Wedgwood 'Fairyland Lustre', painted by Daisy Makeig-Jones, c.1925. This type of decoration was inspired by the work of such artists as Arthur Rackham and Edward Dulac
Courtesy The Wedgwood Museum Trustees, Barlaston, Stoke-on-Trent

A Wedgwood bone china plate from a set of six silk screen designs, entitled 'Variations on a Geometric Theme', by the sculptor and graphic artist, Eduardo Paolozzi. Issued in a limited edition of 200 sets.
Courtesy The Wedgwood Museum Trustees, Barlaston, Stoke-on-Trent

A 'Chou Dynasty' bowl, in bone china, with printed enamel decoration, designed by Susie Cooper in 1979, for Wedgwood. The design is taken from a Chinese bronze of 11th century BC
Courtesy The Wedgwood Museum Trustees, Barlaston, Stoke-on-Trent

Bone china sculpture of the standing figure of a man, centred on a disc which is a silk screen printed lithograph of pale blue to give a cloud-like effect. Entitled 'Sky Plateau II', designed by Glenys Barton, c.1976-7. Mark, WEDGWOOD/MADE IN ENGLAND/SKY PLATEAU II and facsimile signature of Glenys Barton, all printed in black. D. 22.4cm.
Courtesy City Museum & Art Gallery, Stoke-on-Trent

Among the recent new issues of Doulton figures are 'Images of Nature', allowing the sculptors to 'form artistic impressions rather than detailed observations'. The white bone china figure of the cat and dog is termed 'Friendship' (H. 21cm.) and the shoal of fish 'Serenity' (H. 28cm.), both modelled by John Ablitt   Courtesy Royal Doulton Ltd

Continuing their new range of white bone china 'Images' are these two new issues (1990), entitled 'Happy Anniversary' on the left, modelled by Douglas V. Tootle, together with 'Over the Threshold' by Robert Tabbenor. H. (both) 30.5cm.   Courtesy Royal Doulton Ltd

This well-designed teapot is of Doulton's 'Rondo' shape, first produced in 1987. The overglaze printed design, 'Regalia', in blue and green is the work of Hugh Saunders, who has been with Doulton since 1970. H. 16.5cm.   Courtesy City Museum and Art Gallery, Stoke-on-Trent

Porcelain coffee pot, cup and saucer, decorated in colour. The design was registered in 1934 by T.C. Wild & Sons, under the trade name of 'Royal Albert', now part of Royal Doulton Ltd   Courtesy City Museum & Art Gallery, Stoke-on-Trent

Wedgwood. Due to this reorganisation, the industry was able to re-equip and modernise its factories; no longer were the old bottle kilns to be seen on the skyline of the 'five towns' of Arnold Bennett, they were swept away by the Clean Air Act of 1956, and were gradually replaced by the new low tunnel kilns fired by gas or electricity, with many new methods introduced to improve production.

After the dreary years of restricted decoration in all areas of consumer goods, the word 'contemporary' was widely in use to describe the new fashions, eagerly awaited by the young housewives anxious to set up home. Susie Cooper was one of the fashionable designers whose work was much sought after at this time. She originally worked for A.E. Gray & Co. Ltd. of Hanley and later ran her own pottery which amalgamated with R.H. & S.L. Plant Ltd. (Tuscan), which was later taken over by Josiah Wedgwood & Co., where she remained as a designer. Her work was exhibited at the 'Britain Can Make It' exhibition of 1946, and later she provided wares for the Royal Pavilion at the Festival of Britain in 1951. These exhibitions were designed to boost Britain's trade following the long years of restrictions and 'utility' wares.

During the 1950s unusual shapes were introduced, including plates inspired by the shape of the now popular television screen. Colours began to follow the interior designs which were published in popular magazines such as the *Ideal Home* and *House Beautiful*, with grey and maroon particularly fashionable during this period.

The Council of Industrial Design, which was established in 1944 with the aim of encouraging new and better design in all British products, opened the Design Centre in London in 1956. Products which had received the Council's approval were exhibited there, and bore the 'Design Centre Approval' label, which was intended to inspire confidence in the buying public.

Bone china teacup and saucer of 'Black Velvet' design, from 'Hostess Tableware', Tunstall, from c.1965. This trade name was used by the British Anchor Pottery Company, which after various ownerships, is today W.H. Grindley & Co. Ltd., Tunstall, Staffordshire
Courtesy City Museum & Art Gallery, Stoke-on-Trent

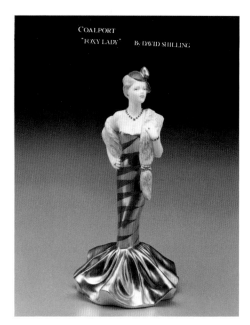

'Foxy Lady', designed by David Shilling, produced by Coalport. This was one of the first figures to be introduced in a limited edition, in the David Shilling Design Collection, in which he depicts a scene of haute couture

Courtesy The Wedgwood Museum Trustees, Barlaston, Stoke-on-Trent

A group of Coalport figures in the 'Debutantes' series, produced in a small size, averaging 12.6cm.

Courtesy The Wedgwood Museum Trustees, Barlaston, Stoke-on-Trent

A popular current design of Spode tablewares is the Stafford Flowers, decorated with a variety of naturalistic flowers in colour and gilt
Courtesy Spode Ltd

Among the many current designs in bone china being made by Spode Ltd. is the Trapnell Sprays, a design which originated c.1900-1 and was reserved to Thomas Goode & Co. the London retailers. The early version of this pattern was very popular, but because it was hand enamelled with gold beading was very expensive and was withdrawn in favour of a new border design on a Chelsea shape
Courtesy Spode Ltd

Spode still find there is a demand for many of their earlier patterns. The reintroduction of this pattern shows the interest in those of the Regency period. The first version is recorded as number 2394 in 1816, and a subsequent revival in 1939 was pattern number Y6179, when the pattern was called 'Regency'. The current pattern illustrated is now known as 'Hallmark' (pattern number Y5799)
Courtesy Spode Ltd

Shelley's tea plate, cup and saucer of bone china in the Queen Anne shape and decorated with the Sunrise and Tall Trees pattern, c.1929
Courtesy Royal Doulton Ltd

Teapot, cup and saucer of bone china, with overglaze printed decoration and gilt. Designed by Harold Holdcroft in 1962, the design is 'Old Country Roses' on Montrose shape, made by Royal Albert, Longton (Doulton)
Courtesy City Museum & Art Gallery, Stoke-on-Trent

Commemorative plate in bone china painted in overglaze enamel colours and gold from the original painting by Jim Mitchell, 'The Battle of Britain 1940-1990 Their Finest Hours'. Made in a limited edition of 326-20,000 world-wide. Made by Hudson & Middleton (Longton) Ltd, Staffordshire, a new company operating under George S. Fairweather since 1975. D 20.6cm.
Issued by the Kingsbury Collection on behalf of The Royal Airforce Museum 1990
Courtesy City Museum & Art Gallery, Stoke-on-Trent

Design for a plate by Reginald Haggar (1905-1988), who was first employed as an Assistant Designer at Minton in 1929 and shortly became the Art Director, a post he held until 1935
Courtesy Minton Museum, Royal Doulton Ltd

This Minton bone china plate is decorated with elaborate raised paste and chased gold, on a Shrewsbury Green ground, a style available in a limited range of table wares. This is probably one of the most expensive modern plates in the world at over £3,500 (1990). D. 27cm.
Courtesy Minton Museum, Royal Doulton Ltd

Lynn Sumner is one of today's talented painters working at Minton, with an example of her work on a special edition of 'Haddon Hall' celebration plates. After her apprenticeship she was trained initially as a figure painter
Courtesy Minton Museum, Royal Doulton Ltd

Wares in the 'Haddon Hall' pattern were first designed in 1949 by John Wadsworth, who was Art Director at Minton from 1935. It is still one of the most popular and best selling tableware patterns, suggested by early embroidery and named after the famous house in Bakewell, Derbyshire. The pattern is applied with lithographic prints on the Bute shape, which they adopted c.1890
Courtesy Minton Museum, Royal Doulton Ltd

Among the many popular designs that Mintons produce today is a range of table wares in the popular 'Jasmine' pattern

A selection of current Minton bone china 'gift-wares' in the 'Fair Isle' pattern, designed by Jean Muir, who is of course a famous fashion designer

Cup and saucer of bone china, decorated in enamel colours and gilding. Made by New Chelsea China Co. Ltd. of Longton, Staffordshire, between 1951 and 1961. D. (saucer) 13.4cm.
Courtesy City Museum and Art Gallery, Stoke-on-Trent

Teacup and saucer of bone china, printed and painted with overglaze colours with a portrait photograph of Queen Elizabeth II, HRH Prince Charles and HRH Princess Anne. Inscribed: 'H M QUEEN ELIZABETH II CROWNED JUNE 2nd 1953'. The photograph is by Marcus Adams. Made by Salisbury China, Longton, Staffordshire. D. (saucer) 14cm.
Courtesy City Museum & Art Gallery, Stoke-on-Trent

Pair of bone china figures of Columbine and Harlequin, painted in the pastel shades currently fashionable, when they were modelled by Peggy Davies in 1956 for Royal Doulton Ltd., these figures were continued in production until 1969. H. 19cm.
Courtesy City Museum & Art Gallery, Stoke-on-Trent

Plate in bone china, printed in colour to celebrate St. Valentine's day, the patron saint of lovers, for 1976. Marked on reverse with an amorous verse and the Royal Doulton Tableware factory mark, ringed with polychrome printed flowers. D. 21cm.
Private Collection

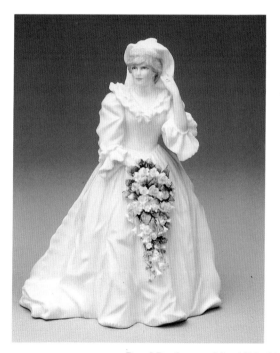

Royal Doulton model published in 1982 of H.R.H. The Princess of Wales, in an edition of 1,500. The modeller, Eric Griffiths, was appointed Head of Doulton's Sculpture Division in 1972. H. 19.6cm.
Courtesy Royal Doulton Ltd

The bone china figure, painted in enamel colours, on the left, is 'Lucinda' from the High Style Collection of Coalport, now part of the Wedgwood Group. H. 22cm. The figure on the right, is the 'Weekend Girl', modelled in 1989 by Timothy Potts, for the Royal Worcester Porcelain Co. H. 21.1cm.
Courtesy City Museum & Art Gallery, Stoke-on-Trent

A wide range of Royal Doulton Fine China Tableware is being made today. The company is particularly proud of 'the sparkling simplicity of pure white octagonal' illustrated here in the Juno pattern, which they claim is oven, freezer, microwave and dishwasher safe, in addition to being chip resistant

Royal Doulton have for many years made wares which have a wide appeal to collectors and they have recently added to their range of ceramic sculptures decorated in rouge flambé, *a glaze perfected by the Chinese potter many centuries ago. Reading from top left to right and then bottom left to right: The Lamp Seller by Robert Tabbenor, H. 23cm; Confucius by Peter Gee, H. 23cm; The Wizard modelled by Alan Maslankowski, H. 25.5cm; a standing Carpet Seller, by William Harper, H. 23cm; The Genie, H. 25cm and the Carpet Seller, H. 17.5cm, by Robert Tabbenor. 'Images of Fire' Series*

Today Royal Doulton are still producing the ever popular 'Real Old Willow' design on a wide variety of table wares in their Majestic shape. Printed in blue with the addition of sparsely applied gilding, the daughter, her lover and the irate father are seen crossing the bridge as related in the romantic love story, but regrettably there does not appear to be any Oriental origin for the tale

Part tea service of bone china, made by Shelleys of Fenton, in their Queen Anne shape, painted in enamel colours of yellow, black and grey with the 'Sunrise and Tall Tree' pattern, introduced c.1929

Courtesy Bearnes, Torquay

Selection of pieces from a bone china tea service made by Shelleys of Fenton, Staffordshire. Painted with flowers in enamel colours with a pink ground on their Queen Anne shape, c.1930

Courtesy Bearnes, Torquay

Part tea service of bone china, made by Shelleys of Fenton, Staffordshire, painted on their Queen Anne shape, with garden and cottage scene, one of over 170 patterns used on this shape, c.1930

Courtesy Bearnes, Torquay

410

Modelled after the famous Walt Disney characters of Snow White and the Seven Dwarfs, these figures were made by the Burslem firm of George Wade & Son Ltd., who are famous for a wide range of minor collectables which include 'Whimsies' and 'Whoppas'. H. 25.5cm.

Courtesy Bearnes, Torquay

A Wedgwood bone china plate painted in brown enamels against a yellow ground, c.1900
Courtesy Wedgwood Museum Trustees, Barlaston, Stoke-on-Trent

This Wedgwood service was ordered for the White House, during the Presidency of Theodore Roosevelt, in 1903. Decorated with the 'Colonnade' border, printed in gold, and with a hand painted representation of the Great Seal of the U.S.A. in polychrome enamels. The service was the work of John Goodwin and Herbert A. Chollerton
Courtesy Wedgwood Museum Trustees, Barlaston, Stoke-on-Trent

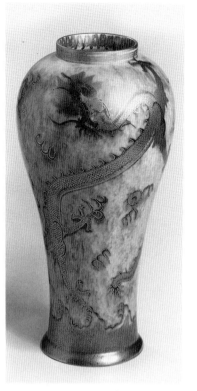

A vase of Chinese baluster form, made by Wedgwood and decorated with a dragon in lustre by Daisy Makeig-Jones, c.1925
Courtesy Wedgwood Museum Trustees, Barlaston, Stoke-on-Trent

A Wedgwood loving cup made in 1936 to commemorate the Coronation of George VI and Queen Elizabeth II. Designed by Dame Laura Knight (1877-1970)
Courtesy Wedgwood Museum Trustees, Barlaston, Stoke-on-Trent

This Coronation pattern was designed by Cecily Stella (Star) Wedgwood, for the Coronation of George VI in 1937, and produced by Wedgwood
Courtesy Wedgwood Museum Trustees, Barlaston, Stoke-on-Trent

This shape and pattern known as 'Sylvia' was designed by Paul Follot and produced by Wedgwood in 1923
Courtesy Wedgwood Museum Trustees, Barlaston, Stoke-on-Trent

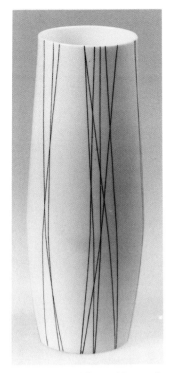

Vase of bone china with overglaze printed decoration, from the range of Queensberry Tableware, designed by David Queensberry when he was designing for Crown Staffordshire Ltd. of Fenton during the 1950s. H. 25cm. Crown Staffordshire China Co. Ltd. are today part of the Wedgwood Group, having been taken over in 1948   Courtesy City Museum & Art Gallery, Stoke-on-Trent

Plate produced by Wedgwood for H.M. The Queen's Coronation Banquet, printed in gold with the design 'Persephone' by Eric Ravilious (1953)
Courtesy Wedgwood Museum Trustees, Barlaston, Stoke-on-Trent

Two plates designed by Laurence Whistler in 1955, entitled 'Outlines of Grandeur', produced by Wedgwood   Courtesy Wedgwood Museum Trustees, Barlaston, Stoke-on-Trent

A plate, designed by Laurence Whistler in 1955 for Wedgwood, entitled 'Dolphins'
Courtesy Wedgwood Museum Trustees, Barlaston, Stoke-on-Trent

The industry seemed to be flourishing during the 1960s and '70s and responded to the fashions of the day with allusions to the contemporary scene, such as a table ware range called 'Flower Power', an oblique reference to the 'Flower People', a young people's peace movement then currently fashionable. These wares were introduced by Washington Pottery (in earthenware). New trends were inspired by such people as Laura Ashley, who created the nostalgic 'country look'. Table wares that could be stacked easily into a small space were introduced, intended to fit into small flats with limited storage space. One of the most successful innovations must have been the introduction of the coffee mug, which fitted in so well with the new casual style of living, as did the oven-to-table wares also introduced about this time. As well as the large dinner services, boxed sets of place settings for four people were also made, which could be added to as required.

A group of bone china wares, using the first lithographed design, multicoloured, with gold edging, entitled 'Charnwood', produced by Wedgwood in the 1960s
Courtesy Wedgwood Museum Trustees, Barlaston, Stoke-on-Trent

A group of wares in bone china designed by Susie Cooper for Wedgwood in 1969, entitled 'Diabolo', painted overglaze   Courtesy Wedgwood Museum Trustees, Barlaston, Stoke-on-Trent

'Apollo', a bone china bowl, 'Shape 225', designed in 1984 by Jerome Gould. The surface pattern of overglaze printing was designed by computer in 1985. Produced by Wedgwood at Barlaston, Stoke-on-Trent
Courtesy City Museum & Art Gallery, Stoke-on-Trent

Coffee pot of bone china, decorated with an overglaze printed design of 'Concerto'. Made by R.H. & S.L. Plant of Longton, c.1987. Established c.1881, this pottery became part of the Wedgwood Group in 1966; the factory was recently renamed Royal Tuscan
Courtesy City Museum & Art Gallery, Stoke-on-Trent

This popular pattern known as the 'Indian Tree' was introduced by Wedgwood in 1801. The pieces shown here are of bone china which are still in current production
Courtesy Wedgwood Museum Trustees, Barlaston, Stoke-on-Trent

A group of porcelain wares, designed by Tom Kellog and Gerome Gould in 1984, entitled 'Tranquillity'. Made by Wedgwood, shape 225
Courtesy Wedgwood Museum Trustees, Barlaston, Stoke-on-Trent

A group of wares in Traditional Shape still in current production
Courtesy Wedgwood Museum Trustees, Barlaston, Stoke-on-Trent

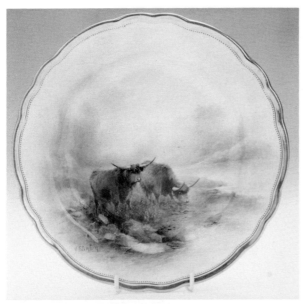

This plate from Royal Worcester is painted with a scene typical of John Stinton, jun. From a family of painters, he is considered to be one of the finest of the landscape painters on china. Printed mark and date code for 1923. D. 22.8cm.

Courtesy Bearnes, Torquay

Vase with pierced neck, painted with enamel colours and gilt by Raymond Rushton. The scene is titled 'Ripple' and the base bears the Worcester mark and date code for 1929. H. 22cm.

Courtesy Bearnes, Torquay

A pair of Royal Worcester baluster vases and covers, decorated with swans in flight amidst reeds, painted against a light blue background. The artist, who specialised in bird studies, was Charles Henry Baldwyn. Printed mark and date code for 1900. H. 23cm.

Courtesy Bearnes, Torquay

A pair of fine Royal Worcester plates, painted by Charles Henry Clifford Baldwyn, who specialised in bird painting, showing swans and fan-tailed pigeons against a light blue ground. Printed mark and date code for 1906. D. 21.8cm.

Courtesy Bearnes, Torquay

417

A pair of Hadley vases, painted by William Jarman, made in 1905, the year in which the firm was amalgamated with the major Worcester Company. Printed marks and date code for 1905. H. 25cm.
Courtesy Bearnes, Torquay

Worcester porcelain vase with pierced decoration, designed to simulate Japanese ivory carving, painted with enamel colours and gilt. The base is also painted and gilt to imitate a wooden stand. Worcester Royal Porcelain factory mark, dating to c.1900. H. 18.5cm.
Courtesy Bearnes, Torquay

Royal Worcester porcelain dish with pierced decoration, painted with enamel colours and gilding. The Highland cattle are painted by John Stinton, jun. (1846-1956). Mark, the Worcester Royal Porcelain Co. with date code for 1906. W. 25cm. The plate on the left is the work of Harry Davis, 1939, who was foreman painter at the Worcester factory, 1928-54. The signature of H. Sivad, which is Davis spelt backwards, was used on the work he prepared to instruct new painters. D. 27cm. The dish on the right shows a view of Ann Hathaway's cottage and was painted by Raymond Rushton, 1940, who specialised in painting seascapes, fine buildings and castles. D. 27cm.
Courtesy Bearnes, Torquay

Very rare Worcester porcelain cup, with enamel painting of a misty view of Venice by Harry Davis; the interior of the cup is entirely gilded. Worcester factory mark and date code for 1926.
Courtesy Bearnes, Torquay

This pair of Royal Worcester vases were painted by Albert Shuck, who is also noted for his paintings of orchids, and fruit. Printed mark and date code for 1914. H. 51cm.

Courtesy Bearnes, Torquay

Part of a Royal Worcester dessert service, possibly painted by Albert Shuck, who was known to have specialised in depicting orchids. Printed mark and date code for 1910

Courtesy Bearnes, Torquay

Plaque of Royal Worcester porcelain, painted in enamel colours and signed by E. Townsend who, despite retiring from the factory at the age of sixty-seven, continued to paint. Edward Townsend became foreman of the male painters in 1954 when Harry Davis retired. This plaque is typical of one of his favourite subjects. W. 36cm.

Courtesy Phillips, London

The small pair of Royal Worcester vases painted with highland cattle on an ivory ground, are signed 'Stinton', and were probably painted by Harry Stinton. Printed mark and date code for 1935. The cylindrical vase in the centre, painted with pheasants in an autumnal landscape, is signed by James Stinton, who specialised in painting game birds. Printed mark and date code for 1935. H. 15cm.

Courtesy Bearnes, Torquay

The Royal Worcester plaque on the left was painted by Harry Stinton (1882-1968) who came from a family of painters, specialised in highland cattle and was a fine watercolourist. A similar plaque, painted with partridges, is on the right. D. (both) 7cm. The central oval plaque, painted with a duck flying out of the reeds is 9.8cm.

Courtesy Bearnes, Torquay

The Royal Worcester plaque in the centre is signed 'SIVAD', which is the reverse name used by Harry Davis, who was well known for his painting of game birds and animals, c.1910. H. 7cm. Of the two smaller plaques, the one on the left is signed by Jack Stanley

Courtesy Bearnes, Torquay

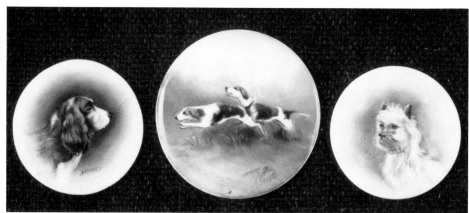

Dessert service of bone china made by the Worcester Royal Porcelain Company and painted in 1933 by Richard Sebright, a highly talented painter of fruit from nature, who also had his watercolours of flowers accepted by the Royal Academy

Courtesy Phillips, London

420

Dorothy Doughty's figures of birds were modelled from life, and are in natural colours. This Moorhen Chick on a Water-Lily Leaf is one of a series of British birds, made at Royal Worcester. Dorothy Doughty completed this series shortly before her death in 1962, they were signed by her, and issued in a limited edition of 500, of life-like size   Courtesy Royal Worcester

Eva L. Soper was first involved as a modeller for Worcester during the 1930s. She initially produced a range of small birds, but went on to model a series of seven models of children in wartime Britain. The 'Evacuees', issued in 1941, is rare. H. 13cm.   Courtesy Phillips, London

Three Royal Worcester bone china figures painted in enamel colours. Modelled by Ruth Van Ruyckevelt, the 'Nursing Sister of The London Hospital' was issued in 1958, 'Melanie' from her Victorian Ladies series, issued in 1962 and the 'Nursing Sister from St. Thomas's Hospital' in 1958; all three were in limited editions of 500. H (Melanie) c.21.5cm.

Courtesy Phillips, London

Two chinoiserie porcelain figures, made by the Worcester Royal Porcelain Company Ltd., and modelled by Miss Pinder-Davies, who was a free-lance modeller for Worcester during the 1940s and '50s; this pair were issued in 1954   Courtesy Phillips, London

Two Royal Worcester porcelain figures modelled by Ruth van Ruyckevelt in her series of Victorian and Edwardian figures; 'Alice' is in the swing (No. 3887) and 'Cecilia' sits on a tree reading a letter (No. 3892), both were modelled in 1969 and were made in editions of 750. H. c.20cm. The Worcester plate painted with birds is from a set of twelve dessert plates painted after original models by Dorothy Doughty. H. 23.5cm.   Courtesy Bearnes, Torquay

This figure of a Green Winged Teal, was modelled by Ronald Van Ruyckevelt for Royal Worcester, from a series of American game birds, produced in a limited edition of 500. Van Ruyckevelt studied the habits of these birds, both in the United States and also at the Wildfowl Trust at Slimbridge, Gloucestershire   Courtesy Royal Worcester

A pair of Pintail Ducks, modelled by Ronald Van Ruyckevelt, from the series of American game birds, produced by Royal Worcester. The task of supporting these bone china figures during the firing process required considerable skill

Courtesy Royal Worcester

Royal Worcester figure of Her Majesty The Queen, when she was HRH Princess Elizabeth, seated on 'Tommy', modelled by Doris Lindner, who is world famous for her ceramic sculptures. The figure is in lifelike colours, and was made at the special wish of Her Majesty Queen Elizabeth, The Queen Mother. Permission was given for 100 copies to be made, and the edition was completed in 1947. H. 38.5cm. L. 28cm.   Courtesy Royal Worcester

Doris Lindner modelled these two Royal Worcester groups. On the left, 'Princess Grace & Foal', H. 24cm., and on the right a model of the racehorse, 'Nijinsky', H. 28cm. Both were issued in limited editions, during the 1960s. Much painstaking care went into the production of these groups
        Courtesy Bearnes, Torquay

Two Royal Worcester groups, on the left the 'Huntsman and Hounds', H. 23.5cm, on the right 'At the Meet', H. 22.8cm. Probably modelled between 1960 and 1970   Courtesy Bearnes, Torquay

This figure of Wellington is one of a series of great Generals on horseback, modelled by Bernard Winskill, in bone china, and issued in 1969 in a limited edition of 750, by Royal Worcester
        Courtesy Royal Worcester

Monteith of bone china, printed with overglaze decoration and gilt, from the Worcester Heritage Collection, 1989, made by The Worcester Royal Porcelain Company Ltd. H. 10.8cm.
Courtesy City Museum & Art Gallery, Stoke-on-Trent

Part of a Royal Worcester coffee service, painted by various artists. This type of ware is lavish and expensive, but still in production today. The interiors of the cups are painted in gold
Courtesy Bearnes, Torquay

By the 1980s and '90s so much more was demanded of the industry as ceramics were required to withstand the stresses of automatic dish-washers, microwave ovens and freezers. We have come a long way from the first proud mid-eighteenth century claim of the Worcester Porcelain Company that their secret recipe would produce wares to withstand hot liquid without cracking or crazing, and the statement of Richard Chaffers of Liverpool advertising on 10th December, 1756, that 'All the ware is proved with boiling water'.

Today the names of industrial designers are little known to collectors. Fortunately their work is recorded by scholars such as Kathy Niblett of the City Museum & Art Gallery, Stoke-on-Trent, where in 1990 she produced an excellent catalogue for an exhibition held there in that year, entitled 'Dynamic Design', which covered British industrial potteries from 1940. Important movements in the industry are also published by Rodney Hampson, a member of the Northern Ceramic Society, in their quarterly News Letter, which is circulated to all members. It is due to the dedication of such enthusiasts that the continuing history of twentieth century industrial wares will be available for future generations.

20th CENTURY STUDIO POTTERS WORKING IN PORCELAIN

Today the studio potter is no longer satisfied with making traditional wares, which in nearly every case calls for the earthenwares and stonewares as used from medieval times. The refined material of porcelain calls for new ideas, enabling the potter to express himself or herself in clay, as a painter might on canvas, for no longer is it considered essential to make purely functional wares. Art objects have for many centuries been created from a wide variety of materials, wood, glass, metals of every type from iron to gold, stone and marble. Today many artists and sculptors are turning from painting and creating works of art in these materials, to the ideal medium of clay; here we are only concerned with those who work in porcelain, perhaps now best referred to as ceramists, who in many cases make only one example of a form, or achieve an unusual and exciting glaze, with most shunning repetitive work, although at times 'bread-and-butter' easy selling wares for marketing commercially have to be produced alongside the art objects.

During most of the nineteenth century there were many industrially made porcelains and these gave many talented painters an opportunity to produce

A bowl with a green glaze decorated with a landscape in brown, black and green. Impressed marks D.E. within a circle. D. 29.2cm. David Eeles (b.1933), works with his family Simon, Caroline and Benjamin, all potters, at the Shepherds Well Pottery in Mosterton, Dorset; they also have three retail shops at Bridport, Watergore and Lyme Regis. Many themes from the countryside are shown on his wares, often taken from sketches of nearby scenes. David Eeles was a founder member of the Craftsmen Potters Association, and his wares can be seen in major museums
Courtesy City Museum & Art Gallery, Stoke-on-Trent

Wall lamp of semicircular form, thinly slip cast in bone china, which is fired to 1260°C, after which the highly translucent form is decorated with the use of an airbrush through a series of masks, in this instance in blue, lilac and turquoise, then it is again fired and polished by hand to achieve an eggshell matt finish. This lamp, made in 1987, is unmarked, but most of the wares made in this technique by Sasha Wardell bear her initials 'SKW'. She studied for her degrees in art in Staffordshire and Bath, where she is at present teaching part-time at Bath College of Higher Education. W. 18.5cm. Courtesy City Museum & Art Gallery, Stoke-on-Trent

wares of beauty, which although identical in form, having been produced with the aid of moulds and machines, were painted with landscapes, figures, floral subjects or designs of entirely original work. As the industry moved into the twentieth century, these expensive art wares became rarer, and competition was so keen, that cheaper forms of decoration, such as transfer printing, became essential to cater for the masses.

Today, it is pleasing to see that once again the industry is endeavouring to provide for the more discerning buyer, and is employing more talented designers, though unfortunately not enough. There is very little hand painting to be seen in today's factories, and the potter now working in the industry never

Prior to becoming a sculptor in ceramics in 1950, Mrs Audrey Blackman (d.1990) worked in bronze. It is only in recent years that she abandoned working in earthenware with underglaze decoration and had favoured porcelain. Her unique technique of using rolls and sheets of clay is best told in her own words in her book Rolled Pottery Figures, *published by Pitman in 1978 and subsequently in a revised edition in 1982 by A. & C. Black. Her pieces were all one-off, hand built creations. This white and coloured biscuit porcelain group is entitled 'A Seat in the Sun'. Marked with 'A. Blackman 1983 Op.5' incised*

Courtesy City Museum & Art Gallery, Stoke-on-Trent

Probably the most widely known and appreciated of present day studio potters is Lucie Rie, who has been producng fine wares since she started her career in Vienna in 1921. She moved to London in 1937, where for a time she worked with the late Hans Coper (d.1981); her much admired porcelains were not produced until after 1949. Today her pieces are much sought after and fetch record prices in the salerooms, something few potters achieve in their lifetime. D. 23cm.

Courtesy City Museum & Art Gallery, Stoke-on-Trent

Marianne de Trey shows her love of both form and bold pattern in this porcelain bowl. She is pictured in the 1989 edition of Potters, the directory of the Craftsmen Potters Association of Britain, as having potted at Dartington, Devon, since 1947 and today she concentrates on 'one-off' creations, mostly in porcelain. D. 20cm.   Courtesy City Museum & Art Gallery, Stoke-on-Trent

Four porcelain dishes made by Derek Emms, a member of the Craftsmen Potters Association. His work is undoubtedly inspired by the wares made in China during the Yuan and Song dynasties and consists primarily of porcelain or stoneware fired in a propane gas kiln to 1280°, in a reducing atmosphere. His clever use of iron oxide is seen in these porcelain dishes: top left with no addition of oxide to the glaze, bottom left with 0.5% red iron oxide, top right 2% and bottom right using a copper oxide. D. 14cm.

Courtesy *The Ceramic Review*, July-August, 1990

Two individual pieces modelled in porcelain: a large globular vessel with a tree frog (H. 12cm), and a small covered box, by Ruth and Alan Barrett-Danes. Unmarked, but initials are sometimes found. Much of their work shows rather grotesque animal forms. Alan Barrett-Danes and his wife Ruth established a studio in Abergavenny, Wales, where they produce wares in both stoneware and porcelain; their work is exhibited in many private collections and major museums. Ruth Barrett-Danies trained at Plymouth College of Art

Courtesy City Museum & Art Gallery, Stoke-on-Trent

A carved porcelain bowl with a mother-of-pearl glaze, in flower form, seemingly influenced by the Ding wares produced in China during the Song dynasty. Made by Tina Sargeant. D. 15cm.

Courtesy City Museum & Art Gallery, Stoke-on-Trent

A porcelain cup with elaborate pierced handles in pale grey with a semi-matt glaze with a pink tinge, the surface of which is crazed. Janet Hamer works in Wales, sharing a studio with Frank Hamer. H. 7.5cm.

Courtesy City Museum & Art Gallery, Stoke-on-Trent

A vessel in stoneware with an attached porcelain ribbon, in an unusual incorporation of the two materials. Made in 1984 by Ian Perie, who trained at the Grays School of Art, Aberdeen, 1969-73, where he now lectures. At one time he worked in partnership with Bill Brown at the Rosebank Pottery where he produced both stoneware and porcelain, drawing inspiration from the landscape and natural imagery. Mark, I.P., monogram within a circle

Courtesy City Museum & Art Gallery, Stoke-on-Trent

This bowl, thrown by Julian Bellmont, has a tin glaze overpainted in gold lustre by Alan Caiger-Smith, treating the ceramic form in the maiolica tradition with broad flowing brush strokes. Caiger-Smith founded the Aldermaston Pottery in 1955 where Julian Bellmont is one of his assistants. After studying painting at Camberwell, Caiger-Smith studied pottery at the Central School of Art and Design. Many major museums have examples of his work. Marks, impressed 'J. Julian Bellmont', painted 'A.C.S.' Year Mark for 1982. H. 5.5cm. D. 21cm.

Courtesy City Museum & Art Gallery, Stoke-on-Trent

Eileen Lewenstein has been potting for over forty years; she moved from London to Hove in 1976, where she has a studio on the shore. She works in stoneware and porcelain and often bases her forms on the sea and its natural effect on the beach. Her work is represented in many major museums and private collections throughout the world. The sculpture shown here is entitled 'Diptych-Connecting', 1988. H. 13.5cm.

Courtesy City Museum & Art Gallery, Stoke-on-Trent

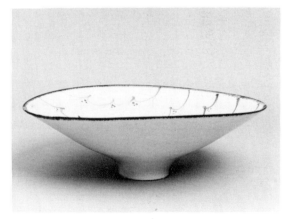

This kettle and bottle with a cream glaze, a pink crackle, and handle of bamboo, are the work of David Leach, who worked with his father Bernard Leach at the Leach Pottery in St. Ives until 1956. Later he moved to Bovey Tracey in Devon and started the Lowerdown Pottery there. He has three sons, all potters, who are carrying on the family tradition. Much of his work is on show in museums both here and on the Continent. He initiated the Dartington Pottery Training Workshop in 1975 with the late David Canter, and spends part of each year giving lectures, demonstrations, and workshops chiefly in the U.S.A., Canada and on the Continent. Impressed marks. H. (bottle) 7.8cm.

Courtesy City Museum & Art Gallery, Stoke-on-Trent

A porcelain bowl, the work of David Leach at Bovey Tracey, Devon, in 1978 (see previous illustration). Impressed marks

Courtesy City Museum & Art Gallery, Stoke-on-Trent

Since 1971 Patrick O'Hara has been creating scientifically accurate porcelain sculptures of flowers and butterflies in their natural habitat. In December 1990 he was engaged in his 453rd composition. He has held exhibitions of his work throughout the world and in 1989 when the European heads of government attended the E.C. summit meeting in Dublin, Ireland, Charles Haughey, the Irish Prime Minister, presented them each with a gift of Patrick O'Hara's work, featuring an endangered species of flower from their own country. Each of his sculptures is single and unrepeated.

'Shooting Stars' is in hard-paste porcelain, painted in enamel colours. The specimens depicted are related to the primulas and cyclamens, 'these aptly named flowers were once common throughout Canada and the Northern States, growing in close association with the Yellow Puccoon also portrayed'. At the base of the plant is a Buckeye butterfly. Made in 1974, it is now in the collection of the Chicago Horticultural Society Museum. H.19cm. Courtesy Patrick O'Hara

has the pleasure of preparing the clay and nursing the creation until its removal from the oven.

The authors' first experience of the creative potter within the industry was in 1959, when the exhibition of 'Three Centuries of Swedish Pottery, Rörstrand', was staged at the Victoria & Albert Museum. The exhibition included the wide variety of wares made at the factory since its beginnings in 1729, together with the work of Scandinavian potters who had been given facilities within the factory from about 1932, by Fredrik Wehtje, the Director at the time, to create individual art objects. This was a most successful venture resulting in beautiful shapes and glazes in hard-paste porcelain from the hands of such famous potters as Hertha Bengston and Carl Harry Stålhane.

By comparison, on a recent visit to a large industrialised English pottery, press-moulded handles were being attached to 'jam-jar' shaped machine produced cylinders by yet another machine, quick maybe, but the operative was certainly missing the pleasure one has, of stroking a rod of wet clay through the fingers to fashion the required section, and then applying and shaping by hand, to produce a 'comfortable' mug.

In their excellent book *New Ceramics*, Eileen Lowenstein and Emmanuel Cooper point out that prior to about 1920, there was a great divide between the work of the studio potter, which was at the time considered to be merely a craft, and was only shown at exhibitions or shops, and that of the painter, whose work was exhibited in art galleries. . . 'it was not until the early 1920s that one English potter, William Staite Murray (1881-1962), was able to cross the barrier between craft and fine art by having his vigorously thrown pieces exhibited at the Lefevre Galleries in London. Each of his pots was given a title, and the prices were comparable with those asked for paintings and sculptures. His aim was for the acceptance of pottery as a medium for expression, on a par with other fine arts'.

In *A Collector's History of English Pottery,* Griselda Lewis well covers the work of the studio potter to the present day, in stoneware and earthenware, but now an increasing number of potters are finding the finesse available in porcelain forms, where at times the advantage of translucency can be exploited, and a new and wide range of exciting art objects is offered. Lucie Rie's work in porcelain has been universally acclaimed for over twenty years; it is amazing that one potter can produce so many pieces without repetition, yet her particular use of the material produces wares of such striking individuality that they need no label, as a Rie creation could only have come from her hands.

A beautiful hand thrown porcelain bowl with deep red copper glaze, acquired by firing in a reduction kiln, which well illustrates the aim of James Walford, which was to 'produce pieces that one can live with and that approach the serenity of the Chinese tradition but with my own variations'. James Walford's 'Retrospective Exhibition' was staged in July, 1990, at Leigh Gallery, 17 Leigh Street, London. D. 15.3cm.   Courtesy Leigh Gallery

A porcelain bowl decorated in underglaze blue, and marked with the initials 'DE' on the base. Made by Derek Emms (b.1929), who studied at Accrington, Burnley and Leeds Colleges of Art and later worked at the Leach Pottery, St. Ives, under Bernard and David Leach. From 1955 to 1985 he was a lecturer in the Department of Three-Dimensional Design (Ceramics) at the North Staffordshire Polytechnic (formerly Stoke-on-Trent College of Art). He retired in 1985 from full-time teaching and is now producing wares in porcelain or stoneware at his own pottery at Stone in Staffordshire. D. 24.5cm. Courtesy City Museum & Art Gallery, Stoke-on-Trent

A porcelain bowl carved and pierced, with a cream glaze and a cream and black crackle, with an incised mark. D. 24cm. The work of Peter Lane is mainly in oxidised porcelain, and are often translucent bowls springing from narrow foot rings such as this bowl. The main inspiration for his work was the natural landscape or other forms found in nature. Peter Lane, who trained at the Bath Academy of Art, is a Fellow of the Society of Designer-Craftsmen and was awarded the Society's Silver Medal in 1981. He was Senior Lecturer in Art Education & Ceramics at the University of East Anglia, Norwich. He is also the author of several books on ceramics and has given many lectures in Britain, and the Continent as well as Australia and North America. His work is represented in many public and private collections Courtesy City Museum & Art Gallery, Stoke-on-Trent

Fine bone china vessels, made c.1978 by Angela Verdon, who has her own studio at Longton, Staffordshire, where she has developed a wide range of unique and delicate, often lace-like, wares. Mark, AV monogram Courtesy City Museum & Art Gallery, Stoke-on-Trent

Porcelain vase made by Mrs Mary Rogers, whose original hand built ceramic wares are to be seen in many major museums in Britain and the U.S.A. Her mark is 'MER' incised or an impressed seal with the initials in monogram form. This undulating vase was made in her studio in 1984 at Loughborough, Leicestershire Courtesy City Museum & Art Gallery, Stoke-on-Trent

A studio potter must consider that he has 'arrived' when fakes of his work appear on the market, as was the case with wares pretending to have been made at St. Ives by the famous Bernard Leach. It was Shoji Hamada, who came from

A hand built porcelain bowl made by Karin Hassenberg at her studio in Walsall, Staffordshire in 1982
Courtesy City Museum & Art Gallery, Stoke-on-Trent

'Sea Holly on the Shore' (Erngium maritimum *with* Melitaea cinxia, *shells and pebbles*), *mounted on an onyx plinth. Hard-paste porcelain painted in enamel colours after nature. Produced by Patrick O'Hara in 1973 and now in a private collection in London. H. 22.5cm.*
Courtesy Patrick O'Hara

Japan with Leach in 1920, who when questioned whether he was worried about other potters making reproductions of his wares, replied 'no', not if it was a good fake, then he would take the credit, but if he made a bad pot, it could always be blamed on the faker. (It is not easy to reproduce the work of a master, as I well know. My own evening class pottery Astbury figure was immediately recognised as 'a fake' by the late W.B. Honey, when head of the Ceramics Department at the Victoria & Albert Museum.)

We illustrate the work of some of the creative potters in porcelain, and it would be unfair to suggest whose work we find the most pleasing. One can only draw the reader's attention to the Craftsmen Potters Association of Great Britain, whose constantly changing display and exhibitions of their members' work are to be seen at William Blake House, 7 Marshall Street, London, W1N 1FD. Those further afield can keep abreast of what is happening in the world of creative clay by subscribing to *Ceramic Review,* the well produced and informative journal, which appears six times a year and is available from the above address.

FURTHER READING:
Ross, Muriel, *Artist Potters in England,* Faber & Faber, 1970.
Lewenstein, Eileen and Cooper, Emanuel, *New Ceramics,* Studio Vista, 1974.

20th CENTURY INDEPENDENT DECORATORS

It was in 1871 that Mintons first set up their 'Art-Pottery Studio' in Kensington, London, adjacent to the Royal Albert Hall, under the direction of William Stephen Coleman, one of their outstanding painters who specialised in figure compositions. It was the company's ambition to attract students from the London schools of art to learn to apply fine decoration on the ceramic 'blanks' supplied by their Staffordshire factory. Among the students who enrolled was Hannah Barlow, who was to achieve recognition through her association with Doultons.

Porcelain plate, painted in enamel colours by Peter Graves, the present Chairman of the British China & Porcelain Artists' Association. From 1975-80 Mr Graves was employed as a painter at Coalport China Ltd. in their Prestige Art Department, since when he has furthered his career as a watercolour artist, and a china painter, favouring decorating miniature boxes and perfume bottles. He also demonstrates at the Gladstone Pottery Museum, Longton, Staffordshire. Both Princess Margaret and former President Jimmy Carter of the U.S.A. own examples of his work. D. 25.5cm.
Courtesy Peter Graves

Cup, painted in enamel colours with fruit and gilded with 22ct gold, by Marie Graves, who between 1975 and 1980 was a still life painter on the porcelains made by Coalport China Ltd. Since 1980 she has, like her husband Peter, also been a self-employed artist working both in watercolour and china painting. She is a tutor for the British China & Porcelain Artists' Association by whom she was commissioned to paint a gift made by the association for ex-Prime Minister Margaret Thatcher. H. 11.5cm.
Private Collection

Plate of porcelain painted by Milwyn Holloway, an artist of traditional hand painted china, now working independently. He started as a modeller and painter at the Worcester Royal Porcelain Co. Ltd. in 1955 at the age of fifteen, as an apprentice to the famous Worcester painter Harry Davis, whose influence on Mr. Holloway can be clearly seen in this painting. We are told by Henry Sandon in his book on Royal Worcester Porcelain, *that Mr. Holloway's hobby was motor racing and that he left the factory to become a freelance painter and teacher in 1971. D. 21.2cm.*

Private Collection

Four porcelain trinket boxes painted in enamel colours by Wanda Sutton, who is a teacher of ceramic painting to members of the British China & Porcelain Artists' Association in the South-Eastern Region. D. 6cm. Courtesy Mrs Wanda Sutton

Porcelain plaque of 'Little Dorritt' painted in enamel colours by Mrs Pat Norman, a teacher of ceramic painting to members of the B.C.P.A.A. in the Yorkshire area and Chairman of the Diploma Committee. Mrs. Norman was at one time a college art teacher Courtesy Mrs Pat Norman

This theatrical design plate, with the novel representation of the audience around the border, was painted to commemorate the retirement of a musical producer by Sheila Southwell, who has written three books on her art. She is Founder President of the Southern China Painting Club and recently produced five murals for the VIP Terminal at Gatwick Airport

The London firm of Howell and James supplied 'blanks' and all the necessary colours, brushes, etc., for the non-industrial painters, who were not always amateurs, and arranged exhibitions where they could exhibit their work.

Many so-called 'easel painters' were attracted to this form of art, appreciating that the colours used in this form of painting would remain permanent after firing. It was the late Bernard Rackham, a former Keeper of the Department of Ceramics at the Victoria & Albert Museum, who when writing of fifteenth and sixteenth century Italian maiolica commented on this fact and that the high temperature colours fired on the tin-glaze were a much truer picture of the original work than that seen and greatly admired today on the painting and murals of the same period, many of which have deteriorated to a great extent over the last four or five hundred years.

Today there has been a great revival in this form of art, both as a profession and also as a hobby and there are hundreds of enthusiastic earthenware or porcelain painters, many of whom are members of the British China & Porcelain Artists Association. The Association is in its eleventh year and has approximately 1,000 members who are able to attend local classes, where professional tuition is available for both beginners and advanced painters from teachers who hold the Association Diploma. Weekend workshops are held in the various regions and an annual convention is held over a Spring weekend, usually attended by hundreds of members. Many of these members contribute to an exhibition of their work which often shows great originality and is so much more satisfying than the commercially sold limited editions of flowers or scenes by a well-known artist, for which the advertisements so often forget to mention that the decoration is merely a form of transfer print. The newest technology under development consists of a full colour design transferred on to the glazed ware in one print, and it is very difficult to distinguish from original work.

REGISTRATION OF DESIGNS & FORMS

Prior to the publication of the first post-war *Handbook of Pottery & Porcelain Marks* (J.P. Cushion in collaboration with W.B. Honey, Faber & Faber, 1956), the deciphering of the mysterious lozenge or 'diamond' mark seen on many pieces of pottery or porcelain was a puzzle to many collectors. From the tables and diagrams published in that first edition could be determined the day, month and year the design or form had first been registered with the Patent Office. The name of the potter, wholesaler, agent or retailer could be obtained by sending an accurate reading of the mark to the Patent Office, with a fee which at that time was one shilling. In later editions of the handbook, now in its fourth edition, and the *Pocket Book of British Ceramic Marks,* by the same author, the authorities of the Patent Office kindly gave permission for the entries relevant to pottery and porcelain to be extracted from the Class IV index (which at the time was kept in the Victoria & Albert Museum), to be published, enabling the reader to not only check the date but also the name and location of the firm or person who applied for the copyright to be registered.

The first Act of Parliament concerning the protection of designs was in 1787, but this was primarily for the protection of the expanding textile industry and only gave protection for three months. Further Acts and amendments were later introduced and in 1797 a Copyright Act was passed concerned with sculpture, which sometimes was used by the pottery firms producing relief moulded jugs and similar high relief wares, when the manufacturer merely printed a mark 'Published by...' followed by the name, address and date of the first publication, but no records relating to these wares were kept.

The two acts passed in 1839, the Copyright of Designs Acts, covered almost all materials, which were protected for a twelve month period, with the exception of metalwork, which was for three years.

Under the Copyright of Design Act of 1842, when thirteen different classes of wares were named, ceramics were included in Class IV and given protection against 'piracy' for a period of three years. The applicant was required to send full details of the application in the form of a drawing, painting or print and the appropriate symbol was allocated to the firm or person concerned to apply to the ware now registered and protected for the three year period. The mark gives a number or letter in the four corners of the device, which by consulting the appropriate table gives the date, the 'parcel' or 'bundle' number relating to the pack of relevant drawings, etc., deposited with the Patent Office, where sometimes as many as twenty-seven designs or forms were registered on the same day. This service was not free and between 1852 and 1880 the Commission for Patents showed a profit of £2,000,000. This method of illustrating the copyright continued until 1883, after which time a simple Registered Number was shown on the wares and the period of protection extended to five years, which was extended yet again in 1907 to another five years, with a further five years at the Comptroller's direction.

The long list of numbers and year dates from 1884 to 1990 indicate the first number taken up on 1st January of that year; these numbers continue progressively until August, 1989, when the series was terminated at 1,061,406 and from August 1st a new sequence of numbers was started at 2,000,000. This system enables the enquirer to check the actual year in which their item was first registered, but if the name of the manufacturer, retailer, dealer or agent responsible for registering the design is required, then one has to approach the Public Record Office, Ruskin Avenue, Kew, Richmond, Surrey, TW9 4DU, where the design records from 1839 until 1910 are kept in a department open to the public. For information regarding registrations from 1910 to the present, the records are preserved in the Patent Office Library, 25 Southampton Buildings, London, WC2A 1AY. This department is not open to the public and prior arrangements are essential (tel: 071 405 8721).

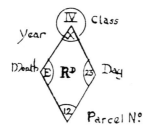

Example of ceramic design registered on 23rd May 1842

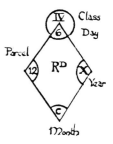

Example of ceramic design, registered on 6th January 1868

1842-67

IV = the Class number (Ceramics)
Top letter = year
Left letter = month
Right number = day
Lower number = parcel or bundle number

1868-83

IV = the Class number
Top number = day
Left number = parcel or bundle number
Right letter = year
Lower letter = month

A	=	1845	N	=	1864		
B	=	1858	O	=	1862		
C	=	1844	P	=	1851		
D	=	1852	Q	=	1866		
E	=	1855	R	=	1861		
F	=	1847	S	=	1849		
G	=	1863	T	=	1867		
H	=	1843	U	=	1848		
I	=	1846	V	=	1850		
J	=	1854	W	=	1865		
K	=	1857	X	=	1842		
L	=	1856	Y	=	1853		
M	=	1859	Z	=	1860		

A	=	1871	L	=	1882
C	=	1870	P	=	1877
D	=	1878	S	=	1875
E	=	1881	U	=	1874
F	=	1873	V	=	1876
H	=	1869	X	=	1868
I	=	1872	Y	=	1879
J	=	1880			
K	=	1883			

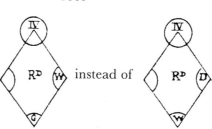

instead of

From 1st to 6th March, 1878, the above Registration Mark was issued.

The months for both periods:

A	=	December	D	=	September	H	=	April	M	=	June
B	=	October	E	=	May	I	=	July	R	=	August
C/O	=	January	G	=	February	K	=	November	W	=	March

Note: K also used December, 1860 and R used 1-19 September, 1857.

Registration numbers used within the year:

1	=	1884	666128	=	1919	872531	=	1954
19754	=	1885	673750	=	1920	876067	=	1955
40480	=	1886	680147	=	1921	879282	=	1956
64520	=	1887	687144	=	1922	882949	=	1957
90483	=	1888	694999	=	1923	887079	=	1958
116648	=	1889	702671	=	1924	891665	=	1959
141273	=	1890	710165	=	1925	895000	=	1960
163767	=	1891	718057	=	1926	899914	=	1961
185713	=	1892	726330	=	1927	904638	=	1962
205240	=	1893	734370	=	1928	909364	=	1963
224720	=	1894	742725	=	1929	914536	=	1964
246975	=	1895	751160	=	1930	919607	=	1965
268392	=	1896	760583	=	1931	924510	=	1966
291241	=	1897	769670	=	1932	929335	=	1967
311658	=	1898	779292	=	1933	934515	=	1968
331707	=	1899	789019	=	1934	939875	=	1969
351202	=	1900	799097	=	1935	944932	=	1970
368154	=	1901	808794	=	1936	950046	=	1971
385180	=	1902	817293	=	1937	955342	=	1972
403200	=	1903	825231	=	1938	960708	=	1973
424400	=	1904	832610	=	1939	965185	=	1974
447800	=	1905	837520	=	1940	969249	=	1975
471860	=	1906	838590	=	1941	973838	=	1976
493900	=	1907	839230	=	1942	978426	=	1977
518640	=	1908	839980	=	1943	982815	=	1978
535170	=	1909	841040	=	1944	987910	=	1979
552000	=	1910	842670	=	1945	993012		1980
574817	=	1911	845550	=	1946	998302	=	1981
594195	=	1912	849730	=	1947	1004456	=	1982
612431	=	1913	853260	=	1948	1010583	=	1983
630190	=	1914	856999	=	1949	1017131	=	1984
644935	=	1915	860854	=	1950	1024174	=	1985
653521	=	1916	863970	=	1951	1031358	=	1986
658988	=	1917	866280	=	1952	1039055	=	1987
662872	=	1918	869300	=	1953	1047478	=	1988
						1056076	=	1989
						2003698	=	1990

The numbering sequence stopped with 1061406 in August 1989 and the new sequence for designs filed after 1st August, 1989, started with 2,000,000.

FURTHER READING:

Cushion, John P. in collaboration with W.B. Honey, *Handbook of Pottery & Porcelain Marks* (4th Edn.), Faber & Faber, 1990.
Cushion, John P., *Pocket-Book of British Ceramic Marks* (3rd Edn.), Faber & Faber, 1988.

Antique Societies

Antique Societies where members can further their knowledge of British Porcelain and other fields of collecting:

Antique Collectors' Club, Regional Clubs of the. The monthly Journal of this club, *Antique Collecting,* lists full details of over one hundred home and overseas clubs, a list which is constantly being updated. The current Journal even lists a new club in Japan.

Belleek Collectors' Society, which publishes a magazine, *The Belleek Collector.* Apply to The Belleek Pottery Ltd., Belleek, Co. Fermanagh, Northern Ireland. Tel: Belleek 501.

Derby Porcelain International Society. A very successful, comparatively new society formed by members whose main ceramic interest is concerned with those made at the Derby factories since the mid-18th century. Hon. Secretary, Marilyn Swain, Westgate Hall, Westgate, Grantham, Lincolnshire, NG31 6LT.

English Ceramic Circle. Started in 1927 as the English Porcelain Circle. Monthly meetings are held in London when papers are read by some of the foremost scholars in the field. Applications for membership from Mrs Joan E. Bennett, 5, The Drive, Beckenham, Kent, BR3 1EE.

The Friends of the Museum and Art Gallery, Hanley, Stoke-on-Trent. A very active group of Museum Friends, who participate in a wide range of museum activities, including many lectures and seminars held in the midst of the finest ceramic collections in Britain. Applications for membership to The Membership Secretary, Friends of the Museum and Art Gallery, c/o City Museum and Art Gallery, Bethesda Street, Hanley, Stoke-on-Trent, ST1 3DE.

Goss and other crested China. There are two major societies catering for collectors of wares decorated with enamel crests, in the south: The Crested Circle: The Editor, Bob Southall, 42 Douglas Road, Tolworth, Surbiton, Surrey, and for northern collectors: The Goss Collectors' Club, The Secretary, Mrs M. Latham, 3 Carr Hall Gardens, Barrowford, Nelson, Lancashire.

Morley College Ceramic Circle. A group which was started in 1967 by ceramic collectors who had previously been attending the author's evening classes on the 'History of Pottery & Porcelain', sponsored by the University of London Extra-Mural Department, which ran from 1960-80. Today the Circle, with still a few founder members, meets on alternate weeks during term-time to either hear a lecture or participate in a 'Masterclass' on a special subject. Annually a weekend seminar is held in late autumn at which outstanding scholars in the chosen field are invited to lecture; the year 1990 saw the 20th seminar. For membership write to The Secretary, Morley College Ceramic Circle, Morley College, 61, Westminster Bridge Road, London, SE1.

Northern Ceramic Society. A group founded in 1972, which shares many interests with the Hanley Museum, mentioned above. Frequent meetings and seminars are held, all relating to some aspect of the study and appreciation of pottery and porcelain, nearly all the meetings being in and around the Potteries. Their main annual event is a week's Summer School run in association with the University of Keele, usually held in August. Membership Secretary, Mrs Hilary Thomas, 'Bramdean' Jacksons Lane, Hazel Grove, Stockport, Cheshire.

Royal Doulton International Collectors Club. A flourishing organisation devoted to meeting the needs and special interests of Royal Doulton enthusiasts. Application forms for membership are available from Royal Doulton International Collectors Club, Royal Doulton Ltd. Minton House, London Road, Stoke-on-Trent, ST4 7QD.

Spode Society. An enthusiastic group of Spode collectors, with many meetings and visits to various venues to study Spode wares throughout the country. Membership Secretary, Mrs Rosalind Pulver, P.O. Box 1812. London NW4 4NW.

The Wedgwood Society. The membership of the Wedgwood Society extends throughout the world, a very active organisation with many well attended meetings catering for collectors of the many types of ware made by the factory of Josiah Wedgwood since 1759. For information on membership write to The Wedgwood Society, Hon. Sec. Mrs B. Jarvis, The Roman Villa, Rockbourne, Fordingbridge, Hampshire.

Associates of the Wedgwood Museum. A wide range of activities are annually arranged at the fine Wedgwood Museum, at Barlaston, Stoke-on-Trent, to where the production was moved from Etruria. For the casual visitor there are also showrooms of today's productions and demonstrations and a nearby 'seconds shop'. For membership write to Associates of the Wedgwood Museum, Curator, Gaye Blake Roberts, The Wedgwood Museum, Barlaston, Stoke-on-Trent, ST12 9ES.

Glossary

ACID GILDING   A decorative process usually applied to the borders of plates by which a design is etched on the porcelain glaze through a wax with hydrofluoric acid, gold is then applied overall and after burnishing, the bright raised areas contrast with the slightly sunken matt areas. A style of decoration used in England from about 1870 on very expensive wares.

ARBOUR GROUP   A bower of trees or climbing plants sometimes used as a background to two or more ceramic figures, more popular on Continental porcelains than in England.

BALUSTER   A thrown ceramic form similar in shape to the upright supports used in the construction of a stone balustrade.

BAROQUE   An art style based on classical symmetrical sources, popular in Europe from the late 16th century to about 1730. Seen on early English porcelain figures fashioned after those of the Meissen modeller J.J. Kaendler, which he produced prior to about 1745.

BAS-RELIEF   Low relief, as seen on the *pâte-sur-pâte* wares modelled at Mintons by Marc Louis Solon in the second half of the 19th century.

BAT-PRINTING   A form of printing upon ceramics introduced about 1800. The required image was produced from a series of dots of varying depth and closeness being punched into a copper plate. Oil was then applied to the plate, surface oil was then removed but retained in the dots. A 'bat' or thin pliable slab of glue or gelatine was then used to transfer the picture in the form of minute globules of oil on to the ready fired glaze of the ware to be decorated. A colour pigment, usually black, was then dusted in a dry powder form on to the oil impression which retained the colour ready for the low temperature firing. This process results in a far softer image than line engraving.

BISCUIT   A fired ceramic body with no glaze, such as seen on faulty wares often found on the site of old factories in the form of wasters. Also seen as finished figures such as produced at Derby to imitate statuary from about 1770 and other factories in the early 19th century such as Swansea (*see also* PARIAN WARE).

BLEEDING   A firing defect where underglaze colours run into the glaze into reserves usually intended to be painted with enamel colours. A fault usually only seen on soft-paste porcelains.

BLUE AND WHITE   Could be of any white ceramic body, but primarily is a term used to refer to hard or soft-paste porcelain decorated with a blue pigment derived from the metallic oxide of cobalt which is sandwiched between the body and the glaze. A form of decoration first used in China from the early 14th century, then being one of only two colours capable of withstanding the high temperature necessary to fire hard-paste porcelain. This form of decoration became very popular in England in many factories during the second half of the 18th century.

BOCAGE   From the French, meaning 'Little wood' and used to describe a backing of a leafy tree with flowers, added to a ceramic figure or group.

BODY   The name used to describe the composite materials used for the production of any particular type of ceramic ware.

BONE-ASH   Calcined animal bone, used in the production of porcelain at the Bow factory from about 1747. Later used in large quantities in the production of bone china. Bone is rich in lime and phosphoric acid.

BONE-CHINA   A form of soft-paste porcelain, thought to have been perfected by Josiah Spode II, shortly after 1796, when the New Hall patent giving them the exclusive right to produce a hard-paste porcelain from china clay and china stone expired. Today Spode's bone china is produced from 50% bone, 25% china clay and 25% china stone and fired at 1220°C. The latter two ingredients are quarried near St Austell, in Cornwall.

BOTTLE KILN   The old type of kiln in the shape of a milk bottle, used when firing with coal, a method of firing now replaced with gas or electric tunnel kilns. The outer shell of the bottle kiln is referred to as the hovel and the inner beehive shaped chamber as the oven.

CABARET SERVICE   A set of porcelain vessels comprising a small breakfast or tea service, often including a matching tray.

CALCINE   To heat to a temperature which will render a substance easier to crush or refine.

CASTING SLIP   A mixture of clay and water with a high clay to water ratio, enabling the cast to be a sufficient thickness before the moulds are saturated with water.

CERAMIC   The word derived from the Greek word Keramos and applied to the wide range of products based on high temperature treatment of silica compounds.

CHEESE-HARD   A word often used to describe the condition of the clay after sufficient of the moisture content has evaporated, but it is still soft enough to handle and for any additional work to be done.

CHINA   The name given in the 18th century to many types of white porcelain especially when decorated in the Chinese manner with underglaze blue decoration. Now usually restricted to meaning bone china.

CHINA CLAY   Known in China as *kaolin,* meaning 'high-ridge', it is a very refractory white clay formed by the decomposition of granite rocks. Used in the production of hard-paste

CHINA STONE   porcelain and bone china, but also used today for many other industrial manufactures.

Known in China as *pai-tun-tzu,* meaning 'little white bricks', the form in which it is dried after being washed and prepared for use, a refined non-plastic felspathic material derived from decayed granite and used together with china clay for the production of hard-paste porcelain and from the last years of the 18th century in the making of bone china.

CHINESE LOWESTOFT   An erroneous term formerly applied to Chinese export porcelain of 18th and 19th century date.

CHINOISERIE   Generic term for Chinese ornamental motifs, particularly for those executed by European craftsmen with a rather distant knowledge of Oriental art.

CLIP HANDLE   A form of handle used at New Hall where the moulded handle would appear to be in two sections, a short upper section clipping over the lower part and so providing a form of thumb-rest.

CLOBBERING   Overpainting in enamels on previously decorated porcelain, sometimes seen on late 18th century Worcester formerly decorated in only underglaze blue, but more common on blue and white Chinese wares.

COBALT   *See:* BLUE AND WHITE.

COMPORT   A form of raised dessert dish on a stem base, popular in the 19th century.

CORRUGATED MOULDING   A form of moulding such as seen on New Hall porcelain, where there is a space between each raised rib, in the manner of corrugated iron or cardboard.

CURVED OR SPIRAL FLUTING   Wares, usually tea or coffee, moulded with ogee shaped concave flutes.

CRAZING   Minute cracks in the glaze caused by the glaze shrinkage differing from that of the body during cooling, a particularly bad fault with soft-paste porcelains as such a faulty glaze no longer protects the body, allowing moisture and impurities to discolour the ware.

DRY BLUE   A brilliant enamel blue firing with a dry appearance, usually seen on Worcester porcelain when attributed to the outside decorator James Giles, or some Derby.

DRY EDGE   An unglazed edge around the base of a figure or a group, usually an indication of early Derby.

ENAMEL   A colouring pigment usually on a lead base which is fired to the glaze for decorating in a low temperature kiln ranging between 750°C-850°C offering an almost unlimited range of colours today, due to the improvement in the knowledge of ceramic chemistry during the 19th and 20th centuries.

FACETED MOULDING   A form of moulded decoration usually seen on tea or coffee wares comprising numbers of connected plane surfaces.

FELSPATHIC GLAZE   A glaze containing felspar (a group of alumino-silicates found as natural rocks).

FETTLING   Fused at a high temperature on hard-paste porcelains.

The removal of any seam or casting marks on a vessel or figure prior to the initial firing, especially necessary on slip cast wares.

FINIAL   An ornament finishing off the apex of lids, etc.

FIRE CRACK   A crack or split in the porcelain, usually occuring in the first firing when the clay shrinks, usually seen as an indication of an early ware when production troubles were being encountered.

FLUX   A material which lowers the temperature at which a mixture of ceramic substances melts.

FOOT RIM   Bottom edge of a cup, mug or similar shape, as distinct from foot ring.

FRIT   An ingredient used in many soft-paste porcelains composed of soluble and fusible alkaline salts of soda and potash which are processed to form a type of finely ground glass.

GILDING (honey)   The application of ground gold leaf or precipitated gold powder in honey, which was then fired at a temperature of approximately 790°C, after which it was burnished with a bloodstone made from naturally occuring haematite, or kidney stone, which is solid iron oxide.

GILDING (mercury)   A type of gilding using an amalgam of gold and mercury used in the later 18th century. Later replaced by some factories with the very inferior 'liquid gold', which did not require burnishing.

GLOST KILN   The kiln used to fire the wares after the application of the glaze to the biscuit. Today the glaze on bone china would be fired at about 1100°C, about 120°C lower than the biscuit firing.

GREEN WARE   Potters' term for unfired pottery.

GROUND LAYING   The application of an even colour ground to a glazed porcelain ware, often achieved by applying a thin coating of oil on to which the colour is dusted in dry powder form and so avoiding a variation in the depth of colour if applied by brush.

HARD-PASTE PORCELAIN   First produced by the Chinese potter by at least the middle of the 9th century, using china clay and china stone. First made at the Plymouth factory of William Cookworthy in England in 1768.

HARDENING-ON   The process of a low firing to fasten printed or painted underglaze colours to the biscuit before the application and firing of the glaze, a measure which volatilises the printing oil and also helps to conserve the fine detail of decoration which at times bleeds into the glaze.

INDEPENDENT DECORATOR   A painter of ceramics not employed regularly at a factory but who obtained wares in the white glazed or partially decorated condition, and then added

JEWELLED DECORATION

colours or gilding in his own studio. Also termed an 'outside decorator'. Today there are many members of the British China & Porcelain Artists Association who decorate wares in a similar manner as a craft.

The application of opaque or translucent drops of enamel, sometimes over gilt or silver foil, to the surface of the glaze to simulate inset precious stones. A form of decoration which originated at Sèvres about 1773 and was copied at Worcester in the mid-19th century. A favourite form of decoration on fake Sèvres.

KAKIEMON

The name of a Japanese family of potters who introduced a style of decoration in Arita in the late 17th century, now known as Kakiemon and which was imitated in many Continental and English porcelain factories

KILN FURNITURE

The name given to the wide range of refractory clay items used to support wares during firing.

LEADLESS GLAZE

In the early 19th century John Rose of the Coalport factory introduced a glaze in which borax was used in place of the earlier glaze which contained lead oxide, which was an extreme health hazard to those potters involved with glazing the wares. In 1894 fritted lead was introduced into glaze to reduce solubility and so minimise lead poisoning and in 1900 the use of raw lead oxide was prohibited to the industry.

LUSTRE DECORATION

A form of decoration first used by the Mesopotamian potter from about the 9th century on his tin glazed earthenwares. Certain metallic pigments such as silver or copper are applied to the glaze before firing in a reduction kiln leaving a fine metallic film on the glaze, which if correctly fired has an iridescent appearance. Copper gives a copper tone, silver a brassy yellow, gold a pink, and platinum a silver.

LUTING

The use of watered down clay or slip, to assemble the sections of a figure or to attach spouts, handles or applied clay decorations to a thrown or moulded form.

MONOCHROME

Painting or other decoration using only a single colour as opposed to polychrome, when a variety of colours is used.

MOULDING

Press moulding is the process of pressing plastic clay into the various sections of a mould, usually of plaster-of-Paris, after which the casts are luted together with slip to make a finished figure or vessel.

MUFFLE KILN

A lower temperature kiln in which enamel colours are fired c.750°-850°C.

OBCONICAL

An inverted conical form attached by the point, a common shape seen on New Hall jugs.

OVEN

The inner chamber of the old type kiln, made of bricks, into which the wares were placed in saggars and stacked. No longer necessary in present day tunnel kilns.

OXIDISING KILN

A kiln where during the firing the air is freely allowed into the kiln, as opposed to a reduction kiln. The resulting kiln atmospheres have varying colour results on the clays, glazes and metallic decoration.

PARIAN CHINA

A porcelain body so named due to its similarity in appearance to the white marble quarried on the island of Paros in Greece. First called 'Statuary Porcelain' by Copeland & Garrett who appear to be one of the first potteries to produce the ware in about 1842.

PATCH MARK

Small circular blemishes on the underside of some figures or wares, caused by their being stood on small clay pads in the glost firing to prevent adhesion to the inside base of the saggar (see DERBY).

PÂTE-SUR-PATE

A very costly type of porcelain decorated with the application of layers of contrasting colour slip, usually white, upon a coloured unfired body, giving the artist sufficient thickness of clay to model as a bas-relief (see MINTONS for the work of Marc Louis Solon).

PHOSPHATIC PORCELAIN

An artificial porcelain containing phosphoric acid as a result of including bone ash as an ingredient.

PORCELAIN

A white ceramic body, which if fired at the correct temperature and is not excessively thick has varying degrees of translucency. A variety of different ingredients are used depending on the type of porcelain being produced, such as a hard-paste or a soft-paste.

POUNCED

A form of stencilling with powdered charcoal through a pricked paper or thin metal sheet to providing guiding outlines for the painter.

PRESS MOULDING

In this process the clay is rolled into sheets of a convenient thickness, after which it is hand pressed into an earthenware, alabaster, metal or plaster-of-Paris open mould, which may be either smooth or decorated with intaglio ornamentation. Vessels may be made by luting with slip the various sections made in this way together. Relief decoration can also be press moulded for applying to the surface of the ware, such as on Wedgwood jasper. Some figures were made in this same way and the various sections, arms, heads, legs, etc., were then luted together to produce the complete figure, the clay having to remain very moist during all this work. This is an alternative method of producing wares to slip casting, where the vessels or figures usually have thinner walls and are much lighter in weight.

PRINT AND ENAMEL

Decoration which has been hand coloured on a printed outline.

PRINTING

A very economic form of multiple decoration by transferring a pigment, or ink, from engraved wood or copperplates by means of a thin tissue paper. (See MATERIALS AND TECHNIQUES for the fully explained process.)

443

RAISED GOLD	An effect obtained by applying a special paste, which after being fired, is covered with gold.
REDUCTION KILN	A kiln firing, in which a reducing atmosphere is acquired by controlling the intake of air and so creating a low oxygen and smoky atmosphere, which has the effect of changing the colour of the glaze. For example a glaze containing copper in an oxidising kiln produces a green, whilst in a reduction kiln the result is a red. Likewise, iron in an oxidising kiln gives a brown (rust-like), whilst in a reduction kiln the much admired 'Celadon' grey-green is acquired.
REEDED MOULDING	Moulding seen on various table wares composed of convex columns. The converse of fluting.
REFRACTORY	Ceramic materials which will withstand being fired at high temperatures without deforming.
REGISTERED	From 1842 a ceramic form of decoration could be patented, giving the firm or individual three years' protection against 'piracy'. From 1842-84 the mark used to indicate the day, month, year and 'parcel' number was in the form of a diamond shaped panel, headed with the class number IV. From 1884 to the present, wares if registered merely bear 'R^d No' followed by a number as listed under REGISTERED DESIGNS giving the date of manufacture within the year.
REPAIRER	The rather inappropriate title of the potter who assembles the various casts necessary to make a complete figure or highly decorated useful wares with relief decoration, etc.
RETICULATED	Having a pattern of pierced work forming a net-like design, often seen on a double walled vessel such as a teapot, with the piercing in the outer wall.
ROCOCO	An assymetrical style of decoration usually involving scrollwork, foliage, rockwork and shells. Rococo became fashionable in about 1755 on English porcelain and was revived about 1830 on Coalport and many other porcelain factories. Taken from the French *rocaille,* meaning shell-shaped.
SAGGAR (or SAGGER)	The refractory fire clay container in which the wares were placed within the oven to prevent direct contact with the flames.
SILK SCREEN	A transfer, printed with solid colours and/or gold through a fine mesh stencil.
SLIP CASTING	The process of pouring watered down clay (slip) into plaster-of-Paris moulds to produce a thin cast which is formed on the inside wall of the mould by the rapid absorption of the water in which the particles of clay are suspended. After a short period the surplus slip is poured off and in a short while the mould can be parted and the cast removed.
SPRIGGING	The application of separately moulded decoration to the surface of wares prior to firing.
STEAM HOLE	An erroneous name for the small hole in lids of tea or coffee pots, the actual purpose being to permit air into the pot when the contents are being poured.
STILT or SPUR MARKS	The small blemishes found on the underside of some wares caused by the fire clay stilts or other 'gadgets' to keep the wares free from each other or the base of the saggar, when being placed in the glost oven.
THROWING	The making of a hollow circular form on a rotating wheel, using the centrifugal force against the wet hands of the potter.
TOOLED	Detailed decoration applied with gilders' tools after the application of the gilding.
TOWING	Smoothing the surface and edges of flatwares using tow (flax fibre).
TOYS	A term usually applied to scent bottles, seals, boxes, etc., such as made at Chelsea and the Girl-in-a-Swing factory. Miniatures would be an equally appropriate word.
TUNNEL KILN	The modern type of gas or electric kiln in use at most ceramic factories today, where the wares are stacked on wheeled trollies which run on railway-type lines through a long tunnel in which the temperature reaches its maximum near the centre and gradually diminishes towards the exit.
VENT HOLE	Small hole placed in an otherwise sealed hollow shape to allow the gases or air to escape as the piece shrinks.
WASTERS	Misshapen wares or fragments of broken wares which have not survived the kiln firing and are discarded. Valuable evidence used by archaeologists to indicate the types of wares made on a site.
WATER SLIDE	Method of applying lithograph and silk screen transfers by soaking them from paper backing and sliding them into position on glost ware.
WICKER MOULDED	A vessel moulded with a surface meant to resemble wicker basket work.
WREATHING	Spiral indentations, a fault sometimes seen on the sides of hard-paste porcelain wares at Plymouth, Bristol and New Hall.

Index